RECOLLECTIONS OF A TOUR
MADE IN SCOTLAND

Dorothy Wordsworth in her mid-thirties, *c.*1806.
Anonymous silhouette. Courtesy of the Wordsworth Trust, Dove Cottage.

RECOLLECTIONS OF A TOUR MADE IN SCOTLAND

DOROTHY WORDSWORTH

Introduction, Notes and Photographs by

Carol Kyros Walker

YALE UNIVERSITY PRESS
NEW HAVEN & LONDON

Published with assistance from the
Charles S. Brooks Fund.

Set in Bembo by Best-set Typesetter Ltd., Hong Kong

Printed in Hong Kong

Library of Congress Cataloging-in-Publication Data
Wordsworth, Dorothy, 1771–1885.
Recollections of a tour made in Scotland / Dorothy Wordsworth; introduction, notes,
and photographs by Carol Kyros Walker.
p.   cm.
Includes bibliographical references (p.   ) and index.
ISBN 0-300-07155-8 (hardback)
1. Scotland—Description and travel. 2. Wordsworth, Dorothy, 1771–1885—Journeys—
Scotland. 3. Women authors, English—19th century—Journeys—Scotland.
4. British—Travel—Scotland—History—19th century.
I. Walker, Carol Kyros. II. Title.
DA865.W92 1997
914.1104′73—dc21   96-52071
                                                                          CIP

A catalogue record for this book is available from the British Library.

CONTENTS

PREFACE

For so engaging a tale as this, of Dorothy Wordsworth's journey through Scotland in 1803, I have wanted to advance the point of view of the author, releasing her as much as possible from the "sister of" status she too easily assumes into the role of originator. Locating the "I" in her story, however, meant searching beneath the "we" she so persistently employed in her writing. The effort yielded a distinct and inviolate voice.

In photographing Dorothy's journey I was fascinated with the mental process of drawing up images from the past, ever mindful of what loaded terms "remembering" and "recollecting" were in the Wordsworthian ideology Dorothy knew. My decision to use only black-and-white photography reflects my sense of the distinction between on-the-spot reactions and accounts, and recollections. In calling up, and re-collecting the images of a place there must be a moment just before total illumination in the mind when what is there pauses for the final investment of the thinker. For me, that instant is in black and white; Dorothy Wordsworth, whose gift for remembering was extraordinary, was to give the moment its color with her words.

The photographs begin with a tunnelling in through trees to the door of Greta Hall, Coleridge's home, and end with an opening out from the interior of Dove Cottage through an open window. It is the metaphor for Dorothy's journey, to the point where she begins to write about it. The world she recreates in her book is still there for the modern traveller to find to a great extent—with this proviso, that in following her directions one must allow for a modest margin of error and the changes that come inevitably with modernization.

As precise as Dorothy's travel writing might be, I learned I would have to suspend my expectations at times. The once dazzling force of the Falls of the Clyde provides electrical power now. Harnessed, the "astounding Flood" of William Wordsworth's "Cora Linn" endures its reduction with grace. Loch Katrine provides drinking water for all of Glasgow today, and as its water level has been raised by several feet, the contours Dorothy caresses in remembrance are not exactly the ones we see, so that there is guesswork in finding her bays and the Den of the Ghosts, and we recognize that if the loch is still pristine, it is so for different reasons. Thread is no longer carried away by English ladies from Luss, and Jedburgh pears seem to have no name-recognition in Jedburgh.

Following Dorothy Wordsworth today means training oneself to see again—whether with the naked eye or through the lens of a camera. She has

many ways of looking—some (the most interesting) peculiar to her own
aesthetics, some prescribed by notions of the sublime, the beautiful, the
picturesque that had filtered into her consciousness, and some directed by
the impulse to "sightsee," as we would say in our time. Betraying theatrical
awareness, she might invite her reader to see what she is looking at as a
puppet performance or a "raree-show" or a painted scene on the backdrop
of a playhouse, viewed by candlelight. She liked seeing objects at a distance
framed ("screened") and was keenly aware of lines of perspective, observing
a scene "terminating" in mountains. A landscape might be "pensive," fishing
boats covered with drying nets assume a "funereal gloom," and houses are
"huddled up in trees," so that whatever she looked at took on character.
Often she would direct the reader how to move from view to view, as with
the three distinct outlooks from Dumbarton Rock. Panning, magnifying,
closing in, scooping up with a wide angle, her techniques ranged from
painterly to cinematic, and it is interesting to question whether she would
reject, on the grounds of artificiality, or embrace, arguing for accuracy, a
camcorder if she were travelling today.

The spelling in Dorothy Wordsworth's narrative has been preserved as
she gave it. I have used the modern spelling of place names for the new
maps and my own prose. Dorothy uses "Erse" for *Gaelic* and "sate" for *sat*.
The discrepancies between her place name spellings and the modern ones,
such as Loch Ketterine and Loch Katrine, are hardly subtle and need no
explanation.

If I could bring Dorothy back to life for a conversation, I would begin by
apologizing for calling her by her first name as often as I do. A practical
consideration, not a sense of familiarity, led to this. If I called her
Wordsworth, readers would assume I meant her brother. *Ms.* seemed anach-
ronistic, *Miss*, condescending. My dilemma was even more pronounced
when I realized I would not correspondingly call Coleridge *Samuel*, because
he didn't like the name, preferring S.T.C. if his surname were not to be
used.

Thanks go to many Scots who extended traveller's aid to me. Mr.
Campbell, who works for the Strathclyde Water Works on Loch Katrine,
drove me in his lorry on his rounds along a road where private traffic is not
permitted to Glengyle, which he had known since boyhood, and led me to
the enclosed burial grounds of the MacGregors, a little plot so hidden by
trees that I would never have found it on my own. Dorothy Leitch of
Carluke charioted me in her "open air car" to the Cartland Bridge (a
Thomas Telford wonder) to show me the hazards of the Cartland Crags and
Wallace's Cave below. Jean McAleer of Closeburn, Thornhill interrupted
her production of currant jam to serve me coffee and tell me how to find
the Brownhill Inn I had been searching for when I knocked on her door.
Margaret McCulloch of Kirkfieldbank, Lanark walked me through a wet

field of tall wild flowers to take me to Stonebyres, the last of the Falls of the Clyde. And my notebook bursts with folksy "maps" drawn by solicitous natives to get me to local spots.

To Jeff Cowton particularly, and the staff of Dove Cottage Library, Grasmere generally, I owe considerable thanks for facilitating my use of manuscripts and other relevant texts in the Wordsworth collection. The silhouette of Dorothy Wordsworth and the maps from her manuscript are reproduced by permission of the Wordsworth Trust, to which I am also grateful for permission to photograph the interior of Dove Cottage.

The resources of the following libraries enabled my research to proceed: Glasgow University Library, Special Collections; Keswick Library, Cumbria; Tullie House, Carlisle; Motherwell Library, Motherwell; Alan Ramsay Library, Leadhills; Regenstein Library, University of Chicago; Newberry Library, Chicago; Bancroft Library and Doe Library, University of California, Berkeley; the Lilly Library, Indiana University; the Harry Ransom Humanities Research Center, University of Texas, Austin.

Ben Harris McClary and Dolores Mitchell gave my Introduction a discerning reading before it went to Yale University Press, and Norman Walker reviewed the text with valuable critical eyes over the long haul. No cartographer could have been more cheerful and at the same time skilled in creating maps for my work than Jörg Metzner. As a translator of Latin John Nolan brought a welcome freshness to Smollett. I appreciate the sabbatical leave granted by the City Colleges of Chicago so that I might begin my work. Many voices in the stellar cast of romanticists who comprised the Wordsworth Summer Conference, 1996 resonated in my thoughts as I ended my work, and I can only thank them collectively. Carl Woodring provided just the smile of reason I needed from a Wordsworth scholar when I first conceived of following Dorothy to Scotland. There is ample reason to thank Jack Stillinger for whatever I do well in romantic studies, and I do. The scholars whose work on Dorothy Wordsworth have influenced me most are Pamela Woof and Susan M. Levin. Amanda Gilroy gave support to my early initiatives in Scotland, looking at them with her own publishing interests in romantic travellers, especially women.

I have been fortunate in having as my editor John Nicoll of Yale University Press, who has designed this book and overseen its production with the special sensitivity of one who can call the Lake District home. As manuscript editor, Sue Jackson provided invaluable refinements and improvements to the text. My photography has been processed by Gamma Photo Labs, Chicago.

INTRODUCTION

I. Place to Place

Dorothy Wordsworth set out on her tour of Scotland on 15 August 1803 as
a vibrant, marvelously capable, discerning single woman of thirty-one with
as much zest for travel as satisfaction in staying at home. The two men who
were to enjoy her company and abilities on this tour were her brother
William and Samuel Taylor Coleridge, with whom she had travelled as a
threesome before. As summer journeys tend to be universally, this one was
undertaken to benefit the health of the travellers while they explored new
places. For Dorothy, who had never been to Scotland, the journey would
confirm the reputed wonders of the land to the north, touted in current
guide books, and by word of mouth, as wild, mysterious, sublime, and
Gaelic to the point of seeming foreign. Though it was part of her own Great
Britain, and she knew the Lowlands through Robert Burns, much of
Scotland was to seem as alien as France or Germany, where she had already
travelled. By the time she returned home to Grasmere six weeks and 663
miles later, her imagination had ranged over such provocative landscapes and
her analytical mind had sorted and stored so many brilliant memories that
she would want to write the account she entitled *Recollections of a Tour Made
in Scotland, A.D. 1803*, the text published here.

Venturing into Scotland was not for the faint of heart. The roads were
poorly surfaced and dangerous, even along the postal routes and the main
highway to the North from London. In some areas a drover's road would be
the best one could find. And of course, there were places where no road
whatsoever existed—only a footpath which, though marked on the map,
required a local guide who knew where the fishermen travelled carrying
their herring across low mountains between Loch Lomond and Loch
Katrine. Guide books always evaluated road conditions as they noted the
mileage. Dorothy Wordsworth does this too, labeling the routes from "most
excellent" (the road to Callander) to "roughish" (to Jedburgh) to "very bad"
(to Hesket Newmarket).

"The Highlands" connoted a certain mysterious strangeness to many early
travellers, who appreciated passage into that part of their own country as
they would arrival into a foreign land—with a mixture of apprehension and
excitement. The tourist travelling north to Scotland by way of Glasgow
considered the village of Luss, on Loch Lomond, the beginning of the
Highlands. Henry Skrine, a Somerset gentleman, wrote in his travel account

in 1795 that after leaving Dumbarton and viewing the Smollett monument at Renton, he proceeded along the Leven to Loch Lomond, and dined at the inn in Luss. "We had now entered the Highlands," he announced, certain of the boundary (*Three Successive Tours*, p. 44). His route to this point had been exactly that of Dorothy Wordsworth. To this day, Luss presents itself to tourists travelling north as the start of the Highland experience.

There is in fact a Highland Boundary Fault which runs through Loch Lomond northeast, separating the entire area of Loch Lomond and the Trossachs, familiar to some today as Rob Roy country. The geological character of the landscape changes with the fault line because, broadly speaking, the rocks to the north are harder than the sandstone south of the fault line. Today a traveller carrying a *Blue Guide* would learn that the division of Scotland into Highlands and Lowlands runs along a diagonal line from "roughly" Dumbarton, some ten miles below Luss, to Stonehaven, on the east coast, below Aberdeen. William Gilpin, travelling in 1776, and taking a route north from Perth to Dunkeld identified the eastern entry point: "What is remarkable, from these high grounds [near Dulkeld] you *descend* into the *Highlands*: for here the country begins, which takes that denomination" (*Observations*, I p. 112).[1]

In Dorothy Wordsworth's time, the boundaries might have been blurred, especially as one travelled northeast, but the distinctions in the culture, dress and language were far more noticeable, and travel accounts announced tartans, bonnets, plaids, huts, cairns, barefootedness, and Gaelic speech with remarkable suddenness as journeys proceeded north. In Luss Dorothy sensed the difference: "Here we first saw houses without windows, the smoke coming out of the open window-places" (p. 84). And two of William's most fundamentally Scottish poems, the eloquent "Stepping Westward" and "To a Highland Girl," have associations with places barely within the border.

Scottish inns and public houses, whether Highland or Lowland, were notoriously lacking in comforts and amenities, as well as cleanliness. Some houses regarded the lodging of horses as their priority and were ill equipped to put up people. Certain inns, like the Saracen's Head in Glasgow, to which Dorothy Wordsworth and her party had been referred, had passed the test of time and discriminating patronage, like that of Samuel Johnson and his loyal Scottish friend Boswell, who stopped there on their Scottish tour of

1. Gilpin was at the starting point of what was known as Pennant's Short Tour (of the Highlands). On this route one entered the Highlands at Dunkeld and exited at Luss. The northern Highlands and the west coast were not included. Peter Womack comments in his *Improvement and Romance* that this was the "standard route for the 'picturesque tour' which became established as a fashionable amusement from about 1760" (p. 62). Thomas Pennant himself travelled beyond the extremes of the Highlands and identified specific points of entry into the Highlands from the north, the south, the east, and the west in his account, *A Tour in Scotland. MDCCLXIX* (p. 197).

1773. The Cairndow Inn, on Loch Fyne in the Highlands, would receive Keats and his friend Charles Brown on their walking tour of Scotland in 1818 and draws informed travellers as well as fishermen to its doors to this day. "The house was clean for a Scotch inn" (p. 158), Dorothy proclaimed at Tyndrum, welcoming as well the sight of well-dressed guests and meals served on white table cloths with glasses and English dishes. But such inns were the exception in 1803. English travellers in the eighteenth century and just after were more likely to censure than praise their Scottish hosts. Fashionable though it had become to travel in Scotland, it seemed more fashionable to return and tell the tale of discomforts endured. Most complaints were well founded, for Scotland overall was simply not geared to provide comforts to visitors. The country was suffering from great poverty. In the Highlands the citizens who remained on the land after so many of their kin and former clansmen had sought new lives in America and other distant places in the great waves of emigration that followed the Battle of Culloden in 1746, with its final blow to the clan system, found themselves without a social or political structure they could trust. The Highland Clearances, which began about 1780 and would continue into the mid-nineteenth century, saw crofters evicted from their homes to make way for English and Lowland sheep farmers, to whom the land was being rented for profit by the very Highland chiefs to whom they had once been loyal. On both the cultural and the personal level, these Scots felt disenfranchised and hopeless.

If Dorothy Wordsworth had been looking for more evidence of prosperity, she might have found it in the thriving city of Glasgow, but she did not enjoy urban bustle and left town without even seeing the renowned Cathedral, giving heavy rain as an excuse. It was rural Scotland she came to see, and this is where dependence on simple people for food and lodging became a matter of critical negotiation as well as luck. On balance, she fared well, her assertive character taking over where chance failed her. "Dorothy had a bed in the Hovel which was varnished *so rich* with peat smoke, an apartment of highly polished [oak] would have been poor to it: it would have wanted the *metallic* Lustre of the smoke-varnished Rafters," Coleridge reported of her quarters on Loch Katrine (*Collected Letters*, II p. 978). But Dorothy relished the simple hospitality of private residences, from the most rustic, like the hut of the ferryman and his wife near Glengyle on Loch Katrine, to the townish quarters of the old woman and her blind husband near the Cathedral in Jedburgh. It could please her to sleep on the floor if she had been made to feel warmly welcome. In a cottage south of Blair she and William were taken in by a kind woman who could offer them only her floor for a bed. "William lay upon the floor on some hay, without sheets; my bed was of chaff; I had plenty of covering, and a pair of very nice strong clean sheets,—she said with some pride that she had good linen" (p. 171).

Dorothy would not exploit a humble situation for either an extravagant metaphor like Coleridge's or an appeal to the reader's sympathy. The integrity of a sincere human gesture was almost sacred to her.

To be sure, Dorothy could cite shortcomings in her hosts quite clearly. Her litany of complaints about King's House in Glen Coe begins with, "Never did I see such a miserable, such a wretched place" (p. 153), and escalates with precise documentation. She came to accept the slowness of service at public houses as a fact of travel in Scotland. But she could neither dismiss nor explain the refusal of a nameless woman at the crude public house near Faskally to take William and her in, twice, on two different nights, "Though we had every reason to believe that she had at least one bed for me" (p. 165). It seems not to have occurred to Dorothy that in this instance the problem may have been the very fact that she and her brother were English and therefore the object of fear and resentment in a Highland setting where the 1746 Battle of Culloden was still fresh in the memories of people who had lost their culture, their clan ways, and their Gaelic tongue to the English. The Wordsworths had come to the area to see the Pass of Killiecrankie, site of a battle in which the English troops were defeated by the Highlanders on 22 July 1689. The surly woman who denied Dorothy, her brother, and their exhausted horse shelter near Fascally may have been executing her own minor defeat of the English. Times were such that not only the economic conditions but the attitude of the Scots might work against the comfort of English travellers.

"A boiled sheep's head, with the hair singed off" (p. 65) was true Scottish fare to Dorothy, and she savored it, along with the barley broth in which the head had been boiled—just as an English tourist should in the Lowland Lanark inn which knew its clientele from the south. Farther north Johnson's dictionary definition of "Oats" as "A grain, which in England is generally given to horses, but in Scotland supports the people" summed up the state of culinary arts as the English visitors found them in the eighteenth century. Not much had changed by 1818, when John Keats walked through Scotland with his friend Charles Brown and complained of a diet of eggs and oat cakes.

Dorothy Wordsworth, however, found pleasure in the simplicity of the food she encountered—so long as it was offered with the genuine artlessness of a native. At Arrochar an upscale pretentious inn offered good dining, "yet would [we] have gladly changed our roasted lamb and pickles, and the gentleman-waiter with his napkin in his pocket, for the more homely fare of the smoky hut at Loch Katrine, and the good woman's busy attentions" (p. 116). Far more to her liking was a chance to chat with other women, over a fire, cooking for herself some fish they had given her, as she had done at Ballachulish (p. 148). If dining on "moorfowl and mutton-chops" at a house in Tyndrum (p. 158) satisfied her, so did entering the kitchen of her hostess in the village near Loch Lubnaig to talk while she rolled out barley cakes by hand, and even to inquire why she did not take a rolling-pin to her dough as the more efficient women at home in Cumberland did for their oat cakes. She did not find a ready listener in the Scotswoman, and Dorothy resigned herself to waiting for food—the cakes as well as the main course—again, but this time with some understanding of slow service. Dorothy Wordsworth was at an advantage as a woman: she could go behind the scenes in Scotland. Unlike Johnson before her or Keats later, or all the male English travellers in between, she could review eating in Scotland without bias or fashionable crankiness.

Indeed, overall it is not surprising that Dorothy occasionally criticized as she travelled; it is surprising that she criticized so little. She was fortunate in her disposition. Her sensibilities enriched her experiences with rural people and their rustic life and she seemed to share her brother's belief that "in that condition, the essential passions of the heart find a better soil in which they can attain their maturity, are less under restraint, and speak a plainer and more emphatic language" (Preface to the Second Edition of *Lyrical Ballads*, 1800, in *Poetical Works*, II p. 386). With a lively spontaneity she embraced people living close to the land she visited. As she proceeds toward Tarbet after the first visit to Loch Katrine, her sense of being within the boundary of the Highlands is acute. She hears a boy hooting for his cattle. His image haunts her, and as she writes her *Recollections* she recalls "his dress, cry, and appearance all different from anything we had been accustomed to" (p. 114). The lad measured a Scottish dimension of Wordsworthian trust in the sanctity of childhood, the integrity of humans who live close to their origins, uncorrupted by the world of "getting and spending." This boy, in his setting, was "a text . . . containing in itself the whole history of the High-lander's life—his melancholy, his simplicity, his poverty, his superstition, and above all, that visionariness which results from a communion with the unworldliness of nature" (p. 114). From place to place, what was peculiarly Scottish may have changed, but what was human remained the same, residing in the hearts of simple people.

II. The Jaunting Car

Dorothy, William, and Coleridge had talked about the trip throughout the summer. They decided, not entirely to the satisfaction of Coleridge, who would have preferred to make a pedestrian tour, to travel in an Irish jaunting car, an open air two-wheeled cart drawn by a single horse and suited to country life. It was, compared to the kind of elaborately fitted out chaise more fashionable travellers took to Scotland, plain and exposed. On the other hand, it was ideally suited to the principle of being close to the people of another place and open to the experience of nature that particularly guided the art of the Wordsworths.

The purchase of the cart and procurement of a horse fell upon Coleridge, for whom such simple business proved troublesome. He fretted to William (23 July 1803): "What the Devil to do about a Horse!" (*Collected Letters*, II p. 957). The impossibility of locating in Keswick, the kind of car they had decided upon distressed him too. He tried to negotiate the purchase of one in the South, where he had lived before moving north to be close to Wordsworth, and even then, he haggled about the cost, fifteen pounds, and finally confessed to William: "I begin to find that a Horse & Jaunting Car is *an anxiety*—& almost to wish that we had adopted our first thought, & *walked*: with one pony & side saddle for our Sister Gift-of-God [Dorothy]." (pp. 957–58)

Yet when the transportation finally materialized Coleridge seems to have taken some pride in it. The day before the threesome took off, he wrote to his brother-in-law, Robert Southey:

> We have bought a stout Horse—aged but stout & spirited—& an open vehicle, called a Jaunting Car—there is room in it for 3 on each side, on hanging seats—a Dicky Box for the Driver / & a space or hollow in the middle, for luggage—or two or three Bairns.—It is like half a long Coach, only those in the one seat sit with their *back* to those in the other / instead of face to face.—Your feet are not above a foot—scarcely so much—from the ground / so that you may get off & on while the Horse is moving without the least Danger / there are all sorts of Conveniences in it. (p. 975)

Dorothy and the two poets were obliged to focus much attention on the jaunting car and horse. Mishaps, from the minor early ones of backing into water and being stymied by a narrow bridge in Grisdale, to the later appalling crossings of water in the Highlands, endangered the horse and created unexpected tensions for the travellers. There was an ongoing concern for where the horse was to be housed, what it would be fed, and whether its stamina would hold out, as well as where it could be left during the periods when the travellers wanted to explore the country on foot, as they did in the Trossachs.

Travellers meeting other travellers often make sharp impressions on each other. If they happen to have literary status as well, some fortunate records come out of the encounters. Samuel Rogers, who was travelling with his sister, leaves a vital account of meeting the Wordsworth–Coleridge party in Dumfries and spending about quarter of an hour with them. Dorothy emerges as the one who had to take charge oftener than not:

> During our excursion we fell in with Wordsworth, Miss Wordsworth, and Coleridge, who were, at the same time, making a tour in a vehicle

that looked very like a cart. Wordsworth and Coleridge were entirely occupied in talking about poetry; and the whole care of looking out for cottages where they might get refreshment and pass the night, as well as of seeing their poor horse fed and littered, devolved upon Miss Wordsworth. She was a most delightful person,—so full of talent, so simple-minded, and so modest! (*Table-Talk*, pp. 208–209)

After Rogers saw them William would have to get over his awkwardness in unyoking a horse, learn to mend a wheel and create a makeshift harness, and deal with a blacksmith in remote Scotland. Coleridge would bow out of the tour altogether after two weeks, but while he was still in the party he complained of the grating of the cart's wheels, and left the driving to William, because, according to Mrs. Coleridge, "poor Samuel is too weak to undertake the fatigue of driving—he was very unwell when he went off . . ." (*Collected Letters*, II p. 975n). But Dorothy remained the woman she was when Rogers praised her; she, more than anyone, would worry about the welfare of the horse.

In their Irish car the travellers from Westmorland cut an amusing picture for urban Scots. As they rode through Glasgow, "in spite of the rain, every person as we went along stayed his steps to look at us; indeed, we had the pleasure of spreading smiles from one end of Glasgow to the other" (p. 75). Children were fascinated, following the odd English party and longing to climb up for a ride, with such winning charm that the adults got off to allow four of the boys to experience the jaunting car. "I would have walked two miles willingly," Dorothy wrote, "to have had the pleasure of seeing them so happy" (p. 76). As they proceeded up Loch Lomond the disparity between their style of travel and that of the more fashionable visitor, arriving at an inn in a smart carriage with servants, struck Dorothy, and she acknowledged that their "outlandish Hibernian vehicle" set them apart.

A turning point in the events of the Irish car was the crossing at Connel, which outraged Dorothy and irremediably terrified the horse. Dorothy's account brilliantly indicts the ferrymen who perpetrated the abuse of her animal, who was "harshly driven over rough stones" to reach the boat, then beaten and pushed onto a ferry boat. "A blackguard-looking fellow, blind of one eye, which I could not but think had been put out in some strife or other, held him by force like a horse-breaker, while the poor creature fretted, and stamped with his feet against the bare boards, frightening himself more and more with every stroke" (p. 140). Nor did the unfortunate creature make it to shore without further assaults. "All the while the men were swearing terrible oaths, and cursing the poor beast, redoubling their curses when we reached the landing-place, and whipping him ashore in brutal triumph" (p. 140). The horse was never the same after this treatment, and his consequent fear of water would require special consideration for the duration of the journey. An accident only a day after his traumatic ferry ride confirmed his vulnerability:

> We travelled close to the water's edge, and were rolling along a smooth road, when the horse suddenly backed, frightened by the upright shafts of a roller rising from behind the wall of a field adjoining the road. William pulled, whipped, and struggled in vain; we both leapt upon the ground, and the horse dragged the car after him, he going backwards down the bank of the loch, and it was turned over, half in the water, the horse lying on his back, struggling in the harness, a frightful sight! I gave up everything; thought that the horse would be lamed, and the car broken to pieces. (p. 147)

There were to be no more jocular references to the horse and cart after the crossing and the subsequent accident. Dorothy's concern for the "poor horse" is always serious.

III. Times and Ties

The timing of Dorothy's journey is in some respects puzzling. The summer of 1803 was marked by external conflicts and internal bonds. In May the Peace of Amiens was broken and England resumed war with France. Travel in Great Britain was generally favored over journeys abroad, where the Napoleonic campaigns presented real danger. In Scotland the presence of British troops at the ancient fortress at Dumbarton, near Glasgow, revealed a nation apparently poised for invasion. Yet Dorothy played down the significance of the military presence in her recollections, reducing the interplay between an armed, red-coated sentinel pacing the ramparts and grazing sheep to a puppet show (p. 78), and once atop Dumbarton Rock, claiming, "[W]e could not help looking upon the fortress, in spite of its cannon and soldiers, and the rumours of invasion, as set up against the hostilities of wind and weather rather than for any other warfare" (p. 79). Her sophistication about the realities of a war that had already touched her brother's life led to some scoffing here at the idea of a military strategy that would draw the French to this western inlet of Scotland.

William's responses to France, both as a nation struggling for freedom and later as a power hostile to his own country, had taken him down a painful moral and psychological path. A student at St. John's College, Cambridge when the storming of the Bastille occurred on 14 July 1789, he shared with other young men the kind of liberal political thought that would endorse a show of force to achieve liberty.[2] In 1790, at the start of a walking tour with

2. For a detailed examination of Wordsworth's political views from his Cambridge days through the entire Revolution, see Nicholas Roe, *Wordsworth and Coleridge: The Radical Years.* Oxford: Clarendon Press, 1988.

his friend Robert Jones through France and the Alps, he landed at Calais on 13 July and joined in the Bastille Day celebration the next day. "Bliss was it in that dawn to be alive" (*The Prelude* (1805) Book Tenth, l. 693). After finishing his B.A. he returned to France (1791–92), remaining mostly in Orléans and Blois, though with a significant visit to Paris, as the French Revolution progressed in an orderly fashion. There were two legacies of that visit. One was a friendship with an army officer, Michel Beaupuy, who took William's political inclinations much further in support of the Revolution. The other was a love affair with a woman named Annette Vallon, with whom he conceived a child. When war broke out between England and France in 1793, William found his loyalties tested to the extreme:

> It was a grief—
> Grief call it not, 'twas any thing but that—
> A conflict of sensations without name.
> (ll. 263–65)

With his love of France and his strong sense of the moral rectitude of its cause (freedom for the people, and by extension for all humankind), he had rejoiced when Englishmen were defeated by the French and felt grief that in the village churches of his country people prayed for victory over France. By 1796 he had fallen into a kind of mental breakdown, or at least a severe crisis in his moral beliefs. It is impossible to say how much of the breakdown was directly related to his concerns with war, but he remembered

> Dragging all passions, notions, shapes of faith,
> Like culprits to the bar
> (ll. 889–90)

Dorothy's role in restoring his confidence and health as a poet and thinker is inestimable. It was she, he later acknowledged, who

> didst lend a living help
> To regulate my soul.
> (ll. 906–907)

Dorothy became a part of these French legacies. William's daughter remained in the picture. She was baptized Anne Caroline Wordsworth on 15 December 1791, after William had returned to England. If he had intended to return to France to marry Annette and assume the role of a legitimate father to the child, called simply Caroline, the outbreak of war between the two countries prevented him. Dorothy as well as William wrote letters to Annette for some time, but during the war years correspondence was restricted and letters were sometimes confiscated. She would join William in making a trip to France to visit Annette and Caroline at the first opportunity, during the Peace of Amiens in 1802.

In a more general way a cloud of mystery fell over the Wordsworths because of William's association with radical thinkers, William Godwin among them. An odd consequence of this occurred during one of the happiest periods of Dorothy's life, in 1797, when she and her brother resided in a lovely mansion in the village of Holford in the Quantock Hills of northwest Somerset, and at a time when the British government had become particularly repressive. Local people suspected they were French. The company they kept, and indeed entertained at their home, was unconventional, if not radical. Thomas Poole (who had arranged for them to rent this house at an affordable price) and Coleridge, both of whom lived in nearby Nether Stowey, were constant visitors. On one occasion John Thelwall, a friend of Coleridge who had been arrested, but acquitted, under the Treasonable Practices Act, was the guest of honor at a dinner party hosted by the Wordsworths. The Home Secretary was informed, and a detective was sent down from the Home Office to investigate William, who apparently was already on file because of his French sympathies.

Now in Scotland it was wise to look upon the soldiers on Dumbarton rock and betray no interest in the war.

Again, toward the end of their journey, when Dorothy and William sent their Irish jaunting car ahead for the pleasure of walking down the main street of Peebles, "William was called aside in a mysterious manner by a person who gravely examined him—whether he was an Irishman or a foreigner, or what he was; I suppose our car was the occasion of suspicion at a time when every one was talking of the threatened invasion" (p. 202). The background to this confrontation lay to the west as well as the east. An Irish rebel, Robert Emmet, had been plotting to turn Franco-English hostilities to the advantage of Ireland, working through a revolutionary band, known as the United Irishmen, and French officials. The idea, in brief, was to support, with arms, a French invasion of Great Britain, projected for August.[3] Much as Dorothy might want to gloss over the national sense of imminent danger, it was there.

The consideration of war aside, both Dorothy and William had family ties that favored remaining home this summer. It had not been quite a year since William's marriage to Dorothy's friend Mary Hutchinson on 4 October 1802, and only two months since the birth of their first child John, on 18 June. Dorothy lived with her brother and sister-in-law as an integral part of their harmonious household at Dove Cottage, where she and William had lived before his marriage. She had just begun her new role of loving aunt. The journey would take Dorothy and William away from all that was dear to them except each other for some six weeks. Why they would voluntarily

3. Emmet was captured at the end of August (the 20th) and hanged 20 September, not long after William Wordsworth's minor interrogation, when the threat of a French invasion was still in the air.

effect such a long separation when fundamental ties should have bound them to a scene in Grasmere is not easy to fathom.

For Dorothy the time with William outside his domestic context might have been welcomed as a period for redefining her relationship to him. William, for his part, might have viewed the trip as an opportunity to reaffirm his affection for his sister. He had witnessed Dorothy's intense emotional reaction to his betrothal: on the occasion of his wedding she had been too ambivalent to attend the ceremony. Despite her genuine affection for Mary, she in fact seems to have been traumatized by the actual matrimonial union. Her own ingenuous journal account of the event betrayed her disturbance, and possibly, considering his disposition of the wedding ring, William's culpability in complicating her emotions:

> I saw them go down the avenue towards the Church. William had parted from me upstairs. I gave him the wedding ring—with how deep a blessing! I took it from my forefinger where I had worn it the whole of the night before—he slipped it again onto my finger and blessed me fervently . . . I kept myself as quiet as I could, but when I saw the two men [William, and John Hutchinson] running up the walk, coming to tell us it was over, I could stand it no longer & threw myself on the bed where I lay in stillness, neither hearing or seeing any thing, till Sara [Hutchinson] came upstairs to me & said 'They are coming'. This forced me from the bed where I lay & moved I knew not how straight forward, faster than my strength could carry me till I met my beloved William & fell upon his bosom. (*Grasmere Journals* p. 126)

William was hardly obtuse. With the recent birth of his son he would have recognized the potential for Dorothy to feel displaced again and seen the need for Dorothy to have some separate time with him now and the value of investing in the woman who had been so sensitive a partner in the generation of his poems.

Born on Christmas day, 1771, not quite a year and a half after William (7 April 1770), Dorothy was the third child and only girl in a family of five siblings. When her mother died, in 1778, she was sent to live with her aunt, while the boys remained with their father. The death of her father in 1783 left the children orphaned, and Dorothy's longing for closeness to her brothers grew more intense. "We have been endeared to each other by early misfortune. We in the same moment lost a father, a mother, a home . . ." she reflected when she was twenty-one, adding the proclamation: "Neither absence nor Distance nor Time can ever break the Chain that links me to my Brothers" (*Letters*, I p. 88). Her declaration found a parallel in the words of Keats, also orphaned at an early age: "My love for my Brothers from the early loss of our parents and even for earlier Misfortunes has grown into [an] affection 'passing the Love of Women'—" (*Letters of John Keats*, I p. 293).

Dorothy's urgent desire for union with her siblings, like Keats's for his, was central to her life. It accounted especially for her closeness to the one brother with whom she now lived, and for the value they both placed on having a family home. Dorothy and William had a reciprocally warm attachment to each other, one that defied easy explanation and sometimes invited gossip, and certainly one that reflected the complexity of human love in the lives of uncommon people.

Dorothy and William had moved into Dove Cottage shortly before her twenty-eighth birthday, in December 1799. They had lived together before, at Racedown, in Dorset in a house that had been lent to them by a friend of William's, and then had moved to Alfoxden to be near Coleridge. But this snug nest in Grasmere, which had once been a pub, belonged to them, and moving into it marked the beginning of a happy period for the two. For the first time since her mother had died, Dorothy might enjoy a home that felt permanent and was family-owned.

Coleridge, the youngest of the three at thirty years old, figured critically in the decision to travel this summer. He now lived a mere thirteen miles north—an easy walk for him—in an attractive hilltop residence overlooking the River Greta, which Dorothy had found for him when he decided to move with his pregnant wife and their first son Hartley (then almost four years old) from Nether Stowey, Somerset to Cumberland, in July 1800, to be close to the Wordsworths. He and William had already collaborated on *Lyrical Ballads*, and their lives as poets and friends had been united in travel and talk. Dorothy had been a part of their formative experiences, sharing their walking tour along the southern coast of the Bristol Channel, witnessing, if not participating in, their talks on this expedition about dividing their efforts for *Lyrical Ballads* along natural and supernatural emphases; and sailing with them to Germany in 1798, where the three remained together some ten days in Hamburg and then separated, so William and Dorothy might seek more economical quarters in Goslar, in the Hartz Mountains, while Coleridge went to Ratzeburg, and four months later to Göttingen, where he enrolled at the university.

Dorothy, William, and Coleridge had developed into a sort of family unto themselves. Each of them was a writer, though only the two men had wanted to be published. By 1803 *Lyrical Ballads* had been published twice. Coleridge had written in 1797, when the three first began to form a unit as writers, the "Ancient Mariner," "Kubla Khan," and "Cristabel," and the next year "Frost at Midnight," "France: An Ode," "The Nightingale," and "Fears in Solitude." His ode "Dejection," responding to William's "Intimations" ode and to his love for Sara Hutchinson, grew out of his relocation to the neighborhood of the Wordsworths in the north. And yet, at the time of the Scottish tour, Coleridge was searching for a medium other than poetry in which to reconcile metaphysical concerns that had preoccupied him as a sophisticated reader and interpreter of current German philo-sophical works, particularly those of Kant.[4]

Wordsworth, on the other hand, was entirely clear about committing himself to a career as a poet, and was enjoying a period of high creativity. His physical environment was familiar and nourishing to his creative energies; his home life was tranquil and affirmative. He had contributed unforgettable works to *Lyrical Ballads*, composed the famous Preface (incor-porating Coleridge's thoughts), adding "Michael" and "The Brothers" to the second, 1800 volume. His journey to Germany had yielded the Lucy Poems as well as the poetical reminiscences of childhood that would be incorpo-rated into his great autobiographical work *The Prelude*, which was well underway by the time of the Scottish tour.

Dorothy's brilliance with words and images took a more private form: she kept diaries. William knew them well, but they were not meant for other readers—at least not in her lifetime. Today they are read, admired, and written about as much for what they reveal about their author as for what they disclose about the life she shared with her brother. Literary critics and biographers have extolled the riches of the *Alfoxden Journal*, written between 20 January and 22 May 1798 while living with William in Somerset, near Coleridge, and the *Grasmere Journal*, begun 14 May 1800 and "completed" (or set aside) 16 January 1803. These journals, as well as one she kept for a short time while in Hamburg with Coleridge and her brother in 1798, formed her writing portfolio before she left for Scotland.

Of the three travellers Coleridge had the least reason to question—if anyone did question—the timing of the trip and had most to gain by getting away now. All three had health problems. But Dorothy's recurring head-aches and bowel problems were hardly debilitating at this point in her life.[5] She seems, in fact, to have been in a robust state—if the evidence of all she tolerated on the Scottish tour speaks to her health. Wordsworth had a

4. Rosemary Ashton's *Life of Samuel Taylor Coleridge* is especially effective in exposing the German literary and philosophical works with which Coleridge concerned himself in the period before the 1803 Scottish tour, while duly noting the major religious and philosophical questions that had been raised by his readings of British thinkers (Hartley and Godwin, for example), as well as Plato, and by his early involvement in Unitarianism. See chapters 6, "To Germany and Back 1798–1800," and 7, "Greta Hall 1800–1802."
5. Although Dorothy Wordsworth lived a long life, dying in 1855, just after she turned eighty-five (surviving William, who died in 1850), she did not enjoy good health in her later years. In 1829 she suffered a sharp decline, and with some periods of remission, endured severe pain: probably, as biographers Robert Gittings and Jo Manton surmise, the conse-quence of a gall-bladder problem (*Dorothy Wordsworth*, p. 256). At her worst she needed to be transported in the "Family phaeton" or another makeshift carriage, vehicles sadly lacking in the mirthful associations of the Irish jaunting car of her Scottish tour. For the last twenty years of her life she suffered from what today would be diagnosed as Alzheimer's disease. Through this phase, which was characterized by long periods of derangement, she lived at Rydal Mount and, as Pamela Woof notes, was "cared for lovingly by William and Mary and the household at Rydal Mount" (*Dorothy Wordsworth, Writer*, p. 14).

tendency to feel ill without identifying a disease, but again, he was not suffering from a physical problem that necessitated getting away from home. Coleridge, on the other hand, was dealing with both gout and an opium addiction. His marriage was unhappy and he had fallen in love with Sara Hutchinson, Wordsworth's wife's younger sister. And in his creative and literary life he seemed to be floundering. Putting some distance between himself and his combative wife would relieve some of his stress. But more importantly, travelling with Dorothy and William in Scotland might restore not only some health but also a generative collaboration like the one he discovered with them in the South.

IV. "Poor Coleridge"

The charmed friendship of Dorothy, William and Coleridge did not work so well this summer. After all his efforts to supply the horse and Irish jaunting car, the Keswick partner did not complete the journey with the Wordsworths. Far more underlies Dorothy's recurrent epithet "Poor Coleridge" than her characteristic tact and good taste would permit her to betray in her recollections of their time together and of the occasions she thought of Coleridge after he struck out on his own. While the wit and brilliance of his conversation no doubt prevailed much of the time they were together, Coleridge was too physically ill to be thoroughly enjoyable company. He articulated his complaints in vivid detail, with the precision of a medical researcher. Any beneficiary of his reports would be alarmed, if not sickened. If the Wordsworths witnessed only a portion of his suffering, they would have felt some relief at his departure. As for Coleridge, he might have wished for privacy to avoid embarrassment.

Coleridge had been ill before the journey with what he was certain was "Atonic Gout." Shortly before leaving he wrote to Southey: "I have been very ill, & in serious dread of a paralytic Stroke in my whole left Side. Of my disease there now remains no Shade of Doubt: it is a compleat & almost heartless Case of Atonic Gout" (*Collected Letters*, II p. 974), referring Southey to an *Encyclopedia Britannica* article that confirms the diagnosis. His doctor, Mr. Edmondson, advised in favor of the trip, urging that "the Exercise & the Excitement" (p. 975) would offset the dangers of wet and cold and prescribing Carminative Bitters to relieve what Coleridge describes as "this truly poisonous, & body-&-soul-benumming Flatulence and Inflation" (p. 974).

But it is in a letter from Fort William to his wife Sara, sent after he had left the Wordsworths, that he reveals the kind of bodily suffering to which he might have exposed his travelling companions if he had remained with them. He had walked twenty-eight miles that day, he told Sara, when he stopped to scoop up water with his hand, repeatedly, to quench his thirst.

> —Soon after (in less than a furlong)—a pain & intense sense of fatigue fell upon me, especially within my Thighs—& great Torture in my bad Toe—However I dragged myself along; but when I reached the Town, I was forced to lean on the man that shewed me to my Inn . . . Mrs Munroe, the Landlady, had no room at all—and I could not stand— however she sent a boy with me to another little Inn, which I entered— & sitting down . . . an affair altogether of the Body, not of the mind—that I had, it was true, a torturing pain in all my limbs, but that this had nothing to do with my Tears which were hysterical & proceeded from the Stomach—. (p. 980)

He was served a bowl of tea, but "Before I could touch it, my Bowels were seized violently, & there . . . [a] Gallon of nasty water" (p. 981). One cannot help but be glad for Dorothy that she was spared such a crisis, with all its bodily spectacle.

Coleridge's physical condition was also complicated by his addiction to opium.[6] The agonizing bodily disruptions he describes in his letters of this period square all too well with the symptoms of addiction and withdrawal. In recent years Coleridge had been medicating himself, applying laudanum to the joints and taking it internally to relieve what appeared to be symptoms of gout; to this end, he would have purchased the locally manufactured Kendal Black Drop, an extra-strength laudanum solution advertised as a relief for a panoply of health problems. This, of course, was not the first time he had employed an addictive drug—whether labeled laudanum, morphine, or simply opium—prescribed for health reasons; nor was it the first time Coleridge welcomed the legitimacy of a disease like gout to mask a deeper psychological need for sedation. Coleridge had classic symptoms of dependency. On the Scottish tour, however, he appears to have taken a smaller amount of morphine with him, possibly to use the journey as an opportunity to take himself off this drug. His struggle to disguise his addiction from his travelling companions might have influenced his decision to withdraw from their company.

"Coleridge resolves to go home," Dorothy heads the fifteenth day of her table of contents for her journal. On the rainy day of 29 August, following an excursion to Loch Katrine and the Trossachs, the three landed at Tarbet, on Loch Lomond, and proceeded to Arrochar, where they dined at an inn and absorbed the view of The Cobbler across Loch Long. At 4:00, when the rain had stopped, they set out upon independent routes—the Wordsworths

---

6. Molly Lefebure offers a full-length study of Coleridge's struggle with addiction in her *Samuel Taylor Coleridge: A Bondage of Opium.*

to Cairndow and Coleridge, allegedly to Edinburgh and then home to Keswick. "We portioned out the contents of our purse before parting; and, after we had lost sight of him, drove heavily along" (p. 117), Dorothy wrote, not quite concealing the harshness of money matters from her sensibilities about separation.

What Coleridge subsequently gave as his reason for returning depended on his audience. The Wordsworths would have understood that, because dampness was a threat to his health, it was not wise for him to continue to be exposed to the elements in the open jaunting car. But in his letter to his wife (2 September 1803) he reveals: "We returned to E. Tarbet, I with the rheumatism in my head / and now William proposed to me to leave them, & make my way on foot, to Loch Ketterin[e], the Trossachs, whence it is only 20 miles to Stirling, where the Coach runs thro' for Edinburgh . . ." (p. 978). The same letter betrays both defensiveness and acrimony: "I eagerly caught the Proposal: for the *sitting* in an open Carriage in the Rain is Death to me, and somehow or other I had not been quite comfortable" (p. 978). The way the money had been divided did not set well with him either: "The worst thing was the money—they took 29 Guineas, and I six—all our remaining Cash!" (p. 978). When accounting to Sir George and Lady Beaumont for his departure from his companions, and their mutual friends, he gallantly took the blame entirely on himself: "I left Wordsworth & his Sister at Loch Lomond / I was so ill that I felt myself a Burthen on them / & the Exercise was too much for me, & yet not enough" (p. 994). In writing to Thomas Poole, Coleridge shifted some blame to Wordsworth: "I soon found that I was a burthen on them / & Wordsworth, himself a brooder over his painful hypochondriacal Sensations, was not my fittest companion . . ." (p. 1010).

Dorothy must have witnessed disturbing behavior: the polarizing of the two such distinct personalities could not have been easy to overlook. Yet she does not allude to their rift in her writing. On the contrary, her references to Coleridge suggest that she was concerned about his well being and often that she missed his company. In an odd way, Coleridge emerges as an *éminence grise* in her text—turning up in unexpected places in a kind of ghostly pattern. After the Arrochar separation, Coleridge continued to pop up—not live, but in reports from inns in the Highlands. When the Wordsworths arrived, they learned Coleridge had already had been there— perhaps just a few days before. He was like the child who runs away from home but leaves a distinct trail so that his family can still find him.

There were more surprises. Coleridge had not, after all, headed immediately to Edinburgh for a comfortable retreat to Keswick. Instead, he marshalled extraordinary strength and pursued his own journey, apparently welcoming the solitude and freedom. From Ballachulish he wrote to his wife that "having found myself so happy alone—such blessing is there in perfect

Liberty!— . . . I walked off" (p. 979). As Dorothy would later learn, his was a pedestrian journey to boast of. He walked 263 miles in eight days, averaging, he made clear to readers of his letters, over thirty a day. He accumulated adventures that made good tales, like being taken for a spy and clapped into jail in Fort Augustus (p. 982), or burning his shoes at a fire while trying to dry them and then facing the prospect of travelling barefoot until money arrived from home to buy new ones. On the dark side, his lonely if athletic excursion was haunted by opium-related nightmares. He described his pain to Southey: "[M]y spirits are dreadful, owing entirely to the Horrors of every night—I truly dread to sleep / it is no shadow with me, but substantial Misery foot-thick, that makes me sit by my bedside of a morning, & *cry*—" (p. 982). Having professed abstinence ("I have abandoned all opiates except Ether be one; & that only in *fits*" (p. 982)), he offers "a true portrait of my nights" (p. 984) in the form of a poem later to be called "The Pains of Sleep." The work is a veritable exposition of his anguish and agony, weaving fear, guilt, shame, terror, screaming, crying, self-loathing, and powerlessness in verse that signals alarm to a stable reader.

Dorothy would not learn of Coleridge's actual troubles and travels until they were reunited in the Lakes. For the duration of her own journey, with her brother as sole companion, her thoughts of "poor Coleridge" could only have been complex. What was he doing in the Highlands when his health dictated rest? Had she contributed to the problem between the two men because she sometimes recited her brother's poems but never Coleridge's? While she may not have known a clinical term for Coleridge's addiction, or possessed a framework for examining a bi-polar personality, she was far too sensitive a human to misread the portrait of a troubled man.

She might have examined another parting of the ways on a journey. This was when they visited Germany, to study the language and immerse themselves in the culture. After they arrived money matters determined that the Wordsworths would live in the Hartz Mountains, while Coleridge settled ultimately at the university in Göttingen. Coleridge enjoyed a better social life and was able to enter into an intellectual environment; the Wordsworths were not invited to socialize with the better class of Germans and kept to themselves. The disparity was noted by Dorothy when she wrote to her brother Christopher, but seemed not to have been an open wound among the friends.

On the contrary, from the letters they exchanged it appeared most of all that they missed each other. Dorothy wept and kissed the letter when one arrived from Coleridge. And Coleridge wrote of his loneliness without them. However, when this sentiment came from Coleridge, it was laced with some self pity, an awe of Wordsworth, and an envy of the closeness between Dorothy and William—a sad, undignified package from so gifted a man. When Dorothy read the last lines of a poem Coleridge sent, she should have sensed a vulnerability: "William, my head and my heart! Dear William and dear Dorothea! / You have all in each other; but I am lonely, and want you!" (*Collected Letters*, I p. 452). But Dorothy would have been busy copying the new poems her brother was writing—that and keeping warm this coldest of winters in Germany.

It is fortunate she could not know the content of letters Coleridge sent to others. It would have hurt her to be cited as the cause of her brother's social rejection and to realize how their relationship had been perceived. For to his wife Coleridge had written: "His taking his Sister with him was a wrong Step—it is next to impossible for any but married women or in the suit of married women to be introduced to any company in Germany. Sister . . . is considered as only a name for Mistress" (p. 459).

If she had been able to look more deeply into the implications of Coleridge's excessive admiration for William she might have seen a need to spread her attentions as a literary friend a little more generously. In July 1797 Coleridge told Southey, "Wordsworth is a very great man—the only man, to whom at all times & in all modes of excellence I feel myself inferior . . ." (p. 334). His idolatry of William had worried his friends—Charles Lamb, Thomas Poole, the Wedgwood brothers (Thomas and Josiah); when the Wordsworths and Coleridge went their separate ways in Germany, these friends rejoiced. Yet the tendency continued, and even when toward the end of his stay in Germany Coleridge was weighing William's invitation to move north he still held to the feeling: as he told Poole, "It is painful to me too to think of not living near him; for he is a *good* and a *kind* man, & the only one whom in all things I feel my Superior . . ." (p. 491).

The hints of the moment when Coleridge would break away from the Wordsworths at Arrochar were there in the German episode. But the intervening years, with the growing complexity of their lives and friendships, may have obscured this past time. Dorothy accepted the darker side of Coleridge. Certainly, by the time she began writing her *Recollections*, her "poor Coleridge" were words with compound interest.

V. *The Crafting of her "Journal"*

Dorothy Wordsworth wrote her account of the Scottish tour over a period of some twenty months, starting in September 1803, soon after she returned to Dove Cottage. When her *Recollections of a Tour Made in Scotland*, A.D. *1803* was completed its style betrayed remarkable coherence, with a concern for ordering the entire work and providing it with a unity that would be both pleasing to and convenient for the reader. Still, traces of a change in tone and density that corresponded to an affecting event in her life—the death of her brother John at sea—gave the final third of her work a different complexion. The immediate audience she had in mind was one of friends and family. She wrote to her dear friend Mrs. Clarkson: "I had written it for the sake of Friends who could not [be] with us at the time, and my Brother John had been always in my thoughts, for we wished him to know every thing that befel us" (11 June 1805; *Letters*, I p. 598). It is hard to imagine that she did not conceive of a later generation of readers as well, considering that William was becoming well known as a poet and she was an acknowledged partner in his success.

In the first stretch of crafting her recollections she wrote from September until late December, when a long visit from Coleridge with his three-year-old son Derwent brought a hiatus. "Poor Coleridge" exhibited health problems after arriving and extended what was meant to be a social visit of a few days to a recovery period of a few weeks, during which time Dorothy took on extra nursing responsibilities. Her work proceeded through stops and starts from 2 February through July of 1804. She began the last third of it in April 1805. In a "memorandum" at the end of her manuscript she notes rather precisely: "Finished this journal May 31st 1805 in the Moss Hut at the top of the orchard" (DC MS 54).

No doubt the lively population under the roof of Dove Cottage took her away from her writing often enough. Little John, the firstborn, was developing into a toddler; a niece, Dorothy's namesake and the only girl, was born in August of 1804; her sister-in-law, so often described as "thin" during this period, depended upon her for help with the children; and William needed her to copy his poems, including parts of *The Prelude* on which he was currently working. A cat was introduced into the household as a companion for Johnny and a deterrent to the growing number of rats. If Rover and the kitten mentioned in the sonnet Dorothy wrote as she neared Grasmere at the end of the Scottish tour were still under the roof, animals abounded. Servants came and went—"old Molly" easing out of the picture and a younger woman, Sally Ashburner, entering to take her place. Visitors came and went, including Mrs. Coleridge with her three children. And one wonders how often the following scene was re-enacted: Dorothy must stop writing a letter to a friend because, "William is calling to me every instant to hear some lines he is writing" (21 November 1803; *Letters*, I p. 423). Had the shed—the "Moss Hut"—not been erected above the cottage, Dorothy, without a retreating spot, might have taken even longer with her journal.

"Journal" was the name she used only after qualifying it, explaining to Mrs. Clarkson: "By the bye I am writing not a journal, for we took no notes, but *recollections* of our Tour in the form of a journal" (13 November 1803; p. 421). If she had some criteria to work with, they were in the negative: she was *not* going to produce travel writing. "I think journals of Tours except as far as one is interested in the travellers are very uninteresting things. Wretched, wretched writing! I can hardly read it myself" (p. 421). What she did write then, she hoped, was consciously about the travellers more than about the places and routes, not realizing, perhaps, at this early stage of her book that sometimes the one may not be separated from the other and that the fusion made for some of her most entertaining prose.

Her protestations to Mrs. Clarkson to the contrary, Dorothy did take occasional notes. A Dove Cottage Library manuscript (Journal MS 7 DC MS 54) of a single folded sheet of paper, 10.5 × 8.5 cm., written in pencil, records some events of the early part of the tour: "4th, 5th and 6th Days of Tour. Brownhill to Leadhills. Aug. 18th to 20th." She notes that they "Dined drank tea and supped and slept at Brownhill—a lone house—fine Beechtree—Thursday . . . Shepherd reading under his plaid." No doubt there were many more such jottings in rough form. Her sense of not having kept a consistent record *did* trouble her as she wrote *Recollections*. When she cannot summon distinct images of hills she passed travelling along the Tweed she writes, "I now at this distance of time regret that I did not take notes" (p. 202). And earlier, in recounting her experience with a Highland driver who could rattle off the names of "every hill; almost every rock" (p. 151), she feels compelled to confess, "partly from laziness, and still more because it was inconvenient, I took no notes, and now I am little better for what he told me" (p. 151). The rocks and hills would have filled a scrap of paper had her stamina been at its peak and writing conditions favorable. Her propensity to be specific demanded documentation.

She had a map to work from as well, and at least one guide book in reconstructing her tour. Discussing the area of Blair she writes, "Being come to the most northerly point of our destined course, we took out the map . . ." (p. 167). Maps had engaged her imagination even before she began the journey. When she arrived at the first sea-loch she had ever seen, she measured reality against anticipation: "Often have I, in looking over a map of Scotland, followed the intricate windings of one of these sea-lochs, till, pleasing myself with my own imaginations, I have felt a longing, almost painful, to travel among them by land or by water" (p. 117).

Recognizing the evocative powers of cartography, she made her own sketches, integrating them into her manuscript. Drawn freehand, they especially particularized bodies of water, giving full value to their curves and sweeps. One is a simple, continuous, wildly sweeping line entitled "Windings of the River Tummel." It is an exaggerated depiction of the flow of the river, but Dorothy's sketch is meant to be expressive of a "glassy river" that glided "not in serpentine windings, but in direct turnings backwards and forwards" (pp. 168, 169). Her drawing is copied from "a rough sketch which I made while we sate upon the hill" and is significant because it raises the question of how many other rough sketches, verbal or pictorial, might have been made on the spot throughout the journey.

The maps she drew, each covering a whole page of her manuscript, tended to combine the correctness that would come from reference to an official map, and the personalization one would expect an author to give places she had visited. Of the six maps, three featured the area of the Trossachs and Loch Katrine which she chose to visit twice, obviously finding it romantic, wild, and exciting. Her sense of its beauty and sublimity seemed to come from an independent vision and anticipated a flood of tourism. Scott had not yet published *The Lady of the Lake* (1810) or *Rob Roy* (1817), both of which popularized the area for generations of readers and travellers. By the 1840s the Trossachs and Loch Katrine were to become major visitors' sites, with the first Cook's tours invading the seclusion with prophetic energy.

In 1803 the area was still relatively untouched. "A laugh was on every face" when William told the residents of Glengyle that they had come to see the Trossachs, and Dorothy realized "no doubt they thought we had better have stayed at our own homes" (p. 97). William had to point out that it "was a place much celebrated in England." Lush, rough, and not easily accessible, the area appealed to the more daring and artistic wayfarer. In fact, John Stoddart, whose *Remarks on Local Scenery and Manners of Scotland during the Years 1799 and 1800*, popularly known as "Stoddart's Tour," Dorothy had read and alluded to, said very little about the Trossachs; he gave more attention to the fact that "noble proprietors" created some paths "at considerable expence" (*Remarks*, II p. 307) so that the traveller might view the lake than to the wonders that might be discovered by a romantic traveller.

Another travel writer, the intrepid Sarah Murray, however, tapped just the resource of wilderness that would have appealed to literary personalities. With the instincts of a professional travel writer she sought out "the surrounding scenes of Loch Catherine, which, I have been informed, were more romantic than any other in Scotland" (*A Companion*, I p. 158), and waxed ecstatic in the account of her visit, which was charged with words like "awfulness," "solemnity," "sublimity," and "gloomy." While no Wordsworth would have approved of Mrs. Murray's style, Dorothy, at least, would have endorsed her enthusiasm. Dorothy's responses to the Trossachs–Loch Katrine area are no less excited than Mrs. Murray's, but they are more thoughtfully authenticated and enlarged by personal interaction with the landscape itself as well as the native residents. Her map labels are the homespun "Den of the Ghosts hereabouts," "Mr. MacFarlane's," "Ferryhouse," and "Resting place." However her cartography might have been influenced by a professional map in her possession, it bears the mark of her humanizing narrative. Her stories about the Macfarlanes, the (misinformed) visit to Rob Roy's grave, the encounters with highland girls, the sight of a solitary reaper—all allowed her readers to experience, as if they were there, the character of genuine Scottish life.

Beyond her narratives, there are her brother's poems: she incorporates into her manuscript early versions of the as yet unpublished works that celebrate the Scottish experience they shared. "To a Highland Girl," "Stepping Westward," and "The Solitary Reaper" preserve, in the inimitable Wordsworth idiom, the particular excellence of a native Highlander, in each case a female. And "Rob Roy's Grave" aligned the writer with the loyalties and lore of the land, as did "Glen Almain," which marked with respect the supposed resting place of Ossian. That later readers would learn that one poem—"The Solitary Reaper"—had been suggested by a line by Thomas Wilkinson, and that another—"Rob Roy's Grave"—was based upon a visit to the wrong burial place does not take away from the fact that Dorothy meant them to be illustrative of her journal.

In crafting the *Recollections* Dorothy provided some structuring and editorial formatting so that though the piece was written over a period of time, it had order. Her role thus shifted from being a journal writer to being the maker of a book. She created a day-place-page directory for the beginning of the book and provided a list of distances from place to place. And she divided the work as a whole into three sections: Part I, Aug. 14–25; Part II, Aug. 26–Sept. 5; and Part III, Sept. 6–26. Perhaps her most intrusive editorial gestures are the "Memorandum" (p. 161) in which she announces the three-part division and the explanatory note dated "April 11th, 1805," in which she accounts for a change in tone and style to come in the pages to follow—in effect, the final third of her book. Both assume an understanding of the fact that her brother, Captain John Wordsworth, went down with his ship, the *Earl of Abergavenny*, on 5 February 1805. His death had weighed heavily on her and both dampened her spirits and stalled her productivity.

As she resumed her writing of the *Recollections* Dorothy was to make a concession to the family tragedy: she would take some shortcuts, giving up her original commitment "to omit no incident, however trifling, and to describe the country so minutely that you should, when the objects were the most interesting, feel as if you had been with us" (p. 162). With the change in intention came the advantage that she could avoid redundancy, since she would be going over some of the same territory (for example, the Trossachs) she had already described. She will write, from the twenty-second day of the journey to the end, about "those scenes which pleased us most, dropping the incidents of the ordinary days" (p. 162).

Yet another device for organizing as well as for condensing the incidents in the last third of her book was to refer to "Stoddart's Tour." This work, some editions of which were illustrated and contained a map, was well known to the Wordsworths and their circle. Stoddart was the mutual friend of Wordsworth, Scott, and Coleridge. He called Wordsworth "much my friend" (*Remarks*, I p. 208) and quoted his poetry in his book. It was he who urged Coleridge to come to Malta, where from 1803 to 1807 Stoddart was the King's and Admiralty's Advocate. When Coleridge writes to his wife from Ballachulish Ferry about his solo Scottish adventures, therefore, it is with confidence in familiarity that he refers to "Stoddart's Tour, where there is a very good view of Dumbarton Rock & Tower" (*Collected Letters*, II p. 977). Dorothy occasionally cites Stoddart's work rather than give her own description. To give a picture of the Fall of Tummel she points out, "Stoddart's print gives no notice of it" (p. 172), assuming all her readers have access to Stoddart's book. Some editions (an example is in the Glasgow University Library) contained hand-tinted prints, and the Wordsworths and their friends would have known or owned these copies. When it came to assessing Stirling Castle Dorothy resorted to another abbreviation, noting: "The rock or hill rises from a level plain; the print in Stoddart's book does indeed give a good notion of its form" (p. 195). Again, rather than tackle Holyrood House in Edinburgh she writes, "you have a description of it in Stoddart's Tour, therefore I need not tell you what we saw there" (p. 198).

If Stoddart provided ellipses for Dorothy's description, Walter Scott offered routing for her return trip from Edinburgh and Midlothian, south through what would eventually come to be known to tourists as the "Scott country." The Wordsworths travelled with an agenda casually determined by Scott, who though not yet *Sir* Walter, was well known, indeed beloved, and as Sheriff of Selkirk, influential. Scott provided not only tips on where to go and what to see, but a "passport" to preferential treatment, and ultimately, accommodations in a private home in Jedburgh, which was crowded with people attending the courts because of the assizes. Visits and encounters with this cordial local celebrity occupied significant space in Dorothy's account and permitted her to write in a documentary mode when sadness over the death of her brother John made the pleasurable recollection of private experience difficult. Attention to Scott, however important it would prove as information for literary scholars, was a kind of avoidance for Dorothy, and certainly a shortcut, since so many of the places visited on account of Scott were too well known to warrant another effort at description.

Recollections was admired by readers almost from the start. Circulating among friends in manuscript form, the verbal pictures, so often compared to Lake District scenes, and the personal accounts of the travel experiences, fascinated an already interested audience. Coleridge looked forward to reading a copy when he returned from Malta. Publication was inevitable, despite Dorothy's apparent reticence about public exposure. One of the first to promote the idea of commercial publication was Samuel Rogers, whom the Wordsworths and Coleridge had met in Scotland in 1803, where he was travelling with his sister. Rogers had read a manuscript, possibly in 1812, when he visited the Wordsworths in the Lake District. In September 1822 William wrote to him to ask that he pursue a publisher for the *Recollections*.

He reminded Rogers that "Some time ago you expressed (as perhaps you will remember) a wish that my Sister would publish her Recollections of the Scotch Tour, and you interested yourself so far in the scheme, as kindly to offer to assist in disposing of it to a Publisher for her advantage" (*Letters*, III p. 152).

Dorothy had been in Scotland again for a second Scottish tour of seven weeks with Joanna Hutchinson when a response from Rogers arrived. On 3 January of the new year she wrote to him to say she was "flattered" by his "thinking so well of my Journal as to recommend (indirectly at least) that I should not part with all power over it till its fortune has been tried," and to ask if he might find a bookseller who would take her copyright for a sum and publish "a given number of copies," adding, "I find it next to impossible to make up my mind to sacrifice my privacy for a certainty *less* than two hundred pounds, a sum which would effectually aid me in accomplishing the ramble [to Italy] I so much, and I hope not unwisely, wish for." With this businesslike proposition—such that Rogers would also receive a share of the profits—Dorothy accepted the idea of publication on practical grounds: it would bring in some money for further travel abroad. Though her most recent Scottish tour would have been freshest in her memory, she began to revise her 1803 "journal" of her first trip for publication. Apparently Rogers was not successful in locating a publisher or working out an arrangement through a bookseller, for her work did not go through the press until after her death.

It was the Scottish principal of United College, St. Andrews, later professor of poetry at Oxford, John Campbell Shairp, LL.D., who first edited the work for commercial publication in 1874. He brought to her manuscript a profound and informed sensitivity to Wordsworth's poetry and a love of the landscape of his own Scotland. More importantly, "Principal Shairp," as later editors referred to him, valued Dorothy herself sufficiently to write the first substantial biographical sketch of her for his Preface. In a critical appraisal of her writing that belies an era so greatly pre-dating feminist awareness, he notes,

> there is the most absolute sincerity, the most perfect fidelity to her own experience, the most single-minded endeavour to set down precisely the things they saw and heard and felt, just as they saw and heard and felt them, while moving on their quiet way. And hence perhaps the observant reader who submits himself to the spirit that pervades this Journal may find in its effortless narrative a truthfulness, a tenderness of observation, a "vivid exactness," a far-reaching and suggestive insight, for which he might look in vain in more studied productions. (Preface to *Recollections*, pp. xxxi–xxxii)

It was not only that she greeted events with her spirit and recorded them with integrity that impressed Shairp; she offered a valuable historical picture of Scotland in 1803. "It [*Recollections*] marks the state of Scotland, and the feeling with which the most finely gifted Englishmen came to it seventy years since, at a time before the flood of English interest and 'tourism' had set across the Border" (p. xxxii).

Shairp's first edition (Edinburgh University Press), with its ample Preface, signed "Cuilaluinn, June 1874," sold so well that a second edition followed soon afterwards, published both in the United States (New York: Putnam's) and Great Britain (Edinburgh: Edmonston and Douglas) with an added Preface signed "Cuilaluinn, August 1874." Twenty years later, a third edition (Edinburgh: David Douglas, 1894) appeared, with the original Preface and the same text as the second edition. At the turn of the century, in 1897, *Recollections* came out again as part of William Knight's *Journals of Dorothy Wordsworth*. Echoing Shairp, though in comparatively limpid prose, Knight claimed, "It will always hold a place of honour in itinerary literature. It possesses a singular charm, and has abiding interest, not only as a record of travel, but also as a mirror of Scottish life and character nearly a hundred years ago" (p. xi). In 1941 another round of critical admiration came from Ernest de Selincourt when he brought out his first edition of *Journals of Dorothy Wordsworth*, which included the Scottish tour. De Selincourt deemed *Recollections* "one of the most delightful of all books of travel, and it is, undoubtedly her masterpiece" (p. vii).

I have adopted here the Shairp edition of Dorothy Wordsworth's tour,[7] as I consider it the most readable of the three published editions. Knight simply reproduces Shairp's work; while de Selincourt makes few significant changes but reverts to an arrangement of the text in the three parts into which Dorothy Wordsworth originally divided it, based on her periods of composition rather than the narrative of the text. Shairp exhibited the kind of good judgment a fine editor must have when considering how to present a travel book for a general audience. It was he who divided her long blocks of prose, which ran without indentation, into paragraphs—a task from which Knight and de Selincourt benefitted without giving credit—, organized her account into a week-by-week structure, and spelled out "William" and "Coleridge" where she had used the abbreviations "Wm" and "C." Shairp also toned down some of her prose by occasionally eliminating her underlining, so that fewer words than originally intended by her ended up in italics, with the result that those that did, seemed more emphatic, and he did not print every sentence she wrote.

Dorothy Wordsworth's first manuscript was lost. Fortunately, she had shared it with her friend Catherine Clarkson, who made a copy of it, and

7. Shairp's Notes and Appendices are not included here: the relevant substance of these has been subsumed into the present author's own notes.

from the Clarkson copy Dorothy made another. This manuscript, DC MS 54 in the Dove Cottage collection, referred to as MS B by editors, is the one Shairp worked from. (Knight printed from Shairp, and de Selincourt returned to MS B, but borrowed some of Shairp's editing). Another copy, MSS C (Ci and Cii), in the hand of Sara Hutchinson, has not been published; nor has a fifth manuscript, MS D, transcribed by Dorothy and revised by William much later, in 1822–23, though MS D was produced with publication in mind.

Ms B is bound in red cardboard, with metal clasps and five stitches at the spine. It measures 23.1 × 19.1 × 2.8 cm., and runs to 242 pages, not including the itinerary at the beginning or notes at the end. Dorothy numbers her pages in the upper left or right, verso or recto, corners. The script, in sepia ink, is clear, with beautiful capital letters. Some corrections she made appear to be in darker ink; a few are in pencil. One sees her editing her own work, correcting herself on the over-use of intensifiers: for example, by crossing out "very" twice in the course of two pages. Her lines are tightly packed on the pages. One page contained 33 lines; most are 30–31 lines, with an average of 13 words per line.

Her hand-drawn maps, never before published, are curiously not even mentioned by Shairp, Knight, or de Selincourt, though they occupy a single page each and are bound with her manuscript and placed near relevant text.

A reconciliation of emendations, variant readings, dates of composition of particular parts, and comparative merits of the five manuscript versions of *Recollections* awaits the scholarly hand of Dorothy Wordsworth's present day editor, Pamela Woof.

SELECT BIBLIOGRAPHY

Ashton, Rosemary, *The Life of Samuel Taylor Coleridge*. Oxford: Blackwell Publishers Ltd, 1996.

Coleridge, Samuel Taylor, *Collected Letters of Samuel Taylor Coleridge*, I, *1785–1800*; II, *1801–1806*. Ed. Earl Leslie Griggs. Oxford: Clarendon Press, 1956. 6 vols., 1956–72.

——, *Notebooks of Samuel Taylor Coleridge*, I. Ed. Kathleen Coburn. Vols. I and II, New York: Pantheon, 1957. 4 vols. 1957—; vols. III and IV, Bollingen Series L. Princeton University Press.

——, *The Watchman*. Ed. Lewis Patton. London: Routledge & Kegan Paul, 1970. Vol. 2 of *The Collected Works of Samuel Taylor Coleridge*. Ed. Kathleen Coburn. Assoc. Ed. Bart Winer. Bollingen Series LXXV. Princeton University Press. 16 vols., 1969—.

Gill, Stephen, *William Wordsworth: A Life*. Oxford: Clarendon Press, 1989.

Gilpin, William, *Observations, Relative Chiefly to Picturesque Beauty, Made in the Year 1776, On Several Parts of Great Britain; Particularly the High-Lands of Scotland*. London: 1789. 2 vols.

Gittings, Robert, and Jo Manton, *Dorothy Wordsworth*. Oxford: Oxford University Press, 1988.

Keats, John, *The Letters of John Keats* 1814–1821. Ed. Hyder Edward Rollins. Cambridge, Mass.: Harvard University Press, 1958. 2 vols.

Knight, William, Prefatory Note to Dorothy Wordsworth: *Journals of Dorothy Wordsworth*, I. Ed. William Knight. London: Macmillan, 1904. 2 vols.; 1st ed. 1897.

Lefebure, Molly, *Samuel Taylor Coleridge: A Bondage of Opium*. London: Victor Gollancz Ltd, 1974.

Levin, Susan M., *Dorothy Wordsworth & Romanticism*. New Brunswick and London: Rutgers University Press, 1987.

Murray, Sarah (Aust), *A Companion and Useful Guide to the Beauties of Scotland, and the Hebrides, to the Lakes of Westmoreland, Cumberland, and Lancashire; and to the Curiosities in the District of Craven, in the West Riding of Yorkshire. Also a Description of Part of Scotland, Particularly of the Highlands; and of the Isles of Mull, Ulva, Staffa, I-Columbkill, Tirii, Coll, Eigg, Rum, Skye, Raza, and Scalpa. To which is Now Added, An account of the New Roads in Scotland, and of a Beautiful Cavern Lately Discovered in the Isle of Skye*. London: published by the author, 1810 (3rd ed.). 2 vols.

Pennant, Thomas, *A Tour in Scotland*. MDCCLXIX. Chester: 1771.

Reed, Mark, *Wordsworth: The Chronology of the Middle Years, 1800–1815*. Cambridge, Mass.: Harvard University Press, 1975.

Roe, Nicholas, *Wordsworth and Coleridge: The Radical Years*. Oxford: Clarendon Press, 1988.

Rogers, Samuel, *Recollections of the Table-Talk of Samuel Rogers*. Ed. Alexander Dyce. New Southgate: H.A. Rogers, 1887.

Selincourt, Ernest de. *See* Wordsworth, Dorothy.

Shairp, John Campbell. *See* Wordsworth, Dorothy.

Skrine, Henry, *Three Successive Tours in the North of England, and Great Part of Scotland*. London: W. Blumer, 1795.

Stoddart, Sir John, *Remarks on Local Scenery and Manners in Scotland during the Years 1799 and 1800*. London: W. Miller, 1801. 2 vols.

Tomes, John, *Blue Guide. Scotland*. London: A. & C. Black, 1986.

Woof, Pamela, *Dorothy Wordsworth, Writer*. Grasmere: The Wordsworth Trust, 1994.

Womack, Peter, *Improvement and Romance: Constructing the Myth of the Highlands*. Basingstoke: Macmillan, 1989.

Wordsworth, Dorothy, DC MS 54, Manuscript, "Recollections of a Tour, Made in Scotland A.D. 1803," Dove Cottage collection.

——, *The Grasmere Journals*. Ed. Pamela Woof. Oxford: Oxford University Press, 1993.

——, *Journals of Dorothy Wordsworth* I. Ed. Ernest de Selincourt. London: Macmillan, 1970. 2 vols.

——, *Recollections of a Tour Made in Scotland, A.D. 1803*. Ed. John Campbell. Shairp. Edinburgh: David Douglas. 3rd ed. 1894.

Wordsworth, William, and Dorothy Wordsworth, *Letters of William and Dorothy Wordsworth*, I, *The Early Years 1787–1805*. Arr. and ed. Ernest de Selincourt; revd. Chester L. Shaver. Oxford: Clarendon, 1967 (2nd ed.). ——, *The Later Years 1821–1828*, Part I. Revd., arr., and ed. Alan G. Hill. Oxford: Clarendon Press, 1978.

Wordsworth, William, *The Fenwick Notes*. Ed. Jared Curtis. London: Bristol Classical Press, 1993.

——, *Poetical Works of William Wordsworth*, I–III. Ed. Ernest de Selincourt and Helen Darbishire. Oxford: Clarendon Press, 1940–49. 5 vols.

——, *The Prelude, 1799, 1805, 1850*. Ed. Jonathan Wordsworth, M.H. Abrams, and Stephen Gill. New York and London: W.W. Norton, 1979.

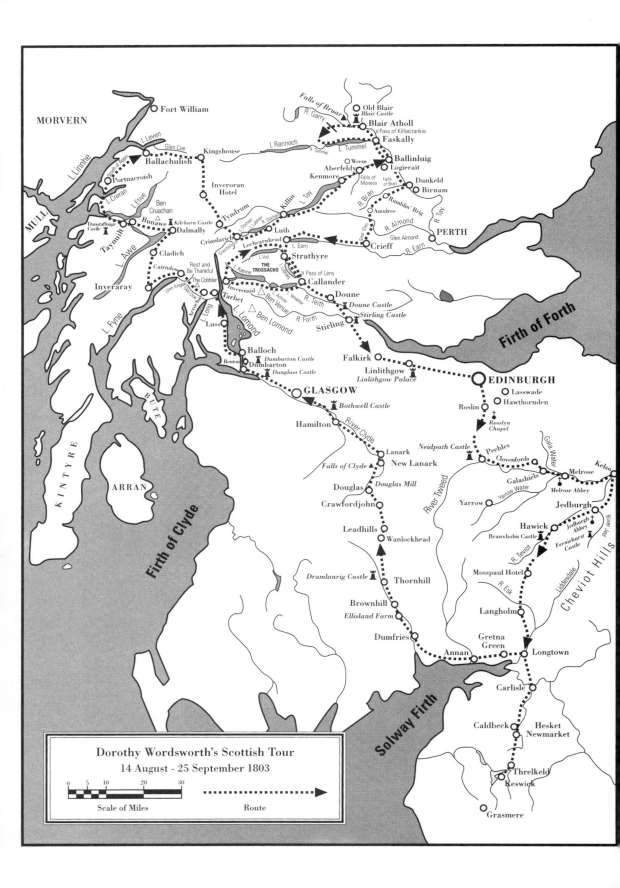

MORVERN

Fort William

L. Linnhe

L. Leven

Glen Coe

Kingshouse

Falls of Bruar

Old Blair
Blair Castle

R. Garry

Blair Atholl

Pass of Killiecrankie

L Rannoch

L. Tummel

Faskally

R. Tummel

MULL

Strath of Appin

Ballachulish

Portnacroish

L. Creran

L. Etive

Ben
Cruachan

Inveroran
Hotel

Ballinluig

Logierait

Aberfeldy

Weem

Kenmore

Falls of Moness

Falls
of Bran

Dunkeld

Birnam

R. Bran

Rumblin' Brig

R. Tay

R. Tay

L. Tay

Tyndrum

Killin

Amulree

R. Almond

PERTH

Dunstaffnage
Castle

Bunawe

Kilchurn Castle

Dalmally

R. Dochart

R. Lochay

R. Dochart

Luib

Glen Ogle

R. Almond

R. Tay

Taynuilt

L. Awe

Cladich

Crianlarich

Lochearnhead

L. Earn

Glen Almond

Crieff

R. Earn

Glen Falloch

Strath Tay

L. Voil

Strathyre

Pass of Leny

L. Katrine

THE
TROSSACHS

L. Achray

Pass of Leny

Cairndow

Rest and
Be Thankful

The Cobbler

Inversnaid

Ben Venue

Callander

Doune

Doune Castle

R. Teith

Glen Kinglas

Glen Croe

Tarbet

Ben Lomond

R. Teith

R. Forth

Stirling Castle

Inveraray

L. Fyne

Arrochar

L. Long

L. Lomond

Luss

Stirling

Falkirk

Firth of Forth

Balloch

Dumbarton Castle

Renton

Dumbarton

Dunglass Castle

Linlithgow

Linlithgow Palace

EDINBURGH

GLASGOW

Bothwell Castle

Roslin

Lasswade

Hawthornden

Hamilton

River Clyde

Rosslyn
Chapel

BUTE

Lanark

New Lanark

Neidpath Castle

Peebles

Clovenfords

Kelso

Falls of Clyde

Galashiels

Melrose

KINTYRE

Douglas

Douglas Mill

River Tweed

Yarrow Water

Melrose Abbey

ARRAN

Crawfordjohn

Yarrow

Jedburgh

Leadhills

Wanlockhead

Hawick

Jedburgh
Abbey

Branxholm Castle

Ferniehurst
Castle

Firth of Clyde

Drumlanrig Castle

Thornhill

Mosspaul Hotel

R. Teviot

Liddesdale

Cheviot Hills

Brownhill

Ellisland Farm

R. Esk

Langholm

Dumfries

Gretna
Green

Annan

Longtown

Solway Firth

Carlisle

Caldbeck

Hesket
Newmarket

Dorothy Wordsworth's Scottish Tour
14 August - 25 September 1803

0   5   10   20   30

Scale of Miles   Route

Threlkeld

Keswick

Grasmere

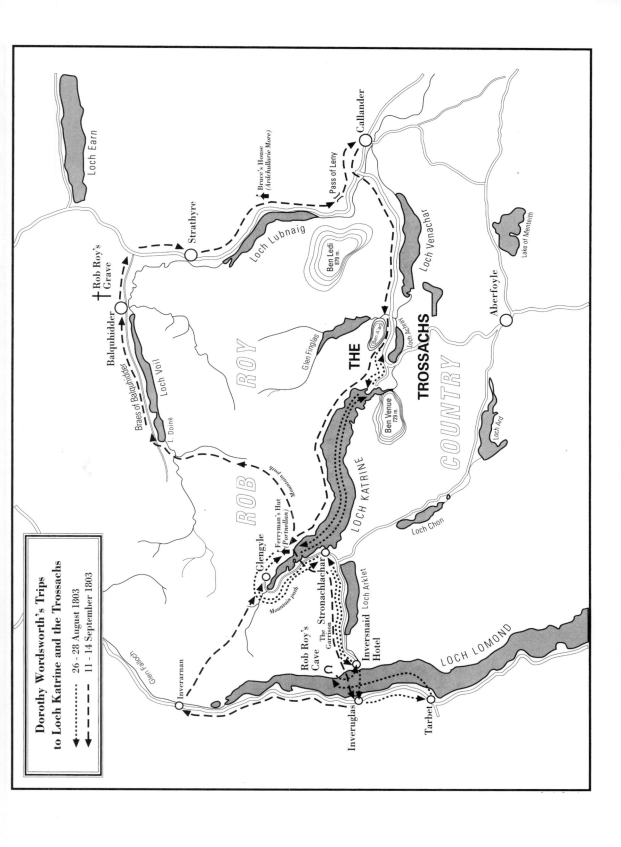

Dorothy Wordsworth's Trips
to Loch Katrine and the Trossachs

- - - - ▶ 26 – 28 August 1803
━━━ ▶ 11 – 14 September 1803

Loch Earn

Strathyre

Bruce's House
(Ardchullarie More)

Pass of Leny

Callander

Loch Lubnaig

Ben Ledi
879 m.

Loch Venachar

Lake of Menteith

Aberfoyle

+ Rob Roy's
Grave

Balquhidder

Loch Voil

Braes of Balquhidder

L. Doine

ROY

Glen Finglas

Ben A'an

Loch Achray

THE

TROSSACHS

Ben Venue
729 m.

COUNTRY

Loch Ard

ROB

LOCH KATRINE

Mountain path

Loch Chon

Glengyle

Ferryman's Hut
(Portnellan)

Mountain path

Stronachlachar

Loch Arklet

Inversnaid
Hotel

Rob Roy's
Cave

The Garrison

Glen Falloch

Inverarnan

Inveruglas

Tarbet

LOCH LOMOND

RECOLLECTIONS OF A TOUR MADE IN SCOTLAND A.D. 1803

DOROTHY WORDSWORTH

CONTENTS

FIRST WEEK

SECOND WEEK

THIRD WEEK

FOURTH WEEK

FIFTH WEEK

SIXTH WEEK

DISTANCES FROM PLACE TO PLACE

	MILES		MILES
Grasmere to Keswick	3	Suie (road excellent)	13
Hesket Newmarket (road very bad)	15	Killin (tolerable)	7
		Kenmore (baddish)	15
Carlisle (bad road)	14	Blair (bad)	23
Longtown (newly mended, not good)	8	Fascally (wretchedly bad)	18
		Dunkeld (bad)	12
Annan (good)	14	Ambletress (hilly—good)	10
Dumfries (good)	15	Crieff (hilly—goodish)	11
Brownhill (pretty good)	12	Loch Erne Head (tolerable)	20
Leadhills (tolerable)	19	Callander (most excellent)	14
Douglass Mill (very bad)	12	Trossachs	16
Lanark (baddish)	9	Ferryman's House (about 8)	8
Hamilton (tolerable)	15	Callander to Falkirk (baddish road)	27
Glasgow (tolerable)	11		
Dumbarton (very good)	15	Edinburgh (good)	24
Luss (excellent)	13	Roslin (good)	6
Tarbet (not bad)	8	Peebles (good))	16
Arrochar (good)	2	Clovenford (tolerable)	16
Cairndow (middling)	12	Melrose (tolerable)	8
Inverary (very good)	10	Dryburgh (good)	4
Dalmally (tolerable)	16	Jedburgh (roughish)	10
Taynuilt (excellent)	13	Hawick (good)	12
Portnacroish (tolerable)	15	Langholm (very good)	24
Ballachulish (part most excellent)	12	Longtown (good)	12
		Carlisle	8
King's House (bad)	12	Grasmere	36
Tyndrum (good)	18		

FIRST WEEK

William and I parted from Mary on Sunday afternoon, August 14th, 1803; and William, Coleridge, and I left Keswick on Monday morning, the 15th, at twenty minutes after eleven o'clock. The day was very hot; we walked up the hills, and along all the rough road, which made our walking half the day's journey. Travelled under the foot of Carrock, a mountain covered with stones on the lower part; above, it is very rocky, but sheep pasture there; we saw several where there seemed to be no grass to tempt them. Passed the foot of Grisdale[1] and Mosedale, both pastoral valleys, narrow, and soon terminating in the mountains—green, with scattered trees and houses, and each a beautiful stream. At Grisdale our horse backed upon a steep bank where the road was not fenced, just above a pretty mill at the foot of the valley; and we had a second threatening of a disaster in crossing a narrow bridge between the two dales; but this was not the fault of either man or horse. Slept at Mr. Younghusband's public-house, Hesket Newmarket.[2] In the evening walked to Caldbeck Falls, a delicious spot in which to breathe out a summer's day—limestone rocks, hanging trees, pools, and water breaks—caves and caldrons which have been honoured with fairy names, and no doubt continue in the fancy of the neighbourhood to resound with fairy revels.

Tuesday, August 16th.—Passed Rose Castle upon the Caldew, an ancient building of red stone with sloping gardens, an ivied gateway, velvet lawns, old garden walls, trim flower-borders with stately and luxuriant flowers. We walked up to the house and stood some minutes watching the swallows that flew about restlessly, and flung their shadows upon the sunbright walls of the old building; the shadows glanced and twinkled, interchanged and crossed each other, expanded and shrunk up, appeared and disappeared every instant; as I observed to William and Coleridge, seeming more like living things than the birds themselves. Dined at Carlisle; the town in a bustle with

1. "Mungrisdale" today. Coleridge gives the route of the first day's journey as: "up the steep Hill to Threlkeld—turned off at the White Horse, under Saddleback to Grisdale . . . [and] so on to Carrock and Heskett Newmarket" (*Notebooks*, 1 p. 1426 16.7).
2. They spent the night at the Queen's Head, which Coleridge remembered in detail: "The sanded stone floor with the spitting Pot full of Sand Dust, two Pictures of Young Master & Miss with their round Birds' Eye & and parlour Dress, he with a paroquet on his hand, horizontal, the other hand pushed forward just below it—she with a rose in her uplifted perpend. hand, the other hand grasping it to support it in that Posture. The whole Room struck me as Cleanliness quarreling with Tobacco Ghosts—" (*Notebooks*, 1 p. 1426 16.7). Dickens also slept here, in 1857.

the assizes; so many strange faces known in former times and recognised, that it half seemed as if I ought to know them all, and, together with the noise, the fine ladies, etc., they put me into confusion. This day Hatfield was condemned.[1] I stood at the door of the gaoler's house, where he was; William entered the house, and Coleridge saw him; I fell into conversation with a debtor, who told me in a dry way that he was 'far over-learned,' and another man observed to William that we might learn from Hatfield's fate 'not to meddle with pen and ink.' We gave a shilling to my companion, whom we found out to be a friend of the family, a fellow-sailor with my brother John 'in Captain Wordsworth's ship.'[2] Walked upon the city walls, which are broken down in places and crumbling away, and most disgusting from filth. The city and neighbourhood of Carlisle disappointed me; the banks of the river quite flat, and, though the holms are rich, there is not much beauty in the vale from the want of trees—at least to the eye of a person coming from England, and, I scarcely know how, but to me the holms had not a *natural* look; there was something townish in their appearance, a dulness in their strong deep green. To Longtown—not very interesting, except from the long views over the flat country; the road rough, chiefly newly mended. Reached Longtown after sunset, a town of brick houses belonging chiefly to the Graham family. Being in the form of a cross and not long, it had been better called Crosstown. There are several shops, and it is not a very small place; but I could not meet with a silver thimble, and bought a halfpenny brass one. Slept at the Graham's Arms, a large inn. Here, as everywhere else, the people seemed utterly insensible of the enormity of Hatfield's offences; the ostler told William that he was quite a gentleman, paid every one genteelly, etc. etc. He and 'Mary' had walked together to Gretna Green; a heavy rain came on when they were there; a returned chaise happened to pass, and the driver would have taken them up; but 'Mr. Hope's' carriage was to be sent for; he did not choose to accept the chaise-driver's offer.

Wednesday, August 17th.—Left Longtown after breakfast. About half-a-mile from the town a guide-post and two roads, to Edinburgh and Glasgow; we took the lefthand road, to Glasgow. Here saw a specimen of the luxuriance of the heath-plant, as it grows in Scotland; it was in the enclosed plantations—perhaps sheltered by them. These plantations appeared to be not well grown for their age; the tress were stunted. Afterwards the road,

1. See Appendix I.
2. John Wordsworth, Dorothy's beloved younger brother (born 1772), celebrated in some of William's poems, had gone to sea in 1788. By 1791 John was "in the service of the East India Company [and] had sailed to the Orient in the *Earl of Abergavenny*, a merchantman part-owned by John Robinson and commanded by his cousin Captain John Wordsworth" (Stephen Gill, *William Wordsworth: A Life*, Oxford: Clarendon, 1989, p. 51).

treeless, over a peat-moss common—the Solway Moss; here and there an earth-built hut with its peat stack, a scanty growing willow hedge round the kailgarth, perhaps the cow pasturing near,—a little lass watching it,—the dreary waste cheered by the endless singing of larks.

We enter Scotland by crossing the river Sark; on the Scotch side of the bridge the ground is unenclosed pasturage; it was very green, and scattered over with that yellow flowered plant which we call grunsel; the hills heave and swell prettily enough; cattle feeding; a few corn fields near the river. At the top of the hill opposite is Springfield, a village built by Sir William Maxwell—a dull uniformity in the houses, as is usual when all built at one time, or belonging to one individual, each just big enough for two people to live in, and in which a family, large or small as it may happen, is crammed. There the marriages are performed. Further on, though almost contiguous, is Gretna Green, upon a hill and among trees. This sounds well, but it is a dreary place; the stone houses dirty and miserable, with broken windows. There is a pleasant view from the churchyard over Solway Firth to the Cumberland mountains. Dined at Annan. On our left as we travelled along appeared the Solway Firth and the mountains beyond, but the near country dreary. Those houses by the roadside which are built of stone are comfortless and dirty; but we peeped into a clay 'biggin' that was very 'canny,' and I daresay will be as warm as a swallow's nest in winter. The town of Annan made me think of France and Germany; many of the houses large and gloomy, the size of them outrunning the comforts. One thing which was like Germany pleased me: the shopkeepers express their calling by some device or painting; bread-bakers have biscuits, loaves, cakes painted on their window-shutters; blacksmiths horses' shoes, iron tools, etc. etc.; and so on through all trades.

Reached Dumfries at about nine o'clock—market-day; met crowds of people on the road, and every one had a smile for us and our car . . . The inn was a large house, and tolerably comfortable; Mr. Rogers and his sister, whom we had seen at our own cottage at Grasmere a few days before, had arrived there that same afternoon on their way to the Highlands; but we did not see them till the next morning, and only for about a quarter of an hour.

Thursday, August 18th.—Went to the churchyard where Burns is buried. A bookseller accompanied us. He showed us the outside of Burns's house, where he had lived the last three years of his life, and where he died. It has a mean appearance, and is in a bye situation, whitewashed; dirty about the doors, as almost all Scotch houses are; flowering plants in the windows.

Went on to visit his grave. He lies at a corner of the churchyard, and his second son, Francis Wallace, beside him. There is no stone to mark the spot;[1] but a hundred guineas have been collected, to be expended on some sort of monument. 'There,' said the bookseller, pointing to a pompous monument, 'there lies Mr. Such-a-one'—I have forgotten his name,—'a remarkably clever man; he was an attorney, and hardly ever lost a cause he undertook. Burns made many a lampoon upon him, and there they rest, as you see.' We looked at the grave with melancholy and painful reflections, repeating to each other his own verses:—

> Is there a man whose judgment clear
> Can others teach the course to steer,
> Yet runs himself life's mad career
>   Wild as the wave?—
> Here let him pause, and through a tear
>   Survey this grave.
> The poor Inhabitant below
> Was quick to learn, and wise to know,
> And keenly felt the friendly glow
>   And softer flame;
> But thoughtless follies laid him low,
>   And stain'd his name.[2]

The churchyard is full of grave-stones and expensive monuments in all sorts of fantastic shapes—obelisk-wise, pillar-wise, etc. In speaking of Gretna Green, I forgot to mention that we visited the churchyard. The church is like a huge house;[3] indeed, so are all the churches, with a steeple, not a square tower or spire,—a sort of thing more like a glass-house chimney than a Church of England steeple; grave-stones in abundance, few verses, yet there were some—no texts. Over the graves of married women the maiden name instead of that of the husband, 'spouse' instead of 'wife,' and the place of abode preceded by 'in' instead of 'of.' When our guide had left us, we turned again to Burns's house. Mrs. Burns was gone to spend some time by the sea-shore with her children. We spoke to the servant-maid at the door, who invited us forward, and we sate down in the parlour. The walls were coloured with a blue wash; on one side of the fire was a mahogany desk,

1. Burns died 21 July 1796 and was buried in a modest grave in a corner of St. Michael's Churchyard, Dumfries. His funeral was most dramatic, with his pregnant wife going into labor during the ceremony. There was no money for an elaborate tombstone, though some time after Dorothy Wordsworth's visit Mrs. Burns provided a simple stone with the poet's name and age on it, and in 1813 a subscription was opened to raise money for a mausoleum. In 1815 Burns's remains were moved to the conspicuous new monument; the original tombstone was buried under the monument.
2. Stanzas II and IV of Burns's "A Bard's Epitaph."
3. Her reference here is ambiguous. Both churches—the one in Gretna Green and St. Michael's in Dumfries—fit the description.

opposite to the window a clock, and over the desk a print from the 'Cotter's Saturday Night,' which Burns mentions in one of his letters having received as a present. The house was cleanly and neat in the inside, the stairs of stone, scoured white, the kitchen on the right side of the passage, the parlour on the left. In the room above the parlour the Poet died, and his son after him in the same room. The servant told us she had lived five years with Mrs. Burns, who was now in great sorrow for the death of 'Wallace.' She said that Mrs. Burns's youngest son was at Christ's Hospital.

We were glad to leave Dumfries, which is no agreeable place to them who do not love the bustle of a town that seems to be rising up to wealth. We could think of little else but poor Burns, and his moving about on that unpoetic ground. In our road to Brownhill, the next stage, we passed Ellisland at a little distance on our right, his farmhouse. We might there have had more pleasure in looking round, if we had been nearer to the spot; but there is no thought surviving in connexion with Burns's daily life that is not heart-depressing. Travelled through the vale of Nith, here little like a vale, it is so broad, with irregular hills rising up on each side, in outline resembling the old-fashioned valances of a bed. There is a great deal of arable land; the corn ripe; trees here and there—plantations, clumps, coppices, and a newness in everything. So much of the gorse and broom rooted out that you wonder why it is not all gone, and yet there seems to be almost as much gorse and broom as corn; and they grow one among another you know not how. Crossed the Nith; the vale becomes narrow, and very pleasant; corn fields, green hills, clay cottages; the river's bed rocky, with woody banks. Left the Nith about a mile and a half, and reached Brownhill, a lonely inn, where we slept. The view from the windows was pleasing, though some travellers might have been disposed to quarrel with it for its general nakedness; yet there was abundance of corn. It is an open country—open, yet all over hills. At a little distance were many cottages among trees, that looked very pretty. Brownhill is about seven or eight miles from Ellisland. I fancied to myself, while I was sitting in the parlour, that Burns might have caroused there, for most likely his rounds extended so far, and this thought gave a melancholy interest to the smoky walls. It was as pretty a room as a thoroughly dirty one could be—a square parlour painted green, but so covered over with smoke and dirt that it looked not unlike green seen through black gauze. There were three windows, looking three ways, a buffet ornamented with tea-cups, a superfine largeish looking-glass with gilt ornaments spreading far and wide, the glass spotted with dirt, some ordinary alehouse pictures, and above the chimney-piece a print in a much better style—as William guessed, taken from a painting by Sir Joshua Reynolds—of some lady of quality, in the character of Euphrosyne. 'Ay,' said the servant girl, seeing that we looked at it, 'there's many travellers would give a deal for that, it's more admired than any in the house.' We could not but smile; for the rest were such as may be found in the basket of any Italian image and picture hawker.

William and I walked out after dinner; Coleridge was not well, and slept upon the carriage cushions. We made our way to the cottages among the little hills and knots of wood, and then saw what a delightful country this part of Scotland might be made by planting forest trees. The ground all over heaves and swells like a sea; but for miles there are neither trees nor hedgerows, only 'mound' fences and tracts; or slips of corn, potatoes, clover—with hay between, and barren land; but near the cottages many hills and hillocks covered with wood. We passed some fine trees, and paused under the shade of one close by an old mansion that seemed from its neglected state to be inhabited by farmers. But I must say that many of the 'gentlemen's' houses which we have passed in Scotland have an air of neglect, and even of desolation. It was a beech, in the full glory of complete and perfect growth, very tall, with one thick stem mounting to a considerable height, which was split into four 'thighs,' as Coleridge afterwards called them, each in size a fine tree. Passed another mansion, now tenanted by a schoolmaster; many boys playing upon the lawn. I cannot take leave of the country which we passed through to-day, without mentioning that we saw the Cumberland mountains within half a mile of Ellisland, Burns's house, the last view we had of them. Drayton has prettily described the connexion which this neighbourhood has with ours when he makes Skiddaw say—

> Scurfell* from the sky,
> That Anadale† doth crown, with a most amorous eye,
> Salutes me every day, or at my pride looks grim,
> Oft threatning me with clouds, as I oft threatning him.[1]

These lines recurred to William's memory, and we talked of Burns, and of the prospect he must have had, perhaps from his own door, of Skiddaw and his companions, indulging ourselves in the fancy that we *might* have been personally known to each other, and he have looked upon those objects with more pleasure for our sakes. We talked of Coleridge's children and family, then at the foot of Skiddaw, and our own new-born John a few miles behind it; while the grave of Burns's son, which we had just seen by the side of his father, and some stories heard at Dumfries respecting the dangers his surviving children were exposed to, filled us with melancholy concern, which had a kind of connexion with ourselves. In recollection of this, William long afterwards wrote the following Address to the sons of the ill-fated poet:—

*Criffel. [D.W.]   †Annandale. [D.W.]

1. Michael Drayton (1563–1631). From "Poly-Olbion," The Thirtieth Song, ll. 203–206.

Ye now are panting up life's hill,
'Tis twilight time of good and ill,
And more than common strength and skill
      Must ye display,
If ye would give the better will
      Its lawful sway.

Strong-bodied if ye be to bear
Intemperance with less harm, beware,
but if your Father's wit ye share,
      Then, then indeed,
Ye Sons of Burns, for watchful care
      There will be need.

For honest men delight will take
To shew you favour for his sake,
Will flatter you, and Fool and Rake
      Your steps pursue,
And of your Father's name will make
      A snare for you.

Let no mean hope your souls enslave,
Be independent, generous, brave;
Your Father such example gave,
      And such revere,
But be admonished by his grave,
      And think and fear.[1]

Friday, August 19th.—Open country for a considerable way. Passed through the village of Thornhill, built by the Duke of Queensberry; the 'brother-houses' so small that they might have been built to stamp a character of insolent pride on his own huge mansion of Drumlanrigg, which is full in view on the opposite side of the Nith. This mansion is indeed very large; but to us it appeared like a gathering together of little things. The roof is broken into a hundred pieces, cupolas, etc., in the shape of casters, conjuror's balls, cups, and the like. The situation would be noble if the woods had been left standing; but they have been cut down not long ago, and the hills above and below the house are quite bare. About a mile and a half from Drumlanrigg is a turnpike gate at the top of a hill. We left our car with the man, and turned aside into a field where we looked down upon the Nith, which runs far below in a deep and rocky channel; the banks woody; the view pleasant down the river towards Thornhill, an open

1. William Wordsworth's "To the Sons of Burns, after Visiting the Grave of their Father. (August 14th, 1803)."

country—corn fields, pastures, and scattered trees. Returned to the turnpike house, a cold spot upon a common, black cattle feeding close to the door. Our road led us down the hill to the side of the Nith, and we travelled along its banks for some miles. Here were clay cottages perhaps every half or quarter of a mile. The bed of the stream rough with rocks; banks irregular, now woody, now bare; here a patch of broom, there of corn, then of pasturage; and hills green or heathy above. We were to have given our horse meal and water at a public-house in one of the hamlets we passed through, but missed the house, for, as is common in Scotland, it was without a sign-board. Travelled on, still beside the Nith, till we came to a turnpike house, which stood rather high on the hill-side, and from the door we looked a long way up and down the river. The air coldish, the wind strong.

We asked the turnpike man to let us have some meal and water. He had no meal, but luckily we had part of a feed of corn brought from Keswick, and he procured some hay at a neighbouring house. In the meantime I went into the house, where was an old man with a gray plaid over his shoulders, reading a newspaper. On the shelf lay a volume of the Scotch Encyclopædia, a History of England, and some other books. The old man was a caller by the way. The man of the house came back, and we began to talk. He was very intelligent; had travelled all over England, Scotland, and Ireland as a gentleman's servant, and now lived alone in that lonesome place. He said he was tired of his bargain, for he feared he should lose by it. And he had indeed a troublesome office, for coal-carts without number were passing by, and the drivers seemed to do their utmost to cheat him. There is always something peculiar in the house of a man living alone. This was but half-furnished, yet nothing seemed wanting for *his* comfort, though a female who had travelled half as far would have needed fifty other things. He had no other meat or drink in the house but oat bread and cheese—the cheese was made with the addition of seeds—and some skimmed milk. He gave us of his bread and cheese, and milk, which proved to be sour.

We had yet ten or eleven miles to travel, and no food with us. William lay under the wind in a corn-field below the house, being not well enough to partake of the milk and bread. Coleridge gave our host a pamphlet, 'The Crisis of the Sugar Colonies;'[1] he was well acquainted with Burns's poems. There was a politeness and a manly freedom in this man's manners which

1. Published in 1802, the pamphlet was written by James Stephen (1758–1832), master in chancery. Stephen ardently opposed slavery and both spoke and wrote against it. Having briefly visited Barbados, he had first-hand knowledge of how the slaves were treated in the sugar colonies. Coleridge held comparably strong anti-slavery convictions, actively campaigned against the slave trade, and advocated the boycott of sugar and rum. In a piece entitled "On the Slave Trade" for *The Watchman* (No. IV. Friday, 25 March 1796) he argued, "If only one tenth part among you who profess yourselves Christians; if one half only of the Petitioners; instead of bustling about with ostentatious sensibility, were to leave off—not all the West-India commodities—but only Sugar and Rum, the one useless and the other

pleased me very much. He told us that he had served a gentleman, a captain in the army—he did not know who he was, for none of his relations had ever come to see him, but he used to receive many letters—that he had lived near Dumfries till they would let him stay no longer, he made such havoc with the game; his whole delight from morning till night, and the long year through, was in field sports; he would be on his feet the worst days in winter, and wade through snow up to the middle after his game. If he had company he was in tortures till they were gone; he would then throw off his coat and put on an old jacket not worth half-a-crown. He drank his bottle of wine every day, and two if he had better sport than usual. Ladies sometimes came to stay with his wife, and he often carried them out in an Irish jaunting-car, and if they vexed him he would choose the dirtiest roads possible, and spoil their clothes by jumping in and out of the car, and treading upon them. 'But for all that'—and so he ended all—'he was a good fellow, and a clever fellow, and he liked him well.' he would have ten or a dozen hares in the larder at once, he half maintained his family with game, and he himself was very fond of eating of the spoil—unusual with true heart-and-soul sportsmen.

The man gave us an account of his farm where he had lived, which was so cheap and pleasant that we thought we should have liked to have had it ourselves. Soon after leaving the turnpike house we turned up a hill to the right, the road for a little way very steep, bare hills, with sheep.

After ascending a little while we heard the murmur of a stream far below us, and saw it flowing downwards on our left, towards the Nith, and before us, between steep green hills, coming along a winding valley. The simplicity of the prospect impressed us very much. There was a single cottage by the brook side; the dell was not heathy, but it was impossible not to think of Peter Bell's Highland Girl.[1]

pernicious—all this misery might be stopped." The line of thinking that had gained currency among some abolitionists was that in abstaining from the use of sugar and rum British citizens would save the lives of slaves on the sugar plantations. One advocate, William Fox, had worked out a probabilities formula: "A family that uses 5 lb. of sugar per week, with the proportion of rum, will, by abstaining from consumption 21 months, prevent the slavery or murder of one fellow creature; eight such families in $19\frac{1}{2}$ years prevent the slavery or murder of 100, and 38,000 would totally prevent the Slave Trade to supply our islands" (*An Address to the People of Great Britain, on the Propriety of Abstaining from West India Sugar and Rum.* Pamphlet, in its 26th ed. in 1793. See *The Watchman*, p. 138n).

Why Coleridge carried Stephen's pamphlet with him on the Scottish tour is as puzzling as how he selected his host to receive it on this occasion in the manner of the Ancient Mariner: "That moment that his face I see, / I know the man that must hear me."

1. In Wordsworth's tale "Peter Bell" (Part Third) a remorseful Peter remembers "A sweet and playful Highland girl" (l. 888) and her home:

> Her dwelling was a lonely house
> A cottage in a heathy dell.
> (ll. 891–92)

We now felt indeed that we were in Scotland; there was a natural peculiarity in this place. In the scenes of the Nith it had not been the same as England, but yet not simple, naked Scotland. The road led us down the hill, and now there was no room in the vale but for the river and the road; we had sometimes the stream to the right, sometimes to the left. The hills were pastoral, but we did not see many sheep; green smooth turf on the left, no ferns. On the right the heath-plant grew in abundance, of the most exquisite colour; it covered a whole hillside, or it was in streams and patches. We travelled along the vale without appearing to ascend for some miles; all the reaches were beautiful, in exquisite proportion, the hills seeming very high from being so near to us. It might have seemed a valley which nature had kept to herself for pensive thoughts and tender feelings, but that we were reminded at every turning of the road of something beyond by the coal-carts which were travelling towards us. Though these carts broke in upon the tranquillity of the glen, they added much to the picturesque effect of the different views, which indeed wanted nothing, though perfectly bare, houseless, and treeless.

After some time our road took us upwards towards the end of the valley. Now the steeps were heathy all around. Just as we began to climb the hill we saw three boys who came down the cleft of a brow on our left; one carried a fishing-rod, and the hats of all were braided with honeysuckles; they ran after one another as wanton as the wind. I cannot express what a character of beauty those few honeysuckles in the hats of the three boys gave to the place: what bower could they have come from? We walked up the hill, met two well-dressed travellers, the woman barefoot. Our little lads before they had gone far were joined by some half-dozen of their companions, all without shoes and stockings. They told us they lived at Wanlockhead, the village above, pointing to the top of the hill; they went to school and learned Latin, Virgil, and some of them Greek, Homer,[1] but when Coleridge began to inquire further, off they ran, poor things! I suppose afraid of being examined.

When, after a steep ascent, we had reached the top of the hill, we saw a village about half a mile before us on the side of another hill, which rose up above the spot where we were, after a descent, a sort of valley or hollow.

1. Wanlockhead, the highest village in Scotland, enjoyed the reputation of providing literacy, through a Reading Society and a library for the miners, established in 1756, encouraged by the success of the Miners' Library in nearby Leadhills. Miners' children received schooling. "The village had a schoolmaster by 1750. Education in the village followed the highly successful Scottish pattern of giving encouragement to those boys who showed signs of a high ability by preparing them for entry to university and, by the end of the eighteenth century, the village had achieved local renown on account of the singularly keen interests of its menfolk . . . During the first half of the nineteenth century the Rev Thomas Hastings, for forty years minister here assisted in the education of more than forty boys who entered the professions as surgeons, lawyers, teachers, ministers and clerks" (*All about Wanlockhead: A Brief History of Scotland's Highest Village.* Wanlockhead: Wanlockhead Museum Trust, 1989, p. 16).

Nothing grew upon this ground, or the hills above or below, but heather, yet round about the village—which consisted of a great number of huts, all alike, and all thatched, with a few larger slated houses among them, and a single modern-built one of a considerable size—were a hundred patches of cultivated ground, potatoes, oats, hay, and grass. We were struck with the sight of haycocks fastened down with aprons, sheets, pieces of sacking—as we supposed, to prevent the wind from blowing them away. We afterwards found that this practice was very general in Scotland. Every cottage seemed to have its little plot of ground, fenced by a ridge of earth; this plot contained two or three different divisions, kail, potatoes, oats, hay; the houses all standing in lines, or never far apart; the cultivated ground was all together also, and made a very strange appearance with its many greens among the dark brown hills, neither tree nor shrub growing; yet the grass and the potatoes looked greener than elsewhere, owing to the bareness of the neighbouring hills; it was indeed a wild and singular spot—to use a woman's illustration, like a collection of patchwork, made of pieces as they might have chanced to have been cut by the mantua-maker, only just smoothed to fit each other, the different sorts of produce being in such a multitude of plots, and those so small and of such irregular shapes. Add to the strangeness of the village itself, that we had been climbing upwards, though gently, for many miles, and for the last mile and a half up a steep ascent, and did not know of any village till we saw the boys who had come out to play. The air was very cold, and one could not help thinking what it must be in winter, when those hills, now 'red brown', should have their three months' covering of snow.

The village, as we guessed, is inhabited by miners; the mines belong to the Duke of Queensberry. The road to the village, down which the lads scampered away, was straight forward. I must mention that we met, just after we had parted from them, another little fellow, about six years old, carrying a bundle over his shoulder; he seemed poor and half starved, and was scratching his fingers, which were covered with the itch.[1] He was a miner's son, and lived at Wanlockhead; did not go to school, but this was probably on account of his youth. I mention him because he seemed to be a proof that there was poverty and wretchedness among these people, though we saw no other symptom of it; and afterwards we met scores of the inhabitants of this same village. Our road turned to the right, and we saw, at the

1. Scabies, a highly contagious skin disease caused by a mite that burrows under the skin, would have spread easily in the close working and living quarters of the miners and their families. Children are especially prone to it. Other health problems, such as scurvy, the result of vitamin deficiencies, apparently came to the attention of the local physician. "No doubt the immensely popular doctor who practiced in Wanlockhead towards the end of the eighteenth century owed some of his success in diagnosis to his knowledge of the effect of lack of fresh vegetables, as he had once served as a ship's surgeon" (*All about Wanlockhead*, p. 7).

distance of less than a mile, a tall upright building of grey stone, with several men standing upon the roof, as if they were looking out over battlements. It stood beyond the village, upon higher ground, as if presiding over it,—a kind of enchanter's castle, which it might have been, a place where Don Quixote would have gloried in. When we drew nearer we saw, coming out of the side of the building, a large machine or lever, in appearance like a great forge-hammer, as we supposed for raising water out of the mines.[1] It heaved upwards once in half a minute with a slow motion, and seemed to rest to take breath at the bottom, its motion being accompanied with a sound between a groan and 'jike.' There would have been something in this object very striking in any place, as it was impossible not to invest the machine with some faculty of intellect; it seemed to have made the first step from brute matter to life and purpose, showing its progress by great power. William made a remark to this effect, and Coleridge observed that it was like a giant with one idea. At all events, the object produced a striking effect in that place, where everything was in unison with it—particularly the building itself, which was turret-shaped, and with the figures upon it resembled much one of the fortresses in the wooden cuts of Bunyan's 'Holy War.'

After ascending a considerable way we began to descend again; and now we met a team of horses dragging an immense tree to the lead mines, to repair or add to the building, and presently after we came to a cart, with another large tree, and one horse left in it, right in the middle of the highway. We were a little out of humour, thinking we must wait till the team came back. There were men and boys without number all staring at us; after a little consultation they set their shoulders to the cart, and with a good heave all at once they moved it, and we passed along. These people were decently dressed, and their manners decent; there was no hooting or impudent laughter. Leadhills, another mining village, was the place of our destination for the night; and soon after we had passed the cart we came in sight of it. This village and the mines belong to Lord Hopetoun; it has more stone houses than Wanlockhead, one large old mansion, and a considerable number of old trees—beeches, I believe. The trees told of the coldness of the climate; they were more brown than green—far browner than the ripe grass of the little hay-garths. Here, as at Wanlockhead, were haycocks, hay-stacks, potato-beds, and kail-garths in every possible variety of shape, but, I suppose from the irregularity of the ground, it looked far less artificial—indeed, I should think that a painter might make several beautiful pictures in this village. It straggles down both sides of a mountain glen. As I have said, there is a large mansion. There is also a stone building that looks

1. The Watt steam engine, which Dorothy Wordsworth saw, was the second to be built (with the assistance of local engineer George Symington) in Scotland, in 1788; it was to be replaced in 1834 by water pressure engines, of which the beam engine, preserved in Wanlockhead today, is an example.

like a school, and the houses are single, or in clusters, or rows as it may chance.

We passed a decent-looking inn, the Hopetoun Arms; but the house of Mrs. Otto, a widow, had been recommended to us with high encomiums. We did not then understand Scotch inns, and were not quite satisfied at first with our accommodations, but all things were smoothed over by degrees; we had a fire lighted in our dirty parlour, tea came after a reasonable waiting; and the fire with the gentle aid of twilight, burnished up the room into cheerful comfort. Coleridge was weary; but William and I walked out after tea. We talked with one of the miners, who informed us that the building which we had supposed to be a school was a library belonging to the village. He said they had got a book into it a few weeks ago, which had cost thirty pounds, and that they had all sorts of books. 'What! have you Shakespeare?' 'Yes, we have that.' and we found, on further inquiry, that they had a large library,[1] of long standing, that Lord Hopetoun had sub-scribed liberally to it, and that gentlemen who came with him were in the habit of making larger or smaller donations. Each man who had the benefit of it paid a small sum monthly—I think about fourpence.

The man we talked with spoke much of the comfort and quiet in which they lived one among another; he made use of a noticeable expression, saying that they were 'very peaceable people considering they lived so much underground;'—wages were about thirty pounds a year; they had land for potatoes, warm houses, plenty of coals, and only six hours' work each day, so that they had leisure for reading if they chose. He said the place was healthy, that the inhabitants lived to a great age; and indeed we saw no appearance of ill-health in their countenances; but it is not common for people working in lead mines to be healthy; and I have since heard that it

1. Founded in 1741, the Leadhills Miners' Library is the oldest subscription library in Britain, established at a time when the Scots Mining company, close to bankruptcy, hired James Stirling as mine manager. Stirling restored prosperity by improving working conditions for the miners, reducing their work day in the mines to six hours, bringing on a surgeon and instituting a health plan. As the pamphlet *Leadhills Library*, from a paper by Morven Cameron (with additional material by W.S. Harvey. Lanark: n.d.) tells us: "The men were encouraged to build stone cottages and to keep gardens; the school was improved and, so that leisure could be put to good use, the Leadhills Miners' Reading Society was founded in 1741 . . . Of the 23 founding members at Leadhills, all were miners except the minister and the school-master. Prospective members were required to submit written applications to the 'Preses' [the chairman of the Reading Society] and, if voted into the Society, had to pay an entrance fee of 3/—. On a member's death, however, should his heir or legatee seek to join the Reading Society, the fee was waived. The annual subscription was 2/—, no small sum at a time when yearly earnings might be no more than £20" (pamphlet). The library had an impressive breadth of literature, and its borrowing rules were clearly defined by and strictly adhered to by the membership of miners, who also had a vote in acquisitions. Eventually the member-ship allowed non-miners to belong to the Society, and the membership extended to as far away as Glasgow and Edinburgh.

The name of the Leadhills-born poet Allan Ramsay (1686–1758) has been given to the library.

is *not* a healthy place. However this may be, they are unwilling to allow it; for the landlady the next morning, when I said to her 'You have a cold climate,' replied, 'Ay, but it is *varra halesome.*' We inquired of the man respecting the large mansion; he told us that it was built, as we might see, in the form of an H, and belonged to the Hopetouns,[1] and they took their title from thence, and that part of it was used as a chapel. We went close to it, and were a good deal amused with the building itself, standing forth in bold contradiction of the story which I daresay every man of Leadhills tells, and every man believes, that it is in the shape of an H; it is but half an H, and one must be very accommodating to allow it even *so* much, for the legs are far too short.

We visited the burying-ground, a plot of land not very small, crowded with graves, and upright grave-stones, overlooking the village and the dell. It was now the closing in of evening. Women and children were gathering in the linen for the night, which was bleaching by the burn-side;—the graves overgrown with grass, such as, by industrious culture, had been raised up about the houses; but there were bunches of heather here and there, and with the blue-bells that grew among the grass the small plot of ground had a beautiful and wild appearance.

William left me, and I went to a shop to purchase some thread; the woman had none that suited me; but she would send a '*wee* lad' to the other shop. In the meantime I sat with the mother, and was much pleased with her manner and coversation. She had an excellent fire, and her cottage, though very small, looked comfortable and cleanly; but remember I saw it only by firelight. She confirmed what the man had told us of the quiet manner in which they lived; and indeed her house and fireside seemed to need nothing to make it a cheerful happy spot, but health and good humour. There was a bookishness, a certain formality in this woman's language, which was very remarkable. She had a dark complexion, dark eyes, and wore a very white cap, much over her face, which gave her the look of a French woman, and indeed afterwards the women on the roads frequently reminded us of French women, partly from the extremely white caps of the elder women, and still more perhaps from a certain gaiety and party-coloured appearance in their dress in general. White bed-gowns are very common, and you rarely meet a young girl with either hat or cap; they buckle up their hair often in a graceful manner.

1. Dorothy Wordsworth undoubtedly meant the Leadhills Parish Church and Manse, the building of which was sustained by Lord Hopetoun. Photographs in the archives of the Leadhills Miners' Library reveal the building to be shaped like a rather squat short-legged half of the letter "H." Dorothy Wordsworth's original manuscript contains a small drawing of this, followed by the sentence: "This is the shape of the foundation of the building." The Established Church, as it was to be called, was demolished in 1938.

I returned to the inn, and went into the kitchen to speak with the landlady; she had made a hundred hesitations when I told her we wanted three beds. At last she confessed she *had* three beds, and showed me into a parlour which looked damp and cold, but she assured me in a tone that showed she was unwilling to be questioned further, that all *her* beds were well aired. I sat a while by the kitchen fire with the landlady, and began to talk to her; but, much as I had heard in her praise—for the shopkeeper had told me she was a varra discreet woman—I cannot say that her manners pleased me much. But her servant made amends, for she was as pleasant and cheerful a lass as was ever seen; and when we asked her to do anything, she answered, 'Oh yes,' with a merry smile, and almost ran to get us what we wanted. She was about sixteen years old: wore shoes and stockings, and had her hair tucked up with a comb. The servant at Brownhill was a coarse-looking wench, barefoot and barelegged. I examined the kitchen round about; it was crowded with furniture, drawers, cupboards, dish-covers, pictures, pans, and pots, arranged without order, except that the plates were on shelves, and the dish-covers hung in rows; these were very clean, but floors, passages, staircase, every-thing else dirty. There were two beds in recesses in the wall; above one of them I noticed a shelf with some books:—it made me think of Chaucer's Clerke of Oxenforde:—

> Liever had he at his bed's head
> Twenty books clothed in black and red.

They were baking oat-bread, which they cut into quarters, and half-baked over the fire, and half-toasted before it. There was a suspiciousness about Mrs. Otto, almost like ill-nature; she was very jealous of any inquiries that might appear to be made with the faintest idea of a comparison between Leadhills and any other place, except the advantage was evidently on the side of Leadhills. We had nice honey to breakfast. When ready to depart, we learned that we might have seen the library, which we had not thought of till it was too late, and we were very sorry to go away without seeing it.

Saturday, August 20th.—Left Leadhills at nine o'clock, regretting much that we could not stay another day, that we might have made more minute inquiries respecting the manner of living of the miners, and been able to form an estimate, from our own observation, of the degree of knowledge, health, and comfort that there was among them. The air was keen and cold; we might have supposed it to be three months later in the season and two hours earlier in the day. The landlady had not lighted us a fire; so I was

54

obliged to get myself toasted in the kitchen, and when we set off I put on both grey cloak and spencer.[1]

Our road carried us down the valley, and we soon lost sight of Leadhills, for the valley made a turn almost immediately, and we saw two miles, perhaps, before us; the glen sloped somewhat rapidly—heathy, bare, no hut or house. Passed by a shepherd, who was sitting upon the ground, reading, with the book on his knee, screened from the wind by his plaid, while a flock of sheep were feeding near him among the rushes and coarse grass— for, as we descended we came among lands where grass grew with the heather. Travelled through several reaches of the glen, which somewhat resembled the valley of Menock on the other side of Wanlockhead; but it was not near so beautiful; the forms of the mountains did not melt so exquisitely into each other, and there was a coldness, and, if I may so speak, a want of simplicity in the surface of the earth; the heather was poor, not covering a whole hillside; not in luxuriant streams and beds interveined with rich verdure; but patchy and stunted, with here and there coarse grass and rushes. But we soon came in sight of a spot that impressed us very much. At the lower end of this new reach of the vale was a decayed tree, beside a decayed cottage, the vale spreading out into a level area which was one large field, without fence and without division, of a dull yellow colour; the vale seemed to partake of the desolation of the cottage, and to participate in its decay. And yet the spot was in its nature so dreary that one would rather have wondered how it ever came to be tenanted by man, than lament that it was left to waste and solitude. Yet the encircling hills were so exquisitely formed that it was impossible to conceive anything more lovely than this place would have been if the valley and hill-sides had been interspersed with trees, cottages, green fields, and hedgerows. But all was desolate; the one large field which filled up the area of the valley appeared, as I have said, in decay, and seemed to retain the memory of its connexion with man in some way analogous to the ruined building; for it was as much of a field as Mr. King's best pasture scattered over with his fattest cattle.

We went on, looking before us, the place losing nothing of its hold upon our minds, when we discovered a woman sitting right in the middle of the field, alone, wrapped up in a grey cloak or plaid. She sat motionless all the time we looked at her, which might be nearly half an hour. We could not conceive why she sat there, for there were neither sheep nor cattle in the field; her appearance was very melancholy. In the meantime our road carried us nearer to the cottage; though we were crossing over the hill to the left, leaving the valley below us, and we perceived that a part of the building was inhabited, and that what we had supposed to be *one* blasted tree was eight trees, four of which were entirely blasted; the others partly so, and round

1. A spencer is a short jacket, usually woolen; it takes its name from the 2nd Earl of Spencer (1758–1834). The altitude of these mining villages necessitated warm clothes.

First Week
13–20 August

1. Keswick. Approach to Greta Hall.

2. Mosedale valley.
"Passed the foot of Grisdale and Mosedale, both pastoral valleys, narrow . . ." (p. 39)

3. Mungrisdale.
"and we had a second threatening of a disaster in crossing a narrow bridge . . ." (p. 39)

4. Hesket Newmarket. Former public house.
"Slept at Mr. Younghusband's public–house . . ." (p. 39)

5. Caldbeck ("Caldbeck Falls").
"In the evening walked to Caldbeck Falls, a delicious spot in which to breathe out a summer's day—
limestone rocks, hanging trees, pools, and water–breaks . . ." (p. 39)

6. Near Carlisle. Rose Castle.
"Passed Rose Castle upon the Caldew, an ancient building of red stone . . ." (p. 39)

7. Carlisle. Town Hall.
"Dined at Carlisle; the town in a bustle with the assizes; so many strange faces . . ." (pp. 39–40)

8. Carlisle. West Wall of Carlisle.
"Walked upon the city walls, which are broken down in places and crumbling away . . ."
(p. 40)

9. Carlisle. Street scene. (p. 40)

10. Longtown. The Graham Arms.
"Slept at the Graham's Arms, a large inn." (p. 40)

11. Springfield.
"At the top of the hill opposite is Springfield, a village built by Sir William Maxwell—a dull uniformity in the houses . . . each just big enough for two people to live in . . ." (p. 41)

12. Gretna Green. Churchyard.
"There is a pleasant view from the churchyard over Solway Firth to the Cumberland
Mountains." (p. 41)

13. Dumfries. Bridge over River Nith.
"Reached Dumfries at about nine o'clock . . ." (p. 41)

14. Dumfries. St. Michael's Churchyard.
"Went to the churchyard where Burns is buried." (p. 41)

15. Dumfries. Burns's house.
"He showed us the outside of Burns's house . . . It has a mean appearance, and is in a bye
situation . . ." (p. 41)

16. Dumfries. Burns's grave site.
"He lies at a corner of the churchyard . . . There is no stone to mark the spot; but a
hundred guineas have been collected, to be expended on some sort of monument."
(pp. 41–2)

17. Dumfries. Writing on grave marker.
"Over the graves of married women the maiden name instead of that of the husband, 'spouse' instead of
'wife,' and the place of abode preceded by 'in' instead of 'of.'" (p. 42)

18. Dumfries. Burns's house. Interior. Writing desk and pen.
    "The house was cleanly and neat in the inside . . ." (p. 43)

19. Dumfries. Burns's house. Staircase.
    "the stairs of stone, scoured white . . ." (p. 43)

20. Ellisland. Ellisland farmhouse.

"In our road to Brownhill, the next stage, we passed Ellisland at a little distance on our right, his farmhouse." (p. 43)

21. Brownhill. Inn.

"Left the Nith about a mile and a half, and reached Brownhill, a lonely inn, where we slept." (p. 43)

22. Brownhill. Area.

"The ground all over heaves and swells like a sea; but for miles around there are neither trees nor hedgerows . . ." (p. 44)

23. Thornhill.
"Passed through the village of Thornhill, built by the Duke of Queensberry; the 'brother-houses, so small that they might have been built to stamp a character of insolent pride on his own huge mansion of Drumlanrigg . . ." (p. 45)

24. Drumlanrig. Castle. ("Mansion.")
"This mansion is indeed very large; but to us it appeared like a gathering together of little things. The roof is broken into a hundred pieces, cupolas, etc., in the shape of casters, conjuror's balls, cups, and the like."
(p. 45)

25. Approach to Wanlockhead.
"Now the steeps were heathy all around. Just as we began to climb the hill we saw three boys who came down the cleft of a brow on our left . . ." (p. 48)

26. Wanlockhead. Old Schoolhouse.
"They [the boys they met] told us they lived at Wanlockhead . . . they went to school and learned Latin, Virgil, and some of them Greek, Homer . . ." (p. 48)

27. Wanlockhead. Miners' cottages.
    "The village, as we guessed, is inhabited by miners . . ." (p. 49)

28. Wanlockhead. Mining fields.
    ". . . the mines belong to the Duke of Queensberry." (p. 49)

29. Wanlockhead. Beam engine.
    "When we drew nearer we saw . . . a large machine or lever, in appearance like a great forge-hammer, as we supposed for raising water out of the mines." (p. 50)

30. Approach to Leadhills.

"Leadhills, another mining village, was the place of our destination for the night; and soon after we had passed the cart we came in sight of it." (p. 50)

31. Leadhills. Houses.

". . . the houses are single, or in clusters, or rows as it may chance." (p. 51)

32. Leadhills. Hopetoun Arms.
"We passed a decent-looking inn, the Hopetoun Arms . . ." (p. 51)

33. Leadhills. Allan Ramsay Leadhills Miners Library.
"We talked with one of the miners, who informed us that the building which we had supposed to be a school was a library belonging to the village. He said they had got a book into it a few weeks ago, which had cost thirty pounds, and that they had all sorts of books." (p. 51)

34. Leadhills. Graveyard.
"We visited the burying-ground, a plot of land not very small, crowded with graves, and upright grave-stones, overlooking the village and the dell." (p. 52)

35. To Crawfordjohn.
"Our road was along the side of a high moor." (p. 55)

36. The Clyde. Near Hyndford Bridge, on the way to Lanark.
"Crossed the river and ascended towards Lanerk, which stands upon a hill." (p. 59)

37. Lanark. Street scene.
"The town showed a sort of French face . . . The houses are of grey stone, the streets not very narrow . . ." (p. 59)

38. Lanark. The Clydesdale Hotel, formerly the New Inn.
"The New Inn is a handsome old stone building, formerly a gentleman's house." (p. 59)

39. New Lanark. View of mills.
"We passed through a great part of the town, then turned down a steep hill, and came in view of a long range of cotton mills, the largest and loftiest I had ever seen . . ." (pp. 59–60)

about the place was a little potato and cabbage garth, fenced with earth. No doubt, that woman had been an inhabitant of the cottage. However this might be, there was so much obscurity and uncertainty about her, and her figure agreed so well with the desolation of the place, that we were indebted to the chance of her being there for some of the most interesting feelings that we had ever had from natural objects connected with man in dreary solitariness.

We had been advised to go along the *new* road, which would have carried us down the vale; but we met some travellers who recommended us to climb the hill, and go by the village of Crawfordjohn as being much nearer. We had a long hill, and after having reached the top, steep and bad roads, so we continued to walk for a considerable way. The air was cold and clear—the sky blue. We walked cheerfully along in the sunshine, each of us alone, only William had the charge of the horse and car, so he sometimes took a ride, which did but poorly recompense him for the trouble of driving. I never travelled with more cheerful spirits than this day. Our road was along the side of a high moor. I can always walk over a moor with a light foot; I seem to be drawn more closely to nature in such places than anywhere else; or rather I feel more strongly the power of nature over me, and am better satisfied with myself for being able to find enjoyment in what unfortunately to many persons is either dismal or insipid. This moor, however, was more than commonly interesting; we could see a long way, and on every side of us were larger or smaller tracts of cultivated land. Some were extensive farms, yet in so large a waste they did but look small, with farm-houses, barns, etc., others like little cottages, with enough to feed a cow, and supply the family with vegetables. In looking at these farms we had always one feeling. Why did the plough stop there? Why might not they as well have carried it twice as far? There were no hedgerows near the farms, and very few trees. As we were passing along,we saw an old man, the first we had seen in a Highland bonnet, walking with a staff at a very slow pace by the edge of one of the moorland cornfields; he wore a grey plaid, and a dog was by his side. There was a scriptural solemnity in this man's figure, a sober simplicity which was most impressive. Scotland is the country above all others that I have seen, in which a man of imagination may carve out his own pleasures. There are so many *inhabited* solitudes, and the employments of the people are so immediately connected with the places where you find them, and their dresses so simple, so much alike, yet, from their being folding garments, admitting of an endless variety, and falling often so gracefully.

After some time we descended towards a broad vale, passed one farm-house, sheltered by fir trees, with a burn close to it; children playing, linen bleaching. The vale was open pastures and corn-fields unfenced, the land poor. The village of Crawfordjohn on the slope of a hill a long way before us to the left. Asked about our road of a man who was driving a cart; he told us to go through the village, then along some fields, and we should come to a 'herd's house by the burn side.' The highway was right through the vale, unfenced on either side; the people of the village, who were making hay, all stared at us and our carriage. We inquired the road of a middle-aged man, dressed in a shabby black coat, at work in one of the hay fields; he looked like the minister of the place, and when he spoke we felt assured that he was so, for he was not sparing of hard words, which, however, he used with great propriety, and he spoke like one who had been accustomed to dictate. Our car wanted mending in the wheel, and we asked him if there was a blacksmith in the village. 'Yes,' he replied, but when we showed him the wheel he told William that he might mend it himself without a blacksmith, and he would put him in the way; so he fetched hammer and nails and gave his directions, which William obeyed, and repaired the damage entirely to his own satisfaction and the priest's, who did not offer to lend any assistance himself; not as if he would not have been willing in case of need; but as if it were more natural for him to dictate, and because he thought it more fit that William should do it himself. He spoke much about the propriety of every man's lending all the assistance in his power to travellers, and with some ostentation or self-praise. Here I observed a honey-suckle and some flowers growing in a garden, the first I had seen in Scotland. It is a pretty cheerful-looking village, but must be very cold in winter; it stands on a hillside, and the vale itself is very high ground, unsheltered by trees.

Left the village behind us, and our road led through arable ground for a considerable way, on which were growing very good crops of corn and potatoes. Our friend accompanied us to show us the way, and Coleridge and he had a scientific conversation concerning the uses and properties of lime and other manures. He seemed to be a well-informed man; somewhat pedantic in his manners; but this might be only the difference between Scotch and English.

Soon after he had parted from us, we came upon a stony, rough road over a black moor; and presently to the 'herd's house by the burn side.' We could hardly cross the burn dry-shod, over which was the only road to the cottage. In England there would have been stepping-stones or a bridge; but the Scotch need not be afraid of wetting their bare feet. The hut had its little kail-garth fenced with earth; there was no other enclosure—but the common, heathy with coarse grass. Travelled along the common for some miles, before we joined the great road from Longtown to Glasgow—saw on the bare hill-sides at a distance, sometimes a solitary farm, now and then a plantation, and one very large wood, with an appearance of richer ground above; but it was so very high we could not think it possible. Having descended considerably, the common was no longer of a peat-mossy brown heath colour, but grass with rushes was its chief produce; there was sometimes a solitary hut, no enclosures except the kail-garth, and sheep pasturing in flocks, with shepherd-boys tending them. I remember one boy in particular; he had no hat on, and only had a grey plaid wrapped about him. It is nothing to describe, but on a bare moor, alone with his sheep, standing, as he did, in utter quietness and silence, there was something uncommonly impressive in his appearance, a solemnity which recalled to our minds the old man in the corn-field. We passed many people who were mowing, or raking the grass of the common; it was little better than rushes; but they did not mow straight forward, only here and there, where it was the best; in such a place hay-cocks had an uncommon appearance to us.

After a long descent we came to some plantations which were not far from Douglas Mill.[1] The country for some time had been growing into cultivation, and now it was a wide vale with large tracts of corn; trees in clumps, no hedgerows, which always make a country look bare and unlovely. For my part, I was better pleased with the desert places we had left behind, though no doubt the inhabitants of this place think it 'a varra bonny spot,' for the Scotch are always pleased with their own abode, be it what it may; and afterwards at Edinburgh, when we were talking with a bookseller of our travels, he observed that it was 'a fine country near Douglas Mill.' Douglas Mill is a single house, a large inn, being one of the regular stages between Longtown and Glasgow, and therefore a fair specimen of the best of the country inns of Scotland. As soon as our car stopped at the door we felt the difference. At an English inn of this size, a waiter, or the master or mistress, would have been at the door immediately, but we remained some time before anybody came; then a barefooted lass made her appearance, but she only looked at us and went away. The mistress, a remarkably handsome woman, showed us into a large parlour; we ordered mutton-chops, and I finished my letter to Mary; writing on the same window ledge on which William had written to me two years before.

After dinner, William and I sat by a little mill-race in the garden. We had left Leadhills and Wanlockhead far above us, and now were come into a warmer climate; but there was no richness in the face of the country. The shrubs looked cold and poor, and yet there were some very fine trees within a little distance of Douglas Mill, so that the reason, perhaps, why the few low shrubs and trees which were growing in the gardens seemed to be so unluxuriant, might be, that there being no hedgerows, the general appearance of the country was naked, and I could not help seeing the same coldness where, perhaps, it did not exist in itself to any great degree, for the corn crops are abundant, and I should think the soil is not bad. While we

1. Douglas Mill no longer stands, either as a place or an inn. The Mill was powered by Park Burn, which ran into Douglas Water. Nearby were Castlemains, the occasional residence of Lord Douglas-Home, and Millbank, with the former gamekeeper's house. These remain and give today's visitor a good sense of the environs.

were sitting at the door, two of the landlady's children came out; the elder, a boy about six years old, was running away from his little brother, in petticoats; the ostler called out, 'Sandy, tak' your wee brither wi' you;' another voice from the window, 'Sawny, dinna leave your wee brither;' the mother then came, 'Alexander, tak' your wee brother by the hand;' Alexander obeyed, and the two went off in peace together. We were charged eightpence for hay at this inn, another symptom of our being in Scotland. Left Douglas Mill at about three o'clock; travelled through an open corn country, the tracts of corn large and unenclosed. We often passed women or children who were watching a single cow while it fed upon the slips of grass between the corn. William asked a strong woman, about thirty years of age, who looked like the mistress of a family—I suppose moved by some sentiment of compassion for her being so employed,—if the cow would eat the corn if it were left to itself: she smiled at his simplicity. It is indeed a melancholy thing to see a full-grown woman thus waiting, as it were, body and soul devoted to the poor beast; yet even this is better than working in a manufactory the day through.

We came to a moorish tract; saw before us the hills of Loch Lomond, Ben Lomond and another, distinct each by itself. Not far from the roadside were some benches placed in rows in the middle of a large field, with a sort of covered shed like a sentry-box, but much more like those boxes which the Italian puppet-showmen in London use. We guessed that it was a pulpit or tent for preaching, and were told that a sect met there occasionally, who held that toleration was unscriptural, and would have all religions but their own exterminated. I have forgotten what name the man gave to this sect; we could not learn that it differed in any other respect from the Church of Scotland. Travelled for some miles along the open country, which was all without hedgerows, sometimes arable, sometimes moorish, and often whole tracts covered with grunsel.[1] There was one field, which one might have believed had been sown with grunsel, it was so regularly covered with it— a large square field upon a slope, its boundary marked to our eyes only by the termination of the bright yellow; contiguous to it were other fields of the same size and shape, one of clover, the other of potatoes, all equally regular crops. The oddness of this appearance, the grunsel being uncommonly luxuriant, and the field as yellow as gold, made William laugh. Coleridge was melancholy upon it, observing that there was land enough wasted to rear a healthy child.

We left behind us, considerably to the right, a single high mountain;[2] I have forgotten its name; we had had it long in view. Saw before us the river Clyde, its course at right angles to our road, which now made a turn, running parallel with the river; the town of Lanerk in sight long before we came to it. I was somewhat disappointed with the first view of the Clyde:

1. Ragweed.   2. Tinto.

the banks, though swelling and varied, had a poverty in their appearance, chiefly from the want of wood and hedgerows. Crossed the river and ascended towards Lanerk, which stands upon a hill. When we were within about a mile of the town, William parted from Coleridge and me, to go to the celebrated waterfalls. Coleridge did not attempt to drive the horse; but led him all the way. We inquired for the best inn, and were told that the New Inn was the best; but that they had very 'genteel apartments' at the Black Bull, and made less charges, and the Black Bull was at the entrance of the town, so we thought we would stop there, as the horse was obstinate and weary. But when we came to the Black Bull we had no wish to enter the apartments; for it seemed the abode of dirt and poverty, yet it was a large building. The town showed a sort of French face, and would have done much more, had it not been for the true British tinge of coal-smoke; the doors and windows dirty, the shops dull, the women too seemed to be very dirty in their dress. The town itself is not ugly; the houses are of grey stone, the streets not very narrow, and the market-place decent. The New Inn is a handsome old stone building, formerly a gentleman's house. We were conducted into a parlour, where people had been drinking; the tables were unwiped, chairs in disorder, the floor dirty, and the smell of liquors was most offensive. We were tired, however, and rejoiced in our tea.

The evening sun was now sending a glorious light through the street, which ran from west to east; the houses were of a fire red, and the faces of the people as they walked westward were almost like a blacksmith when he is at work by night. I longed to be out, and meet with William, that we might see the Falls before the day was gone. Poor Coleridge was unwell, and could not go. I inquired my road, and a little girl told me she would go with me to the porter's lodge, where I might be admitted. I was grieved to hear that the Falls of the Clyde were shut up in a gentleman's grounds, and to be viewed only by means of lock and key. Much, however, as the pure feeling with which one would desire to visit such places is disturbed by useless, impertinent, or even unnecessary interference with nature, yet when I was there the next morning I seemed to feel it a less disagreeable thing than in smaller and more delicate spots, if I may use the phrase. My guide, a sensible little girl, answered my inquiries very prettily. She was eight years old, read in the 'Collection,' a book which all the Scotch children whom I have questioned read in. I found it was a collection of hymns; she could repeat several of Dr. Watts'. We passed through a great part of the town, then turned down a steep hill, and came in view of a long range of cotton mills,[1]

1. These mills, in New Lanark, where one enters the grounds of the Falls of the Clyde today, are the setting of a remarkable socialistic labor community put into effect by Robert Owen (1771–1858), who purchased the mills with two partners in 1799, married the daughter of the former proprietor, and settled in New Lanark. He set about shaping social and industrial changes based on the values of cooperative living that would later earn him the reputation of utopian socialist and reformer. As manager of the textile mills he improved the output and earnings of the industry as a well as the working conditions and lives of the workers.

the largest and loftiest I had ever seen; climbed upwards again, our road leading us along the top of the left bank of the river; both banks very steep and richly wooded. The girl left me at the porter's lodge. Having asked after William, I was told that no person had been there, or could enter but by the gate. The night was coming on, therefore I did not venture to go in, as I had no hope of meeting William. I had a delicious walk alone through the wood; the sound of the water was very solemn, and even the cotton mills in the fading light of evening had somewhat of the majesty and stillness of the natural objects. It was nearly dark when I reached the inn. I found Coleridge sitting by a good fire, which always makes an inn room look comfortable. In a few minutes William arrived; he had heard of me at the gate, and followed as quickly as he could, shouting after me. He was pale and exceedingly tired.

After he had left us he had taken a wrong road, and while looking about to set himself right had met with a barefooted boy, who said he would go with him. The little fellow carried him by a wild path to the upper of the Falls, the Boniton Linn, and coming down unexpectedly upon it, he was exceedingly affected by the solemn grandeur of the place. This fall is not much admired or spoken of by travellers; you have never a full, breast view of it; it does not make a complete self-satisfying place, an abode of its own, as a perfect waterfall seems to me to do; but the river, down which you look through a long vista of steep and ruin-like rocks, the roaring of the waterfall, and the solemn evening lights, must have been most impressive. One of the rocks on the near bank, even in broad daylight, as we saw it the next morning , is exactly like the fractured arch of an abbey. With the lights and shadows of evening upon it, the resemblance must have been much more striking.

William's guide was a pretty boy, and he was exceedingly pleased with him. Just as they were quitting the waterfall, William's mind being full of the majesty of the scene, the little fellow pointed to the top of a rock, 'There's a fine slae-bush there.' 'Ay,' said William, 'but there are no slaes upon it,' which was true enough, but I suppose the child remembered the slaes of another summer, though, as he said, he was but 'half seven years old,' namely, six and a half. He conducted William to the other fall, and as they were going along a narrow path, they came to a small cavern, where William lost him, and looking about, saw his pretty figure in a sort of natural niche fitted for a statue, from which the boy jumped out laughing, delighted with the success of his trick. William told us a great deal about him, while he sat by the fire, and of the pleasure of his walk, often repeating, 'I wish you had been with me.' Having no change, he gave the boy sixpence, which was certainly, if he had formed any expectations at all, far beyond them; but he received it with the utmost indifference, without any remark of surprise or pleasure; most likely he did not know how many halfpence he could get for it, and twopence would have pleased him more. My little girl was delighted with the sixpence I gave her, and said she would buy a book with it on Monday morning. What a difference between the manner of living and education of boys and of girls among the lower classes of people in towns! She had never seen the Falls of the Clyde, nor had ever been further than the porter's lodge; the boy, I daresay, knew every hiding-place in every accessible rock, as well as the fine 'slae bushes' and the nut trees.

SECOND WEEK

Sunday, August 21st.—The morning was very hot, a morning to tempt us to linger by the water-side. I wished to have had the day before us, expecting so much from what William had seen; but when we went there, I did not desire to stay longer than till the hour which we had prescribed to ourselves; for it was a rule not to be broken in upon, that the person who conducted us to the Falls was to remain by our side till we chose to depart. We left our inn immediately after breakfast. The lanes were full of people going to church; many of the middle-aged women wore long scarlet cardinals, and were without hats: they brought to my mind the women of Goslar as they used to go to church in their silver or gold caps, with their long cloaks, black or coloured.

The banks of the Clyde from Lanerk to the Falls rise immediately from the river; they are lofty and steep, and covered with wood. The road to the Falls is along the top of one of the banks, and to the left you have a prospect of the open country, corn fields and scattered houses. To the right, over the river, the country spreads out, as it were, into a plain covered over with hills, no one hill much higher than another, but hills all over; there were endless pastures overgrown with broom, and scattered trees, without hedges or fences of any kind, and no distinct footpaths. It was delightful to see the lasses in gay dresses running like cattle among the broom, making their way straight forward towards the river, here and there as it might chance. They waded across the stream, and, when they had reached the top of the opposite bank, sat down by the road-side, about half a mile from the town, to put on their shoes and cotton stockings, which they brought tied up in pocket-handkerchiefs. The porter's lodge[1] is about a mile from Lanerk, and the lady's house—for the whole belongs to a lady, whose name I have forgotten[2]—is upon a hill at a little distance. We walked, after we had entered the private grounds, perhaps two hundred yards along a gravel carriage-road, then came to a little side gate, which opened upon a narrow gravel path under trees, and in a minute and a half, or less, were directly opposite to the great waterfall. I was much affected by the first view of it. The majesty and strength of the water,[3] for I had never before seen so large

---

1. Called "Mid Lodge" on maps today, this was once the gate-house for the Bonnington Estate. It is now a private residence.
2. Lady Mary Ross, according to Shairp, and Stoddart.
3. The Falls of the Clyde have changed significantly, with far less water shooting from the dramatic heights of Dorothy Wordsworth's time. Since 1927 a hydro-electric plant has harnessed water from the falls for cheap electrical power, so that one finds a tilting weir above

a cataract, struck me with astonishment, which died away, giving place to more delightful feelings; though there were some buildings that I could have wished had not been there, though at first unnoticed. The chief of them was a neat, white, lady-like house,[1] very near to the waterfall. William and Coleridge however were in a better and perhaps wiser humour, and did not dislike the house; indeed, it was a very nice-looking place, with a moderate-sized garden, leaving the green fields free and open. This house is on the side of the river opposite to the grand house and the pleasure-grounds. The waterfall Cora Linn is composed of two falls, with a sloping space, which *appears* to be about twenty yards between, but is much more.[2] The basin which receives the fall is enclosed by noble rocks, with trees, chiefly hazels, birch, and ash growing out of their sides whenever there is any hold for them; and a magnificent resting-place it is for such a river; I think more grand than the Falls themselves.

After having stayed some time, we returned by the same footpath into the main carriage-road, and soon came upon what William calls an ell-wide gravel walk, from which we had different views of the Linn. We sat upon a bench, placed for the sake of one of these views, whence we looked down upon the waterfall, and over the open country, and saw a ruined tower, called Wallace's Tower, which stands at a very little distance from the fall, and is an interesting object.[3] A lady and gentleman, more expeditious tourists

Bonnington Linn and the power station itself below Corra Linn in that very setting that inspired awe in the Romantics and compelled Turner to paint it. They are still stunning, on a different scale, and are incorporated into a nature reserve in the care of the National Trust for Scotland.

1. Corehouse. "The present Corehouse was completed in 1827 in the Elizabethan manorial style. The grounds were laid out by Sir Walter Scott . . ." (Brochure: *Falls of the Clyde*. Scottish Wildlife Trust. n.d.) Dorothy saw an earlier construction of Corehouse.

2. In his poem "Composed at Cora Linn" (in *Memorials of a Tour in Scotland, 1814*) Wordsworth recalls the impact of this fall in the opening lines,

> Lord of the vale! Astounding Flood;
> The Dullest leaf in this thick wood
> Quakes—conscious of thy power.

3. High above Corra Linn, on the west side of the river and falls, stands Corra Castle, mostly hidden by trees from those standing on the popular viewpoint opposite. It is a ruin built in the fifteenth century by the Bannatyne family, and while current literature does not link it with the famous Scottish hero William Wallace, Gilpin, in his *Observations*. (London, 1789), offers clues as to the thinking that would have carried over into the nineteenth century. He refers to "a solitary tower" on one of two "cheeks" above Corra Linn. Concerning his situation at the falls he writes: "In our travels through Scotland I have mentioned many scenes, which were ennobled by being called the retreats of Wallace. This was one. Among these wild rocks, and in the tower, that adorns them, we were told, he lurked, during a period of distress. These traditional anecdotes, whether true, or fabled, add grandeur to a scene: and the variety of these hiding places, which the Scotts [sic] have every where provided for Wallace in his misfortunes, shew at least their gratitude and affection for one of the noblest heroes, which their own, or any other country had produced" (II p. 73). Such "traditional anecdotes" endured through the visits of the Wordsworths and Coleridge and must form the basis of Wordsworth's "Composed at Cora Linn," which has as a sub-title, "In Sight of Wallace's Tower."

than ourselves, came to the spot; they left us at the seat, and we found them again at another station above the Falls. Coleridge, who is always good-natured enough to enter into conversation with anybody whom he meets in his way, began to talk with the gentleman, who observed that it was a *majestic* waterfall. Coleridge was delighted with the accuracy of the epithet, particularly as he had been settling in his own mind the precise meaning of the words grand, majestic, sublime, etc., and had discussed the subject with William at some length the day before. 'Yes, sir,' says Coleridge, 'it *is* a majestic waterfall.' 'Sublime and beautiful,' replied his friend. Poor Coleridge could make no answer, and, not very desirous to continue the conversation, came to us and related the story, laughing heartily.

The distance from one Linn to the other may be half a mile or more, along the same ell-wide walk. We came to a pleasure-house, of which the little girl had the key; she said it was called the Fog-house, because it was lined with 'fog,' namely moss.[1] On the outside it resembled some of the huts in the prints belonging to Captain Cook's Voyages, and within was like a hay-stack scooped out. It was circular, with a dome-like roof, a seat all round fixed to the wall, and a table in the middle,—seat, wall, roof, and table all covered with moss in the neatest manner possible. It was as snug as a bird's nest; I wish we had such a one at the top of our orchard, only a great deal smaller. We afterwards found that huts of the same kind were common in the pleasure-grounds of Scotland; but we never saw any that were so beautifully wrought as this. It had, however, little else to recommend it, the situation being chosen without judgment; there was no prospect from it, nor was it a place of seclusion and retirement, for it stood close to the ell-wide gravel walk. We wished we could have shoved it about a hundred yards further on, when we arrived at a bench which was also close to the walk, for just below the bench, the walk elbowing out into a circle, there was a beautiful spring of clear water, which we could see rise up continually, at the bottom of a round stone basin full to the brim, the water gushing out at a little outlet and passing away under the walk. A reason was wanted for placing the hut where it is; what a good one would this little spring have furnished for bringing it hither! Along the whole of the path were openings at intervals for views of the river, but, as almost always happens in gentle-men's grounds, they were injudiciously managed; you were prepared for a dead stand—by a parapet, a painted seat, or some other device.[2]

1. "Another romantic feature was the doo-cote on the island at Bonnington Linn. Towards the end of the eighteenth century this was converted to a 'foghouse' which was completely lined with moss, including the bench seats. Dorothy Wordsworth thought that it 'resembled some of the huts in the prints belonging to Captain Cooks's Voyages.' To get to this island a narrow iron bridge was built though it must be assumed that the doo-cote had some other access before this" (Brochure: *Falls of the Clyde.* Scottish Wildlife Trust).
2. It is surprising that Dorothy does not cite in this, or the general context of the falls, the pavilion with mirrors erected in 1708 by Sir James Carmichael of Bonnington for viewing Corra Linn.

We stayed some time at the Boniton Fall, which has one great advantage over the other falls, that it is at the termination of the pleasure-grounds, and we see no traces of the boundary-line; yet, except under some accidental circumstances, such as a sunset like that of the preceding evening, it is greatly inferior to the Cora Linn. We returned to the inn to dinner. The landlord set the first dish upon the table, as is common in England, and we were well waited upon. This first dish was true Scottish—a boiled sheep's head, with the hair singed off; Coleridge and I ate heartily of it; we had barley broth, in which the sheep's head had been boiled. A party of tourists whom we had met in the pleasure-grounds drove from the door while we were waiting for dinner; I guess they were fresh from England, for they had stuffed the pockets of their carriage with bundles of heather, roots and all, just as if Scotland grew no heather but on the banks of the Clyde. They passed away with their treasure towards Loch Lomond. A party of boys, dressed all alike in blue, very neat, were standing at the chaise-door; we conjectured they were charity scholars; but found on inquiry that they were apprentices to the cotton factory; we were told that they were well instructed in reading and writing. We had seen in the morning a flock of girls dressed in grey coming out of the factory, probably apprentices also.[1]

After dinner set off towards Hamilton, but on foot, for we had to turn aside to the Cartland Rocks, and our car was to meet us on the road. A guide attended us, who might almost in size, and certainly in activity, have been compared with William's companion who hid himself in the niche of the cavern. His method of walking and very quick step soon excited our attention. I could hardly keep up with him; he paddled by our side, just reaching to my shoulder, like a little dog, with his long snout pushed before him—for he had an enormous nose, and walked with his head foremost. I said to him, 'How quick you walk!' he replied, '*That* was *not* quick walking,' and when I asked him what he called so, he said 'Five miles an hour,' and then related in how many hours he had lately walked from Lanerk to Edinburgh, done some errands, and returned to Lanerk—I have forgotten the particulars, but it was a very short time—and added that he had an old father who could walk at the rate of four miles an hour, for twenty-four miles, any day, and had never had an hour's sickness in his life. 'Then,' said I, 'he had not drunk much strong liquor?' 'Yes, enough to drown him.' From his eager manner of uttering this, I inferred that he himself was a drinker; and the man who met us with the car told William that he gained a great deal of money as an errand-goer, but spent it all in tippling. He had

1. These were the children of the cotton mills managed by Robert Owen, who was deeply concerned with the education of the young who lived and worked in the mill community, many of whom had been brought in from the workhouses and charities of Edinburgh and Glasgow. Owen was later to establish here (in 1816) an Institute for the Formation of Character, which was to provide not only educational facilities for child laborers but also the first nursery school in Great Britain.

been a shoemaker, but could not bear the confinement on account of a weakness in his chest.

The neighbourhood of Lanerk is exceedingly pleasant; we came to a sort of district of glens or little valleys that cleave the hills, leaving a cheerful, open country above them, with no superior hills, but an undulating surface. Our guide pointed to the situation of the Cartland Crags.[1] We were to cross a narrow valley, and walk down on the other side, and then we should be at the spot; but the little fellow made a sharp turn down a footpath to the left, saying, 'We must have some conversation here.' He paddled on with his small pawing feet till we came right opposite to a gentleman's house on the other side of the valley, when he halted, repeating some words, I have forgotten what, which were taken up by the most distinct echo I ever heard—this is saying little: it was the most distinct echo that it is possible to conceive. It shouted the names of our fireside friends in the very tone in which William and Coleridge spoke; but it seemed to make a joke of me, and I could not help laughing at my own voice, it was so shrill and pert, exactly as if some one had been mimicking it very successfully, with an intention of making me ridiculous. I wished Joanna had been there to laugh,[2] for the echo is an excellent laugher, and would have almost made her believe that it was a true story which William has told of her and the mountains. We turned back, crossed the valley, went through the orchard and plantations belonging to the gentleman's house. By the bye, we observed to our guide that the echo must bring many troublesome visitors to disturb the quiet of the owner of that house, 'Oh no,' said he, 'he glories in much company.' He was a native of that neighbourhood, had made a moderate fortune abroad, purchased an estate, built the house, and raised the plantations; and further, had made a convenient walk through his woods to

1. Stoddart offers the best picture of how rocky haunts along the Mouse Water struck Romantic travellers: "These can only be approached by wading in the channel, or scrambling along the edge of the bank, which is sometimes beset with tangling shrubs, and sometimes formed by naked shelving rocks, while the lofty cliffs shooting to a height, as it is said, of 400 feet, and winding like a labyrinth, involve the whole in obscurity, and form gloomy, and apparently impenetrable recesses . . . [T]he features here possess a . . . savage grandeur, from the superior height of the cliffs, the more frequent and abrupt turns made by the river, the rocks rent as it were by an earthquake, and appearing, at times, like massy pillars naked to the top, at others, wholly shrouded by dark coppices, and ancient pines. Every thing seems to show the hand of desolation, and untameable wildness; and so dreary a spot is a fit haunt for its only inmates, the fox, the badger, wild cats, and birds of prey" (*Remarks*, I p. 162).
2. One of Wordsworth's "Poems on the Naming of Places" (1800) celebrates an incident involving Joanna Hutchinson, his sister-in-law, and a place in the Lake District that produced echoes in an entertaining way. Walking along the banks of the Rotha, they came to a tall rock "That eastward looks." Joanna laughs, and

> The Rock, like something starting from a sleep,
> Took up the Lady's voice and laughed again.
> (ll. 54–55)

the Cartland Crags. The house was modest and neat, and though not adorned in the best taste, and though the plantations were of fir, we looked at it with great pleasure, there was such true liberality and kind-heartedness in leaving his orchard path open, and his walks unobstructed by gates. I hope this goodness is not often abused by plunderers of the apple-trees, which were hung with tempting apples close to the path.

At the termination of the little valley, we descended through a wood along a very steep path to a muddy stream running over limestone rocks; turned up to the left along the bed of the stream, and soon we were closed in by rocks on each side. They were very lofty—of limestone, trees starting out of them, high and low, overhanging the stream or shooting up towards the sky. No place of the kind could be more beautiful if the stream had been clear, but it was of a muddy yellow colour; had it been a large river, one might have got the better of the unpleasantness of the muddy water in the grandeur of its roaring, the boiling up of the foam over the rocks, or the obscurity of its pools.

We had been told that the Cartland Crags were better worth going to see that the Falls of the Clyde. I did not think so; but I have seen rocky dells resembling this before, with clear water instead of that muddy stream, and never saw anything like the Falls of the Clyde. It would be a delicious spot to have near one's house; one would linger out many a day in the cool shade of the caverns, and the stream would soothe one by its murmuring; still, being an old friend, one would not love it the less for its homely face. Even we, as we passed along, could not help stopping for a long while to admire the beauty of the lazy foam, for ever in motion, and never moved away, in a still place of the water, covering the whole surface of it with streaks and lines and ever-varying circles. Wild marjoram grew upon the rocks in great perfection and beauty; our guide gave me a bunch, and said he should come hither to collect a store for tea for the winter, and that it was 'varra halesome:' he drank none else. We walked perhaps half a mile along the bed of the river; but it might *seem* to be much further than it was, owing to the difficulty of the path, and the sharp and many turnings of the glen. Passed two of Wallace's Caves.[1] There is scarce a noted glen in Scotland that had not a cave for Wallace or some other hero. Before we left the river the rocks became less lofty, turned into a wood through which was a convenient path upwards, met the owner of the house and the echo-ground, and thanked him for the pleasure which he had provided for us and other travellers by making such pretty pathways.

It was four o'clock when we reached the place where the car was waiting. We were anxious to be off, as we had fifteen miles to go; but just as we were seating ourselves we found that the cushions were missing. William

1. See Appendix 2.

was forced to go back to the town, a mile at least, and Coleridge and I waited with the car. It rained, and we had some fear that the evening would be wet, but the rain soon ceased, though the sky continued gloomy—an unfortunate circumstance, for we had to travel through a beautiful country, and of that sort which is most set off by sunshine and pleasant weather.

Travelled through the Vale or *Trough* of the Clyde, as it is called, for ten or eleven miles, having the river on our right. We had fine views both up and down the river for the first three or four miles, our road being not close to it, but above its banks, along the open country, which was here occasionally intersected by hedgerows.

Left our car in the road, and turned down a field to the Fall of Stonebyres,[1] another of the falls of the Clyde, which I had not heard spoken of; therefore it gave me the more pleasure. We saw it from the top of the bank of the river at a little distance. It has not the imposing majesty of Cora Linn; but it has the advantage of being left to itself, a grand solitude in the heart of a populous country. We had a prospect above and below it, of cultivated grounds, with hay-stacks, houses, hills; but the river's banks were lonesome, steep, and woody, with rocks near the fall.

A little further on, came more into company with the river; sometimes we were close to it, sometimes above it, but always at no great distance; and now the vale became more interesting and amusing. It is very populous, with villages, hamlets, single cottages, or farm-houses embosomed in orchards, and scattered over with gentlemen's houses, some of them very ugly, tall and obtrusive, others neat and comfortable. We seemed now to have got into a country where poverty and riches were shaking hands together; pears and apples, of which the crop was abundant, hung over the road, often growing in orchards unfenced; or there might be bunches of broom along the road-side in an interrupted line, that looked like a hedge till we came to it and saw the gaps. Bordering on these fruitful orchards perhaps would be a patch, its chief produce being gorse or broom. There was nothing like a moor or common anywhere; but small plots of uncultivated ground were left high and low, among the potatoes, corn, cabbages, which grew intermingled, now among trees, now bare. The Trough of the Clyde is, indeed, a singular and very interesting region; it is somewhat like the upper part of the vale of Nith, but above the Nith is much less cultivated ground—without hedgerows or orchards, or anything that looks like a rich country. We met crowds of people coming from the kirk; the lasses were gaily dressed, often in white gowns, coloured satin bonnets, and coloured silk handkerchiefs, and generally with their shoes and stockings in a bundle hung on their arm. Before we left the river the vale became much less

1. Some distance from Bonnington Linn and Corra Linn but nevertheless part of the same system of the Clyde, these falls are also tapped for electrical power today.

interesting, resembling a poor English country, the fields being large, and unluxuriant hedges.

It had been dark long before we reached Hamilton, and William had some difficulty in driving the tired horse through the town. At the inn they hesitated about being able to give us beds, the house being brim-full—lights at every window. We were rather alarmed for our accommodations during the rest of the tour, supposing the house to be filled with *tourists*; but they were in general only regular travellers; for out of the main road from town to town we saw scarcely a carriage, and the inns were empty. There was nothing remarkable in the treatment we met with at this inn, except the lazy impertinence of the waiter. It was a townish place, with a great larder set out; the house throughout dirty.

Monday, August 22d.—Immediately after breakfast walked to the Duke of Hamilton's house to view the picture-gallery, chiefly the famous picture of Daniel in the Lions' Den, by Rubens.[1] It is a large building, without grandeur, a heavy, lumpish mass, after the fashion of the Hopetoun H, only five times the size, and with longer legs, which makes it gloomy. We entered the gate, passed the porter's lodge, where we saw nobody, and stopped at the front door, as William had done two years before with Sir William Rush's family. We were met by a little mean-looking man, shabbily dressed, out of livery, who, we found, was the porter. After scanning us over, he told us that we ought not to have come to that door. We said we were sorry for the mistake, but as one of our party had been there two years before, and was admitted by the same entrance, we had supposed it was the regular way. After many hesitations, and having kept us five minutes waiting in the large hall, while he went to consult with the housekeeper, he informed us that we could not be admitted at that time, the housekeeper being unwell; but that we might return in an hour: he then conducted us through long gloomy passages to an obscure door at the corner of the house. We asked if we might be permitted to walk in the park in the meantime; and he told us that this would not be agreeable to the Duke's family. We returned to the inn discontented enough, but resolved not to waste an hour, if there were anything else in the neighbourhood worth seeing. The waiter told us there was a curious place called Baroncleugh, with gardens cut out

1. Hamilton Palace was demolished over a period of eight years in the 1920s because of subsidence in the land, which was over a coal mining area. Only the Hunting Lodge, now restored, remains.

The original building was vast and constituted a veritable museum, with immensely valuable interior architecture and furnishings. The dining room, for example, contained a fireplace of white marble and paintings by Van Dyck. The famous Rubens that Dorothy's party sought in vain to view hung in the Picture Gallery, outstanding among primarily portraits. It is interesting to note that the painting, now in the National Gallery of Art, Washington D.C., was sold in 1882 for £5,145, repurchased three years later for £2,100 and sold again in 1919 for £2,520.

in rocks, and we determined to go thither. We had to walk through the town, which may be about as large as Penrith, and perhaps a mile further, along a dusty turnpike road. The morning was hot, sunny, and windy, and we were half tired before we reached the place; but were amply repaid for our trouble.

The general face of the country near Hamilton is much in the ordinary English style; not very hilly, with hedgerows, corn fields, and stone houses. The Clyde is here an open river with low banks, and the country spreads out so wide that there is no appearance of a regular vale. Baroncleugh is in a beautiful deep glen through which runs the river Avon, a stream that falls into the Clyde. The house stands very sweetly in complete retirement; it has its gardens and terraces one above another, with flights of steps between, box-trees and yew-trees cut in fantastic shapes, flower-borders and summer-houses; and, still below, apples and pears were hanging in abundance on the branches of large old trees, which grew intermingled with the natural wood, elms, beeches, etc., even to the water's edge. The whole place is in perfect harmony with the taste of our ancestors, and the yews and hollies are shaven as nicely, and the gravel walks and flower-borders kept in as exact order, as if the spirit of the first architect of the terraces still presided over them. The opposite bank of the river is left in its natural wildness, and nothing was to be seen higher up but the deep dell, its steep banks being covered with fine trees, a beautiful relief or contrast to the garden, which is one of the most elaborate old things ever seen, a little hanging garden of Babylon.

I was sorry to hear that the owner of this sweet place did not live there always. He had built a small thatched house to eke out the old one: it was a neat dwelling, with no false ornaments. We were exceedingly sorry to quit this spot, which is left to nature and past times, and should have liked to have pursued the glen further up; we were told that there was a ruined castle; and the walk itself must be very delightful; but we wished to reach Glasgow in good time, and had to go again to Hamilton House. Returned to the town by a much shorter road, and were very angry with the waiter for not having directed us to it; but he was too great a man to speak three words more than he could help.

We stopped at the proper door of the Duke's house, and seated ourselves humbly upon a bench, waiting the pleasure of the porter, who, after a little time, informed us that we could not be admitted, giving no reason whatever. When we got to the inn, we could just gather from the waiter that it was not usual to refuse admittance to strangers; but that was all: he could not, or would not, help us, so we were obliged to give it up, which mortified us, for I had wished much to see the picture. William vowed that he would write that very night to Lord Archibald Hamilton, stating the whole matter, which he did from Glasgow.

I ought to have mentioned the park, though, as we were not allowed to walk there, we saw but little of it. It looked pleasant, as all parks with fine trees must be, but, as it seemed to be only a large, nearly level, plain, it could not be a particularly beautiful park, though it borders upon the Clyde, and the Avon runs, I believe, through it, after leaving the solitude of the glen of Baroncleugh.

Quitted Hamilton at about eleven o'clock. There is nothing interesting between Hamilton and Glasgow till we came to Bothwell Castle, a few miles from Hamilton. The country is cultivated, but not rich, the fields large, a perfect contrast to the huddling together of hills and trees, corn and pasture grounds, hay-stacks, cottages, orchards, broom and gorse, but chiefly broom, that had amused us so much the evening before in passing through the Trough of the Clyde. A native of Scotland would not probably be satisfied with the account I have given of the Trough of the Clyde, for it is one of the most celebrated scenes in Scotland. We certainly received less pleasure from it than we had expected; but it was plain that this was chiefly owing to the unfavourable circumstances under which we saw it—a gloomy sky and a cold blighting wind. It is a very beautiful district, yet there, as in all the other scenes of Scotland celebrated for their fertility, we found something which gave us a notion of barrenness, of what was not altogether genial. The new fir and larch plantations, here as in almost every other part of Scotland, contributed not a little to this effect.

Crossed the Clyde not far from Hamilton, and had the river for some miles at a distance from us, on our left; but after having gone, it might be, three miles, we came to a porter's lodge on the left side of the road, where we were to turn to Bothwell Castle, which is in Lord Douglas's grounds. The woman who keeps the gate brought us a book, in which we wrote down our names. Went about half a mile before we came to the pleasure-grounds. Came to a large range of stables, where we were to leave the car; but there was no one to unyoke the horse, so William was obliged to do it himself, a task which he performed very awkwardly, being then new to it. We saw the ruined castle embosomed in trees, passed the house, and soon found ourselves on the edge of a steep brow immediately above and overlooking the course of the river Clyde through a deep hollow between woods and green steeps. We had approached at right angles from the main road to the place over a flat, and had seen nothing before us but a nearly level country terminated by distant slopes, the Clyde hiding himself in his deep bed. It was exceedingly delightful to come thus unexpectedly upon such a beautiful region.

The Castle stands nobly, overlooking the Clyde. When we came up to it I was hurt to see that flower-borders had taken place of the natural overgrowings of the ruin, the scattered stones and wild plants. It is a large and grand pile, of red freestone, harmonizing perfectly with the rocks of the river, from which, no doubt, it has been hewn. When I was a little accustomed to the unnaturalness of a modern garden, I could not help admiring the excessive beauty and luxuriance of some of the plants, particularly the purple-flowered clematis, and a broad-leaved creeping plant without flowers, which scrambled up the castle wall along with the ivy, and spread its vine-like branches so lavishly that it seemed to be in its natural situation, and one could not help thinking that, though not self-planted among the ruins of this country, it must somewhere have its natural abode in such places. If Bothwell Castle had not been close to the Douglas mansion we should have been disgusted with the possessor's miserable conception of 'adorning' such a venerable ruin; but it is so very near to the house that of necessity the pleasure-grounds must have extended beyond it, and perhaps the neatness of a shaven lawn and the complete desolation natural to a ruin might have made an unpleasing contrast; and besides, being within the precincts of the pleasure-grounds, and so very near to the modern mansion of a noble family, it has forfeited in some degree its independent majesty, and becomes a tributary to the mansion; its solitude being interrupted, it has no longer the same command over the mind in sending it back into past times, or excluding the ordinary feelings which we bear about us in daily life. We had then only to regret that the castle and house were so near to each other; and it was impossible *not* to regret it; for the ruin presides in state over the river, far from city or town, as if it might have had a peculiar privilege to preserve its memorials of past ages and maintain its own character and independence for centuries to come.

We sat upon a bench under the high trees, and had beautiful views of the different reaches of the river above and below. On the opposite bank, which is finely wooded with elms and other trees, are the remains of an ancient priory, built upon a rock: and rock and ruin are so blended together that it is impossible to separate the one from the other. Nothing can be more beautiful than the little remnants of this holy place; elm trees—for we were near enough to distinguish them by their branches—grow out of the walls, and overshadow a small but very elegant window. It can scarcely be conceived what a grace the castle and priory impart to each other; and the river Clyde flows on smooth and unruffled below, seeming to my thoughts more in harmony with the sober and stately images of former times, than if it had roared over a rocky channel, forcing its sound upon the ear. It blended gently with the warbling of the smaller birds and chattering of the larger ones that had made their nests in the ruins. In this fortress the chief of the English nobility were confined after the battle of Bannockburn. If a man is to be a prisoner, he scarcely could have a more pleasant place to solace his captivity; but I thought that for close confinement I should prefer the banks of a lake or the sea-side. The greatest charm of a brook or river is in the liberty to pursue it through its windings; you can then take it in

whatever mood you like; silent or noisy, sportive or quiet. The beauties of
a brook or river must be sought, and the pleasure is in going in search of
them; those of a lake or of the sea come to you of themselves. These rude
warriors cared little perhaps about either; and yet if one may judge from the
writings of Chaucer and from the old romances, more interesting passions
were connected with natural objects in the days of chivalry than now,
though going in search of scenery, as it is called, had not then been thought
of. I had heard nothing of Bothwell Castle, at least nothing that I remembered, therefore, perhaps, my pleasure was greater, compared with what I
received elsewhere, than others might feel.

At our return to the stables we found an inferior groom, who helped
William to yoke the horse, and was very civil. We grew hungry before we
had travelled many miles, and seeing a large public-house—it was in a
walled court some yards from the road—Coleridge got off the car to inquire
if we could dine there, and was told we could have nothing but eggs. It was
a miserable place, very like a French house; indeed we observed, in almost
every part of Scotland, except Edinburgh, that we were reminded ten times
of France and Germany for once of England.

Saw nothing remarkable after leaving Bothwell, except the first view of
Glasgow, at some miles distance, terminated by the mountains of Loch
Lomond. The suburbs of Glasgow extend very far, houses on each side of
the highway,—all ugly, and the inhabitants dirty. The roads are very wide;
and everything seems to tell of the neighbourhood of a large town. We were
annoyed by carts and dirt, and the road was full of people, who all noticed
our car in one way or other; the children often sent a hooting after us.

Wearied completely, we at last reached the town, and were glad to walk,
leading the car to the first decent inn, which was luckily not far from the
end of the town. William, who gained most of his road-knowledge from
ostlers, had been informed of this house by the ostler at Hamilton; it proved
quiet and tolerably cheap, a new building—the Saracen's Head.[1] I shall never

1. The inn still stands at 209 Gallogate (near the Barras, a few blocks from Glasgow Cross),
and having gone through several incarnations over the years, was recently renovated to open
as an attractive tavern. Established in 1755 by Robert Tennant, brother of the founder of
Tennant's brewery, the inn was Glasgow's first hotel, built on the site of Little Mungo's
church and burial ground. The town council sold the property in 1754 for the purpose of
building the Saracen Head Inn (singular "Saracen"), and the purchaser was allowed to take
building material from the churchyard wall (Sir James D. Marwick, *Early Glasgow*. Ed. Robert
Renwick. Glasgow: James Maclehose and Sons, 1911, p. 250). The new owner passes along
a story that a female skull was included in the deed for the inn. The skull is either the head
of a young woman named Maggie who was the last to be burned as a witch, or the head of
a girl from a nearby leper colony. The deed requires that the skull be placed in the Glasgow
Green if it should ever be removed.

Another tale is that there was a huge (five liter) bowl that men who frequented the inn
passed around and drank out of communally. Boswell and Johnson, Burns, and Adam Smith
belong to the history of the place. For *Jones's Directory to Glasgow 1787* the Saracen's Head
was a "favourite place of resort for travellers and citizens of distinction. It was patronized by

forget how glad I was to be landed in a little quiet back-parlour, for my head was beating with the noise of carts which we had left, and the wearisomeness of the disagreeable objects near the highway; but with my first pleasant sensations also came the feeling that we were not in an English inn—partly from its half-unfurnished appearance, which is common in Scotland, for in general the deal wainscots and doors are unpainted, and partly from the dirtiness of the floors. Having dined, William and I walked to the post-office, and after much seeking found out a quiet timber-yard wherein to sit down and read our letter. We then walked a considerable time in the streets, which are perhaps as handsome as streets can be, which derive no particular effect from their situation in connexion with natural advantages, such as rivers, sea, or hills. The Trongate, an old street, is very picturesque—high houses, with an intermixture of gable fronts towards the street. The New Town is built of fine stone, in the best style of the very best London streets at the west end of the town, but, not being of brick, they are greatly superior. One thing must strike every stranger in his first walk through Glasgow—an appearance of business and bustle, but no coaches or gentlemen's carriages; during all the time we walked in the streets I only saw three carriages, and these were travelling chaises. I also could not but observe a want of cleanliness in the appearance of the lower orders of the people, and a dulness in the dress and outside of the whole mass, as they moved along. We returned to the inn before it was dark. I had a bad headache, and was tired, and we all went to bed soon.

Tuesday, August 23d.—A cold morning. Walked to the bleaching-ground, a large field bordering on the Clyde, the banks of which are perfectly flat, and the general face of the country is nearly so in the neighbourhood of Glasgow.[1] This field, the whole summer through, is covered with women of all ages, children, and young girls spreading out their linen, and watching it while it bleaches. The scene must be very cheerful on a fine day, but it

the Lords of Judiciary on circuit, and by the nobility of several counties, including the sporting Duke of Hamilton. It was in this famous hostelry that Dr. Samuel Johnson took up his quarters after his tour through the Hebrides; and on his arrival, after seating himself in front of the fire, he put a leg on each side of the grate, and with a mock solemnity said: 'Here am I, an Englishman, sitting by a coal fire!'" ("The Rambling Reporter" [Peter Allan]: Introduction to a reprint of *Jones's Directory.* Glasgow: William Love, 1868, p. 13).

1. The bleaching ground, near the city's east end, on the banks of the Clyde, was a public laundry area on what is today called Glasgow Green. The grounds had been given to the people of Glasgow around 1450 by Bishop Turnbull for common grazing land. Coleridge was impressed with the facility: "At Glasgow I was most pleased by the [two] great Washing-Houses & Drying Grounds /—Four Square Cloysters, with an open Square, & the Cauldron in the Middle / each Woman pays a $\frac{1}{2}^{ny}$ for her Tub & $\frac{1}{2}$, sometimes in scarce times 1^{d} for a Tub of hot water / a penny to the Watcher—so that the poorest person who can get Cloathes to wash may earn their living, whereas in other cities those only can do it who can pay for Lodgings with Fire & Washing utensiles &c—I suppose there might be 120 women in each House /—" (*Notebooks,* I p. 1454 7.7).

rained when we were there, and though there was linen spread out in all parts, and great numbers of women and girls were at work, yet there would have been many more on a fine day, and they would have appeared happy, instead of stupid and cheerless. In the middle of the field is a wash-house, whither the inhabitants of this large town, rich and poor, send or carry their linen to be washed. There are two very large rooms, with each a cistern in the middle for hot water; and all round the rooms are benches for the women to set their tubs upon. Both the rooms were crowded with washers; there might be a hundred, or two, or even three; for it is not easy to form an accurate notion of so great a number; however, the rooms were large, and they were both full. It was amusing to see so many women, arms, head, and face all in motion, all busy in an ordinary household employment, in which we are accustomed to see, at the most, only three or four women employed in one place. The women were very civil. I learnt from them the regulations of the house; but I have forgotten the particulars. The substance of them is, that 'so much' is to be paid for each tub of water, 'so much' for a tub, and the privilege of washing for a day, and, 'so much' to the general overlookers of the linen, when it is left to be bleached. An old man and woman have this office, who were walking about, two melancholy figures.

The shops at Glasgow are large, and like London shops, and we passed by the largest coffee-room I ever saw.[1] You look across the piazza of the Exchange, and see to the end of the coffee-room, where there is a circular window, the width of the room. Perhaps there might be thirty gentlemen sitting on the circular bench of the window, each reading a newspaper. They had the appearance of figures in a fantoccine,[2] or men seen at the extremity of the operahouse, diminished into puppets.

I am sorry I did not see the High Church: both William and I were tired, and it rained very hard after we had left the bleaching-ground; besides, I am less eager to walk in a large town than anywhere else; so we put it off, and I have since repented of my irresolution.

Dined, and left Glasgow at about three o'clock, in a heavy rain. We were obliged to ride through the streets to keep our feet dry, and, in spite of the rain, every person as we went along stayed his steps to look at us; indeed, we had the pleasure of spreading smiles from one end of Glasgow to the other—for we travelled the whole length of the town. A set of schoolboys, perhaps there might be eight, with satchels over their shoulders, and, except one or two, without shoes and stockings, yet very well dressed in jackets and

1. The Tontine Hotel and coffee room were just west of the toll booth on Trongate. The coffee room was seventy-two feet long, according to *Vanishing Glasgow* (Heather F.C. Lyall; Queen Mother Library, Aberdeen: AUL Publishing, 1991) and "boasted a wall for advertisements, newspapers, a logbook for the arrival and departure of shipping, and a daily delivery of mail. Amazingly tobacco and liquor were barred!" (p. 10).
2. A show performed by puppets operated by concealed wires or strings.

trousers, like gentlemen's children, followed us in great delight, admiring the car and longing to jump up. At last, though we were seated, they made several attempts to get on behind; and they looked so pretty and wild, and at the same time so modest, that we wished to give them a ride, and there being a little hill near the end of the town, we got off, and four of them who still remained, the rest having dropped into their homes by the way, took our places; and indeed I would have walked two miles willingly, to have had the pleasure of seeing them so happy. When they were to ride no longer, they scampered away, laughing and rejoicing. New houses are rising up in great numbers round Glasgow, citizen-like houses, and new plantations, chiefly of fir; the fields are frequently enclosed by hedgerows, but there is no richness, nor any particular beauty for some miles.

The first object that interested us was a gentleman's house upon a green plain or holm, almost close to the Clyde, sheltered by tall trees, a quiet modest mansion, and, though white-washed, being an old building, and no other house near it, or in connexion with it, and standing upon the level field, which belonged to it, its own domain, the whole scene together brought to our minds an image of the retiredness and sober elegance of a nunnery; but this might be owing to the greyness of the afternoon, and our having come immediately from Glasgow, and through a country which, till now, had either had a townish taint, or at best little of rural beauty. While we were looking at the house we overtook a foot-traveller, who, like many others, began to talk about our car. We alighted to walk up a hill, and, continuing the conversation, the man told us, with something like a national pride, that it belonged to a Scotch Lord, Lord Semple; he added, that a little further on we should see a much finer prospect, as fine a one as ever we had seen in our lives. Accordingly, when we came to the top of the hill, it opened upon us most magnificently. We saw the Clyde, now a stately sea-river, winding away mile after mile, spotted with boats and ships, each side of the river hilly, the right populous with single houses and villages— Dunglass Castle upon a promontory,[1] the whole view terminated by the rock of Dumbarton, at five or six miles distance, which stands by itself, without any hills near it, like a sea-rock.

We travelled for some time near the river, passing through clusters of houses which seemed to owe their existence rather to the wealth of the river than the land, for the banks were mostly bare, and the soil appeared poor, even near the water. The left side of the river was generally uninhabited and

---

1. Dunglass Castle was in the early part of the twentieth century the home of graphic artist Talwin Morris and became a center of the art movement known as the Glasgow Style, attracting to its rooms the group called "The Four": Frances and Margaret Macdonald, Herbert MacNair, and Charles Rennie Mackintosh. Mackintosh, in fact, redesigned the interior of the castle. Long after it ceased to be a dwelling place, it was used as a stationery store. It is now on the grounds of an ESSO oil terminal which is kept under strict security. To visit the castle one must must be escorted by an ESSO guard and agree to don a hard hat.

moorish, yet there are some beautiful spots: for instance, a nobleman's house,[1] where the fields and trees were rich, and, in combination with the river, looked very lovely. As we went along William and I were reminded of the views upon the Thames in Kent, which, though greatly superior in richness and softness, are much inferior in grandeur. Not far from Dumbarton, we passed under some rocky, copse-covered hills, which were so like some of the hills near Grasmere that we could have half believed they were the same. Arrived at Dumbarton before it was dark, having pushed on briskly that we might have start of a traveller at the inn, who was following us as fast as he could in a gig. Every front room was full, and we were afraid we should not have been admitted. They put us into a little parlour, dirty, and smelling of liquors, the table uncleaned, and not a chair in its place; we were glad, however, of our sorry accommodations.

While tea was preparing we lolled at our ease, and though the room-window overlooked the stable-yard, and at our entrance there appeared to be nothing but gloom and unloveliness, yet while I lay stretched upon the carriage cushions on three chairs, I discovered a little side peep which was enough to set the mind at work. It was no more than a smoky vessel lying at anchor, with its bare masts, a clay hut and the shelving bank of the river, with a green pasture above. Perhaps you will think that there is not much in this, as I describe it: it is true; but the effect produced by these simple objects, as they happened to be combined, together with the gloom of the evening, was exceedingly wild. Our room was parted by a slender partition from a large dining-room, in which were a number of officers and their wives, who, after the first hour, never ceased singing, dancing, laughing, or loud talking. The ladies sang some pretty songs, a great relief to us. We went early to bed; but poor Coleridge could not sleep for the noise at the street door; he lay in the parlour below stairs. It is no uncommon thing in the best inns of Scotland to have shutting-up beds in the sitting-rooms.

Wednesday, August 24th.—As soon as breakfast was over, William and I walked towards the Castle, a short mile from the town. We overtook two young men, who, on our asking the road, offered to conduct us, though it might seem it was not easy to miss our way, for the rock rises singly by itself from the plain on which the town stands. The rock of Dumbarton is very grand when you are close to it, but at a little distance, under an ordinary sky, and in open day, it is not grand, but curiously wild. The castle and fortifications add little effect to the general view of the rock, especially since the building of a modern house, which is white-washed, and consequently jars, wherever it is seen, with the natural character of the place. There is a path up to the house, but it being low water we could walk round the rock, which we resolved to do. On that side next the town green grass grows to

1. Probably Erskine House, the seat of Lord Blantyre.

a considerable height up the rock, but wherever the river borders upon it, it is naked stone. I never saw rock in nobler masses, or more deeply stained by time and weather; nor is this to be wondered at, for it is in the very eye of sea-storms and land-storms, of mountain winds and water winds. It is of all colours, but a rusty yellow predominates. As we walked along, we could not but look up continually, and the mass above being on every side so huge, it appeared more wonderful than when we saw the whole together.

We sat down on one of the large stones which lie scattered near the base of the rock, with sea-weed growing amongst them. Above our heads the rock was perpendicular for a considerable height, nay, as it seemed, to the very top, and on the brink of the precipice a few sheep, two of them rams with twisted horns, stood, as if on the look-out over the wide country. At the same time we saw a sentinel in his red coat, walking backwards and forwards between us and the sky, with his firelock over his shoulder. The sheep, I suppose owing to our being accustomed to see them in similar situations, appeared to retain their real size, while, on the contrary, the soldier seemed to be diminished by the distance till he almost looked like a puppet moved with wires for the pleasure of children, or an eight years' old drummer in his stiff, manly dress beside a company of grenadiers. I had never before, perhaps, thought of sheep and men in soldiers' dresses at the same time, and here they were brought together in a strange fantastic way. As will be easily conceived, the fearlessness and stillness of those quiet creatures, on the brow of the rock, pursuing their natural occupations, contrasted with the restless and apparently unmeaning motions of the dwarf soldier, added not a little to the general effect of this place, which is that of wild singularity, and the whole was aided by a blustering wind and a gloomy sky. Coleridge joined us, and we went up to the top of the rock.

The road to a considerable height is through a narrow cleft, in which a flight of steps is hewn; the steps nearly fill the cleft, and on each side the rocks form a high and irregular wall; it is almost like a long sloping cavern, only that it is roofed by the sky. We came to the barracks;[1] soldiers' wives were hanging out linen upon the rails, while the wind beat about them furiously—there was nothing which it could set in motion but the garments of the women and the linen upon the rails; the grass—for we had now come to green grass—was close and smooth, and not one pile an inch above another, and neither tree nor shrub. The standard pole stood erect without a flag. The rock has two summits, one much broader and higher than the other. When we were near to the top of the lower eminence we had the pleasure of finding a little garden of flowers and vegetables belonging to the soldiers. There are three distinct and very noble prospects—the first up

1. The barracks were close to the French Prison.

the Clyde towards Glasgow—Dunglass Castle, seen on its promontory—
boats, sloops, hills, and many buildings; the second, down the river to the
sea—Greenock and Port Glasgow, and the distant mountains at the entrance
of Loch Long; and the third extensive and distant view is up the Leven,
which here falls into the Clyde, to the mountains of Loch Lomond. The
distant mountains in all these views were obscured by mists and dingy
clouds, but if the grand outline of any one of the views can be seen, it is
sufficient recompence for the trouble of climbing the rock of Dumbarton.

The soldier who was our guide told us that an old ruin which we came
to at the top of the higher eminence had been a wind-mill—an inconvenient station, though certainly a glorious place for wind; perhaps if it really
had been a wind-mill it was only for the use of the garrison. We looked
over cannons on the battery-walls, and saw in an open field below the
yeomanry cavalry exercising, while we could hear from the town, which
was full of soldiers, 'Dumbarton's drums beat bonny, O!' Yet while we
stood upon this eminence, rising up so far as it does—inland, and having the
habitual old English feeling of our own security as islanders—we could not
help looking upon the fortress, in spite of its cannon and soldiers, and the
rumours of invasion, as set up against the hostilities of wind and weather
rather than for any other warfare. On our return we were invited into the
guard-room, about half-way down the rock, where we were shown a large
rusty sword, which they called Wallace's Sword, and a trout boxed up in a
well close by, where they said he had been confined for upwards of thirty
years.[1] For the pleasure of the soldiers, who were anxious that we should see
him, we took some pains to spy him out in his black den, and at last
succeeded. It was pleasing to observe how much interest the poor soldiers—
though themselves probably new to the place—seemed to attach to this
antiquated inhabitant of their garrison.

When we had reached the bottom of the rock along the same road by
which we had ascended, we made our way over the rough stones left bare
by the tide, round the bottom of the rock, to the point where we had set
off. This is a wild and melancholy walk on a blustering cloudy day: the
naked bed of the river, scattered over with sea-weed; grey swampy fields on

---

1. "The basement and vaulted cellar of the Wallace Tower may be seen inside the north–east
angle of the battery. This tower stood four stories high above its basement until it was levelled
to make way for a barrack-block (now removed) behind the Duke of York's Battery." (Iain
MacIvor, *Dumbarton Castle*. Historic Scotland).

The trout, not Wallace had been confined. Neither the history of Dumbarton Castle nor
the story of Wallace's life squares with the possibility that Wallace had been imprisoned here.
Wallace Tower on Dumbarton Rock was not erected until 1617, long after his death. It was
levelled toward the end of the eighteenth century and the remains give the appearance of a
well. Wallace himself could certainly not have spent thirty years imprisoned anywhere as he
died before he was thirty-five.

Coleridge notices "Wallace's Sword, & the Trout in the Well 36 years of age / black, &
18 inches long—" (*Notebooks*, I p. 1461 7.14).

the other shore; sea-birds flying overhead; the high rock perpendicular and bare. We came to two very large fragments, which had fallen from the main rock; Coleridge though that one of them was as large as Bowder-Stone,[1] William and I did not; but it is impossible to judge accurately; we probably, without knowing it, compared them with the whole mass from which they had fallen, which, from its situation, we consider as one rock or stone, and there is no object of the kind for comparison with the Bowder-Stone. When we leave the shore of the Clyde grass begins to show itself on the rock; go a considerable way—still under the rock—along a flat field, and pass immediately below the white house, which wherever seen looks so ugly.

Left Dumbarton at about eleven o'clock. The sky was cheerless and the air ungenial, which we regretted, as we were going to Loch Lomond, and wished to greet the first of the Scottish lakes with our cheerfullest and best feelings. Crossed the Leven at the end of Dumbarton, and, when we looked behind, had a pleasing view of the town, bridge, and rock; but when we took in a reach of the river at the distance of perhaps half a mile, the swamp ground, being so near a town, and not in its natural wildness, but seemingly half cultivated, with houses here and there, gave us an idea of extreme poverty of soil, or that the inhabitants were either indolent or miserable. We had to travel four miles on the banks of the 'Water of Leven' before we should come to Loch Lomond. Having expected a grand river from so grand a lake, we were disappointed; for it appeared to me not to be very much larger that the Emont, and is not near so beautiful; but we must not forget that the day was cold and gloomy. Near Dumbarton it is like a river in a flat country, or under the influence of tides; but a little higher up it resembles one of our rivers, flowing through a vale of no extreme beauty, though prettily wooded; the hills on each side not very high, sloping backwards from the bed of the vale, which is neither very narrow nor very wide; the prospect terminated by Ben Lomond and other mountains. The vale is populous, but looks as if it were not inhabited by cultivators of the earth; the houses are chiefly of stone; often in rows by the river-side; they stand pleasantly, but have a tradish look, as if they might have been off-sets from Glasgow. We saw many bleach-yards, but no other symptom of a manufactory, except something in the houses that was not rural, and a want

1. The Bowder Stone, in Borrowdale, at the southern extremity of Derwentwater in the Lake District, is a huge rock that appears to have fallen from the crags and landed at a precarious tilt. It was one of the curiosities tourists were urged to discover in early guide books. *Black's Picturesque Guide to the English Lakes* (13th ed. Edinburgh, 1865) describes it as: "an immense block, which has rolled from the heights above, and now rests on a platform of ground, a short distance to the left of the road [from Keswick]. It is 62 feet long, 36 feet high, 89 feet in circumference, and it has been computed to weigh upwards of 1,900 tons. A branch road through the slate quarry, which rejoins the Borrowdale road further on, has been made to the Stone, and the summit may be gained by means of a ladder, affixed for the use of strangers" (p. 14). One may still approach the Bowder Stone by a road passing the quarry, and the ladder is still propped against the stone, but climbing to the top does not yield much of a view since the "immense block" is now surrounded by tall trees.

of independent comforts. Perhaps if the river had been glittering in the sun, and the smoke of the cottages rising in distinct volumes towards the sky, as I have seen in the vale or basin below Pillsden in Dorsetshire, when every cottage, hidden from the eye, pointed out its lurking-place by an upright wreath of white smoke, the whole scene might have excited ideas of perfect cheerfulness.

Here, as on the Nith, and much more than in the Trough of the Clyde, a great portion of the ground was uncultivated, but the hills being less wild, the river more stately, and the ground not heaved up so irregularly and tossed about, the imperfect cultivation was the more to be lamented, particularly as there were so many houses near the river. In a small enclosure by the wayside is a pillar erected to the memory of Dr. Smollett, who was born in a village at a little distance, which we could see at the same time, and where, I believe, some of the family still reside.[1] There is a long Latin inscription, which Coleridge translated for my benefit. The Latin is miserably bad—as Coleridge said, such as poor Smollett, who was an excellent scholar, would have been ashamed of.[2]

Before we came to Loch Lomond the vale widened, and became less populous. We climbed over a wall into a large field to have a better front view of the lake than from the road. This view is very much like that from Mr. Clarkson's windows: the mountain in front resembles Hallan; indeed, is almost the same; but Ben Lomond is not seen standing in such majestic company as Helvellyn, and the meadows are less beautiful than Ulswater. The reach of the lake is very magnificent; you see it, as Ulswater is seen beyond the promontory of Old Church, winding away behind a large woody island that looks like a promontory. The outlet of the lake—we had a distinct view of it in the field—is very insignificant. The bulk of the river is frittered away by small alder bushes, as I recollect; I do not remember that it was reedy, but the ground had a swampy appearance; and here the vale spreads out wide and shapeless, as if the river were born to no inheritance, had no sheltering cradle, no hills of its own. As we have seen, this does not continue long; it flows through a distinct, though not a magnificent vale. But, having lost the pastoral character which it had in the youthful days of Smollett—if the description in this ode to his native stream be a faithful one—it is less interesting that it was then.[3]

The road carried us sometimes close to the lake, sometimes at a considerable distance from it, over moorish grounds, or through half-cultivated

1. The birthplace of Tobias Smollett (1721–71) is a half mile south of his monument in Renton, at the family home of Dalquharn.
2. See Appendix 3.
3. Smollett's poem "Ode to Leven-Water" has the river's banks filled with pastoral motifs. Here one may see "num'rous herds and flocks" as well as

> lasses chanting o'er the pail,
> And shepherds piping in the dale.

enclosure; we had the lake on our right, which is here so wide that the opposite hills, not being high, are cast into insignificance, and we could not distinguish any buildings near the water, if any there were. It is however always delightful to travel by a lake of clear waters, if you see nothing else but a very ordinary country; but we had some beautiful distant views, one in particular, down the high road, through a vista of over-arching trees; and the near shore was frequently very pleasing, with its gravel banks, bendings, and small bays. In one part it was bordered for a considerable way by irregular groups of forest trees or single stragglers, which, although not large, seemed old; their branches were stunted and knotty, as if they had been striving with storms, and had half yielded to them. Under these trees we had a variety of pleasing views across the lake, and the very rolling over the road and looking at its smooth and beautiful surface was itself a pleasure. It was as smooth as a gravel walk, and of the bluish colour of some of the roads among the lakes of the north of England.

Passed no very remarkable place till we came to Sir James Colquhoun's house, which stands upon a large, flat, woody peninsula, looking towards Ben Lomond. There must be many beautiful walks among the copses of the peninsula, and delicious views over the water; but the general surface of the country is poor, and looks as if it ought to be rich and well peopled, for it is not mountainous; nor had we passed any hills which a Cumbrian would dignify with the name of mountains. There was many a little plain or gently-sloping hill covered with poor heath or broom without trees, where one should have liked to see a cottage in a bower of wood, with its patch of corn and potatoes, and a green field with a hedge to keep it warm. As we advanced we perceived less of the coldness of poverty, the hills not having so large a space between them and the lake. The surface of the hills being in its natural state, is always beautiful; but where there is only a half cultivated and half peopled soil near the banks of a lake or river, the idea is forced upon one that they who do live there have not much of cheerful enjoyment.

But soon we came to just such a place as we had wanted to see. The road was close to the water, and a hill, bare, rocky, or with scattered copses rose above it. A deep shade hung over the road, where some little boys were at play; we expected a dwelling-house of some sort; and when we came nearer, saw three or four thatched huts under the trees, and at the same moment felt that it was a paradise. We had before seen the lake only as one wide plain of water; but here the portion of it which we saw was bounded by a high and steep, heathy and woody island opposite, which did not appear like an island, but the main shore, and framed out a little oblong lake apparently not so broad as Rydale-water, with one small island covered with trees, resembling some of the most beautiful of the holms of Windermere, and only a narrow river's breadth from the shore. This was a place where we should have liked to have lived, and the only one we had seen near Loch Lomond.

How delightful to have a little shed concealed under the branches of the fairy island! the cottages and the island might have been made for the pleasure of each other. It was but like a natural garden, the distance was so small; nay, one could not have forgiven any one living there, not compelled to daily labour, if he did not connect it with his dwelling by some feeling of domestic attachment, like what he has for the orchard where his children play. I thought, what a place for William! he might row himself over with twenty strokes of the oars, escaping from the business of the house, and as safe from intruders, with his boat anchored beside him, as if he had locked himself up in the strong tower of a castle. We were unwilling to leave this sweet spot; but it was so simple, and therefore so rememberable, that it seemed almost as if we could have carried it away with us. It was nothing more than a small lake enclosed by trees at the ends and by the way-side, and opposite by the island, a steep bank on which the purple heath was seen under low oak coppice-wood, a group of houses over-shadowed by trees, and a bending road. There was one remarkable tree, an old larch with hairy branches, which sent out its main stem horizontally across the road, an object that seemed to have been singled out for injury where everything else was lovely and thriving, tortured into that shape by storms, which one might have thought could not have reached it in that sheltered place.

We were now entering into the Highlands. I believe Luss is the place where we were told that country begins; but at these cottages I would have gladly believed that we were there, for it was like a new region. The huts were after the Highland fashion, and the boys who were playing wore the Highland dress and philabeg.[1] On going into a new country I seem to myself to waken up, and afterwards it surprises me to remember how much alive I have been to the distinctions of dress, household arrangements, etc. etc., and what a spirit these little things give to wild, barren, or ordinary places. The cottages are within about two miles of Luss. Came in view of several islands; but the lake being so very wide, we could see little of their peculiar beauties, and they, being large, hardly looked like islands.

Passed another gentleman's house, which stands prettily in a bay, and soon after reached Luss, where we intended to lodge.[2] On seeing the outside of the inn, we were glad that we were to have such pleasant quarters. It is a nice looking white house, by the road-side; but there was not much

---

1. A kilt.
2. A well-preserved village today, Luss was the gateway to the Highlands from the mid-eighteenth century through the Romantic period and beyond. To the readers of his guide book John Stoddart pointed out: "The Highlands are usually distinguished from the Lowlands by the use of the Gaelic, and Scottish languages. According to this rule, Luss might be called the portal of the Highlands, as the former of those tongues is used to the north of it, and the latter to the south. Here also begins the more general use of the plaid, with all its accompaniments. I need scarcely mention the great picturesqueness of this dress . . ." (*Remarks*, 1 p. 228).

promise of hospitality when we stopped at the door: no person came out till we had shouted a considerable time. A barefooted lass showed me up-stairs, and again my hopes revived; the house was clean for a Scotch inn, and the view very pleasant to the lake, over the top of the village—a cluster of thatched houses among trees, with a large chapel in the midst of them. Like most of the Scotch kirks which we had seen, this building resembles a big house; but it is a much more pleasing building than they generally are, and has one of our rustic belfries, not unlike that at Ambleside, with two bells hanging in the open air. We chose one of the back rooms to sit in, being more snug, and they looked upon a very sweet prospect—a stream tumbling down a cleft or glen on the hill-side, rocky coppice ground, a rural lane, such as we have from house to house at Grasmere, and a few out-houses. We had a poor dinner, and sour ale; but as long as the people were civil we were contented.

Coleridge was not well, so he did not stir out, but William and I walked through the village to the shore of the lake. When I came close to the houses, I could not but regret a want of loveliness correspondent with the beauty of the situation and the appearance of the village at a little distance; not a single ornamented garden. We saw potatoes and cabbages, but never a honeysuckle. Yet there were wild gardens, as beautiful as any that ever man cultivated, overgrowing the roofs of some of the cottages, flowers and creeping plants. How elegant were the wreaths of the bramble that had 'built its own bower' upon the riggins in several parts of the village; therefore we had chiefly to regret the want of gardens, as they are symptoms of leisure and comfort, or at least of no painful industry. Here we first saw houses without windows, the smoke coming out of the open window-places; the chimneys were like stools with four legs, a hole being left in the roof for the smoke, and over that a slate placed upon four sticks—sometimes the whole leaned as if it were going to fall. The fields close to Luss lie flat to the lake, and a river, as large as our stream near the church at Grasmere, flows by the end of the village, being the same which comes down the glen behind the inn; it is very much like our stream—beds of blue pebbles upon the shores.

We walked towards the head of the lake, and from a large pasture field near Luss, a gentle eminence, had a very interesting view back upon the village and the lake and islands beyond. We then perceived that Luss stood in the centre of a spacious bay, and that close to it lay another small one, within the larger, where the boats of the inhabitants were lying at anchor, a beautiful natural harbour. The islands, as we look down the water, are seen in great beauty. Inch-ta-vanach, the same that framed out the little peaceful lake which we had passed in the morning, towers above the rest. The lake is very wide here, and the opposite shores not being lofty the chief part of the permanent beauty of this view is among the islands, and on the near shore, including the low promontories of the bay of Luss, and the village; and we saw it under its dullest aspect—the air cold, the sky gloomy, without a glimpse of sunshine.

On a splendid evening, with the light of the sun diffused over the whole islands, distant hills, and the broad expanse of the lake, with its creeks, bays, and little slips of water among the islands, it must be a glorious sight.

Up the lake there are no islands; Ben Lomond terminates the view, without any other large mountains; no clouds were upon it, therefore we saw the whole size and form of the mountain, yet it did not appear to me so large as Skiddaw does from Derwent-water. Continued our walk a considerable way towards the head of the lake, and went up a high hill, but saw no other reach of the water. The hills on the Luss side become much steeper, and the lake, having narrowed a little above Luss, was no longer a very wide lake where we lost sight of it.

Came to a bark hut by the shores, and sate for some time under the shelter of it. While we were here a poor woman with a little child by her side begged a penny of me, and asked where she could 'find quarters in the village.' She was a travelling beggar, a native of Scotland, had often 'heard of that water,' but was never there before. This woman's appearance, while the wind was rustling about us, and the waves breaking at our feet, was very melancholy: the waters looked wide, the hills many, and dark, and far off—no house but at Luss. I thought what a dreary waste much this lake be to such poor creatures, struggling with fatigue and poverty and unknown ways!

We ordered tea when we reached the inn, and desired the girl to light us a fire; she replied, 'I dinna ken whether she'll gie fire,' meaning her mistress. We told her we did not wish her mistress to give fire, we only desired her to let *her* make it and we would pay for it. The girl brought in the tea-things, but no fire, and when I asked if she was coming to light it, she said 'her mistress was not varra willing to gie fire.' At last, however, on our insisting upon it, the fire was lighted: we got tea by candle-light, and spent a comfortable evening. I had seen the landlady before we went out, for, as had been usual in all the country inns, there was a demur respecting beds, not withstanding the house was empty, and there were at least half-a-dozen spare beds. Her countenance corresponded with the unkindness of denying us a fire on a cold night, for she was the most cruel and hateful-looking woman I ever saw. She was overgrown with fat, and was sitting with her feet and legs in a tub of water for the dropsy,—probably brought on by whisky-drinking. The sympathy which I felt and expressed for her, on seeing her in this wretched condition—for her legs were swollen as thick as mill-posts—seemed to produced no effect; and I was obliged, after five minutes' conversation, to leave the affair of the beds undecided. Coleridge had some talk with her daughter, a smart lass in a cotton gown, with a bandeau round her head, without shoes and stockings. She told Coleridge with some pride that she had not spent all her time at Luss, but was then fresh from Glasgow.

It came on a very stormy night; the wind rattled every window in the house, and it rained heavily. William and Coleridge had bad beds, in a two-bedded room in the garrets, though there were empty rooms on the first floor, and they were disturbed by a drunken man, who had come to the inn when we were gone to sleep.

Thursday, August 25th.—We were glad when we awoke to see that it was a fine morning—the sky was bright blue, with quick-moving clouds, the hills cheerful, lights and shadows vivid and distinct. The village looked exceedingly beautiful this morning from the garret windows—the stream glittering near it, while it flowed under trees through the level fields to the lake. After breakfast, William and I went down to the water-side. The roads were as dry as if no drop of rain had fallen, which added to the pure cheerfulness of the appearance of the village, and even of the distant prospect, an effect which I always seem to perceive from clearly bright roads, for they are always brightened by rain, after a storm; but when we came among the houses I regretted even more than last night, because the contrast was greater, the slovenliness and dirt near the doors; and could not but remember, with pain from the contrast, the cottages of Somersetshire, covered with roses and myrtle, and their small gardens of herbs and flowers. While lingering by the shore we began to talk with a man who offered to row us to Inch-ta-vanach; but the sky began to darken; and the wind being high, we doubted whether we should venture, therefore made no engagement; he offered to sell me some thread, pointing to his cottage, and added that many English ladies carried thread away from Luss.

Presently after Coleridge joined us, and we determined to go to the island. I was sorry that the man who had been talking with us was not our boatman; William by some chance had engaged another. We had two rowers and a strong boat; so I felt myself bold, though there was a great chance of a high wind. The nearest point of Inch-ta-vanach is not perhaps more than a mile and a quarter from Luss; we did not land there, but rowed round the end, and landed on that side which looks towards our favourite cottages, and their own island, which, wherever seen, is still their own. It rained a little when we landed, and I took my cloak, which afterwards served us to sit down upon in our road up the hill, when the day grew much finer, with gleams of sunshine. This island belongs to Sir James Colquhoun, who has made a convenient road, that winds gently to the top of it.

We had not climbed far before we were stopped by a sudden burst of prospect, so singular and beautiful that it was like a flash of images from another world. We stood with our backs to the hill of the island, which we

Second Week
21–27 August

40. Falls of the Clyde. Gate House. ("Porter's lodge.")
"The porter's lodge is about a mile from Lanerk . . ." (p. 62)

41. Falls of the Clyde. Corra Linn. ("Cora Linn.")
"The waterfall Cora Linn is composed of two falls, with a sloping space, which *appears* to be about twenty yards between, but is much more." (p. 63)

42. Falls of the Clyde. Ruined bridge to island.
"We came to a pleasure-house, of which the little girl had the key; she said it was called the Fog-house, because it was lined with 'fog,' namely moss . . . It was circular, with a dome-like roof . . ." (p. 64)

43. Falls of the Clyde. Lower Fall of Bonnington Falls. ("Boniton Fall.")
    "We stayed some time at the Boniton Fall . . ." (p. 65)

44. Clyde Valley. "Fall of Stonebyres."
    "It has not the imposing majesty of Cora Linn; but it has the advantage of being left to itself, a grand solitude in the heart of a populous country." (p. 68)

45. Clyde Valley. "The Trough of the Clyde."
"We seemed now to have got into a country where poverty and riches were shaking hands
together . . . Bordering on . . . fruitful orchards perhaps would be a patch, its chief produce being gorse or
broom . . . The Trough of the Clyde is, indeed, a singular and very interesting region . . ." (p. 68)

46. Hamilton. Chatelherault. Hunting lodge of the Duke of Hamilton.
"Immediately after breakfast walked to the Duke of Hamilton's house . . ." (p. 69)

47. Bothwell. Bothwell Castle.
"The Castle stands nobly, overlooking the Clyde." (p. 71)

48. Bothwell. Ruined priory opposite Bothwell Castle.
"We sat upon a bench under the high trees, and had beautiful views of the different reaches of the river
above and below. On the opposite bank, which is finely wooded with elms and other trees,
are the remains of an ancient priory . . . Nothing can be more beautiful than
the little remnants of this holy place . . ." (p. 72)

49. Glasgow. Saracen Head ("Saracen's Head") on Gallowgate.
   "Wearied completely, we at last reached the town, and were glad to walk, leading the car to the first decent inn . . . it proved quiet and tolerably cheap, a new building—the Saracen's Head." (p. 73)

50. Glasgow. "The Trongate."
   "We then walked a considerable time in the streets . . . The Trongate, an old street, is very picturesque . . ." (p. 74)

51. Glasgow. Glasgow Green.
   "Walked to the bleaching-ground, a large field bordering on the Clyde . . ." (p. 74)

52. Bowling. Dunglass Castle.
"Dunglass Castle upon a promontory." (p. 76)

53. Dumbarton. Dumbarton Rock. "At a little distance."
"The rock of Dumbarton is very grand when you are close to it, but at a little
sky, and in open day, it is not grand, but curiously wild." (p. 77)

54. Dumbarton. Portcullis Arch.
"The road to a considerable height is through a narrow cleft, in which a flight of steps is hewn; the steps nearly fill the cleft, and on each side the rocks form a high and irregular wall; it is almost like a long sloping cavern, only that it is roofed by the sky." (p. 78)

55. Dumbarton. French Prison.
"We came to the barracks; soldiers' wives were hanging out linen upon the rails . . ." (p. 78)

56. Dumbarton. First view.
"There are three distinct and very noble prospects—the first up the Clyde towards Glasgow . . ." (pp. 78–9)

57. Dumbarton. Second view.
". . . the second, down the river to the sea . . ." (p. 79)

58. Dumbarton. Third view.
"and the third extensive and distinct view is up the Leven, which here falls into the Clyde, to the mountains of Loch Lomond." (p. 79)

59. Dumbarton. Cannon, battery.
"We looked over cannons on the battery-walls . . ." (p. 79)

60. The Leven.

"We had to travel four miles on the banks of the 'Water of Leven' before we should come to Loch Lomond . . . Near Dumbarton it is like a river in a flat country, or under the influence of tides; but a little higher up it resembles one of our rivers, flowing through a vale of no extreme beauty, though prettily wooded; the hills on each side not very high, sloping backwards from the bed of the vale . . ." (p. 80)

61. Renton. Smollett Monument.

"In a small enclosure by the wayside is a pillar erected to the memory of Dr. Smollett . . ." (p. 81)

62. Loch Lomond. "and woody island opposite."
"We had before seen the lake only as one wide plain of water; but here the portion of it which we saw was bounded by a high and steep, heathy and woody island opposite, which did not appear like an island, but the main shore, and framed out a little oblong lake apparently not so broad as Rydale-water . . . This was a place where we should have liked to have lived . . ." (p. 82)

63. Luss. Colquhoun Arms Hotel.
"On seeing the outside of the inn, we were glad that we were to have such pleasant quarters. It is a nice-looking white house, by the road-side . . ." (p. 83)

64. Luss. Village, with houses.
"Here we first saw houses without windows, the smoke coming out of the open window-places; the chimneys were like stools with four legs, a hole being left in the roof for the smoke . . ." (p. 84)

65. Luss. Island of Loch Lomond.
"The islands, as we look down the water, are seen in great beauty . . . The lake is very wide here, and the opposite shores not being lofty the chief part of the permanent beauty of this view is among the islands . . ." (p. 84)

66. Loch Lomond. View to the foot.
". . . and we looked towards the foot of the lake . . . The sun shone, and the distant hills were visible, some through sunny mists, others in gloom with patches of sunshine; the lake was lost under the low and distant hills, and the islands lost in the lake, which was all in motion with travelling fields of light, or dark shadows under rainy clouds." (p. 87)

67. The Cobbler.
"When we were within about half a mile of Tarbet, at a sudden turning looking to the left, we saw a very craggy-topped mountain amongst other smooth ones; the rocks on the summit distinct in shape as if they were buildings raised up by man, or uncouth images of some strange creature . . . As we conjectured, this singular mountain was the famous Cobbler, near Arrochar." (p. 90)

68. Loch Lomond. Crossing to Inversnaid. Rob Roy's Cave.
"We went a considerable way further, and landed at Rob Roy's Caves, which are in fact
no caves, but some fine rocks on the brink of the lake, in the crevices of which a man
might hide himself cunningly enough; the water is very deep below them, and the hills
above steep and covered with wood." (p. 92)

69. Inversnaid. ("Inversneyde.") Ferry landing.
"We landed at Inversneyde, the ferry-house by the waterfall, and were not sorry to part
with our boatman . . ." (p. 93)

70. Inversnaid. Waterfall.
"The fall is not very high, but the stream is considerable, as we could see by the large
black stones that were lying bare . . ." (p. 93)

71. Loch Katrine. ("Loch Ketterine.")
"There were rocky promontories and woody islands . . ." (p. 95)

72. Glengyle. Glengyle House.
"After a little time the gentleman said we should be accommodated with such beds as they
had, and should be welcome to rest in their house if we pleased." (p. 97)

73. Glengyle. Workhouse.
"After tea William and I walked out; we amused ourselves with watching the Highlanders
at work . . ." (p. 97)

74. Glengyle. Cattle in corral.
". . . they went leisurely about everything, and whatever was to be done, all followed, old men, and
young, and little children." (p. 97)

75. Glengyle. Burying place of the lairds of Glengyle.

"Mrs. Macfarlane told me she would show me the burying-place of the lairds of Glengyle, and took me to a square enclosure like a pinfold, with a stone ball at every corner . . ." (p. 100)

76. Glengyle. Graves in burying place.

". . . it was a dismal spot, containing four or five graves overgrown with long grass, nettles, and brambles." (p. 100)

77. Glengyle. Marble monument.

"Against the wall was a marble monument to the memory of one of the lairds, of whom they spoke with veneration . . ." (p. 100)

78. Loch Katrine. Island.
". . . a small island was near, and the opposite shore, covered with wood, looked soft
through the misty rain." (p. 101)

79. Loch Katrine. Foot, or south end of the loch, with *SS Sir Walter Scott* (steamboat).
". . . the termination of a long out-shooting of the water, pushed up between the steps of the main shore
where huts stand, and a broad promontory which, with its hillocks and points and lesser promontories,
occupies the center of the foot of the lake." (p. 104)

80. Loch Achray and the Trossachs.
"At the opening of the pass we climbed up a low eminence, and had an unexpected prospect suddenly before us—another lake, small compared with loch Ketterine . . ." (p. 105)

were ascending, and which shut out Ben Lomond entirely, and all the upper
part of the lake, and we looked towards the foot of the lake, scattered over
with islands without beginning and without end. The sun shone, and the
distant hills were visible, some through sunny mists, others in gloom with
patches of sunshine; the lake was lost under the low and distant hills, and the
islands lost in the lake, which was all in motion with travelling fields of light,
or dark shadows under rainy clouds. There are many hills, but no commanding eminence at a distance to confine the prospect, so that the land seemed
endless as the water.

What I had heard of Loch Lomond, or any other place in Great Britain,
had given me no idea of anything like what we beheld: it was an outlandish
scene—we might have believed ourselves in North America. The islands
were of every possible variety of shape and surface—hilly and level, large and
small, bare, rocky, pastoral, or covered with wood. Immediately under my
eyes lay one large flat island, bare and green, so flat and low that it scarcely
appeared to rise above the water, with straggling peat-stacks and a single hut
upon one of its out-shooting promontories—for it was of a very irregular
shape, though perfectly flat. Another, its next neighbour, and still nearer to
us, was covered over with heath and coppice-wood, the surface undulating,
with flat or sloping banks towards the water, and hollow places, cradle-like
valleys, behind. These two islands, with Inch-ta-vanach, where we were
standing, were intermingled with the water, I might say interbedded and
interveined with it, in a manner that was exquisitely pleasing. There were
bays innumerable, straits or passages like calm rivers, landlocked lakes, and,
to the main water, stormy promontories. The solitary hut on the flat green
island seemed unsheltered and desolate, and yet not wholly so, for it was but
a broad river's breadth from the covert of the wood of the other island. Near
to these is a miniature, an islet covered with trees, on which stands a small
ruin that looks like the remains of a religious house; it is overgrown with
ivy, and were it not that the arch of a window or gateway may be distinctly
seen, it would be difficult to believe that it was not a tuft of trees growing
in the shape of a ruin, rather than a ruin overshadowed by trees. When we
had walked a little further we saw below us, on the nearest large island,
where some of the wood had been cut down, a hut, which we conjectured
to be a bark hut. It appeared to be on the shore of a little forest lake,
enclosed by Inch-ta-vanach, where we were, and the woody island on
which the hut stands.

Beyond we had the same intricate view as before, and could discover
Dumbarton rock with its double head. There being a mist over it, it had a
ghost-like appearance—as I observed to William and Coleridge, something
like the Tor of Glastonbury from the Dorsetshire hills. Right before us, on
the flat island mentioned before, were several small single trees or shrubs,
growing at different distances from each other, close to the shore, but some

optical delusion had detached them from the land on which they stood, and they had the appearance of so many little vessels sailing along the coast of it. I mention the circumstance, because, with the ghostly image of Dumbarton Castle, and the ambiguous ruin on the small island, it was much in the character of the scene, which was throughout magical and enchanting—a new world in its great permanent outline and composition, and changing at every moment in every part of it by the effect of sun and wind and mist and shower and cloud, and the blending lights and deep shades which took place of each other, traversing the lake in every direction. The whole was indeed a strange mixture of soothing and restless images, of images inviting to rest, and others hurrying the fancy away into an activity still more pleasing than repose. Yet, intricate and homeless, that is, without lasting abiding-place for the mind, as the prospect was, there was no perplexity; we had still a guide to lead us forward.

Wherever we looked, it was a delightful feeling that there was something beyond. Meanwhile, the sense of quiet was never lost sight of; the little peaceful lakes among the islands might make you forget that the great water, Loch Lomond, was so near; and yet are more beautiful, because you know that it is so: they have their own bays and creeks sheltered within a shelter. When we had ascended to the top of the island we had a view up to Ben Lomond, over the long, broad water without spot or rock; and, looking backwards, saw the islands below us as on a map. This view, as may be supposed, was not nearly so interesting as those we had seen before. We hunted out all the houses on the shore, which were very few: there was the village of Luss, the two gentlemen's houses, our favourite cottages, and here and there a hut; but I do not recollect any comfortable-looking farm-houses, and on the opposite shore not a single dwelling. The whole scene was a combination of natural wildness, loveliness, beauty, and barrenness, or rather bareness, yet not comfortless or cold; but the whole was beautiful. We were too far off the more distant shore to distinguish any particular spots which we might have regretted were not better cultivated, and near Luss there was no want of houses.

After we had left the island, having been so much taken with the beauty of the bark hut and the little lake by which it appeared to stand, we desired the boatman to row us through it, and we landed at the hut. Walked upon the island for some time, and found out sheltered places for cottages. There were several woodman's huts, which, with some scattered fir-trees, and others in irregular knots, that made a delicious murmuring in the wind, added greatly to the romantic effect of the scene. They were built in the form of a cone from the ground, like savages' huts, the door being just large enough for a man to enter with stooping. Straw beds were raised on logs of wood, tools lying about, and a forked bough of a tree was generally suspended from the roof in the middle to hang a kettle upon. It was a place that might have been just visited by new settlers. I thought of Ruth and her dreams of romantic love:

> And then he said how sweet it were,
> A fisher or a hunter there,
> A gardener in the shade,
> Still wandering with an easy mind,
> To build a household fire, and find
> A home in every glade.[1]

We found the main lake very stormy when we had left the shelter of the islands, and there was again a threatening of rain, but it did not come on. I wanted much to go to the old ruin, but the boatmen were in a hurry to be at home. They told us it had been a stronghold built by a man who lived there alone, and was used to swim over and make depredations on the shore,—that nobody could ever lay hands on him, he was such a good swimmer, but at last they caught him in a net. The men pointed out to us an island belonging to Sir James Colquhoun, on which were a great quantity of deer.

Arrived at the inn at about twelve o'clock, and prepared to depart immediately: we should have gone with great regret if the weather had been warmer and the inn more comfortable. When we were leaving the door, a party with smart carriage and servants drove up, and I observed that the people of the house were just as slow in their attendance upon them as on us, with one single horse and outlandish Hibernian vehicle.

When we had travelled about two miles the lake became considerably narrower, the hills rocky, covered with copses, or bare, rising more immediately from the bed of the water, and therefore we had not so often to regret the want of inhabitants. Passed by, or saw at a distance, sometimes a single cottage, or two or three together, but the whole space between Luss and Tarbet is a solitude to the eye. We were reminded of Ulswater, but missed the pleasant farms, and the mountains were not so interesting: we had not seen them in companies or brotherhoods rising one above another at a long distance. Ben Lomond stood alone, opposite to us, majestically overlooking the lake; yet there was something in this mountain which disappointed me,—a want of massiveness and simplicity, perhaps from the top being broken into three distinct stages. The road carried us over a bold promontory by a steep and high ascent, and we had a long view of the lake pushing itself up in a narrow line through an avenue of mountains,

1. The simple, unfortunate heroine of Wordsworth's poem "Ruth" (1800), beguiled by an impetuous young man who has served in the military in America (in Georgia), learns in these lines some of the prospects of the new world. Dorothy overlooks the sad outcome of the relationship that promised so much, for Ruth marries the youth and he deserts her.

terminated by the mountains at the head of the lake, of which Ben Lui, if I do not mistake, is the most considerable. The afternoon was showery and misty, therefore we did not see this prospect so distinctly as we could have wished, but there was a grand obscurity over it which might make the mountains appear more numerous.

I have said so much of this lake that I am tired myself, and I fear I must have tired my friends. We had a pleasant journey to Tarbet; more than half of it on foot, for the road was hilly, and after we had climbed one small hill we were not desirous to get into the car again, seeing another before us, and our path was always delightful, near the lake, and frequently through woods. When we were within about half a mile of Tarbet, at a sudden turning looking to the left, we saw a very craggy-topped mountain amongst other smooth ones; the rocks on the summit distinct in shape as if they were buildings raised up by man, or uncouth images of some strange creature. We called out with one voice, 'That's what we wanted!' alluding to the frame-like uniformity of the side-screens of the lake for the last five or six miles. As we conjectured, this singular mountain was the famous Cobbler, near Arrochar.[1] Tarbet was before us in the recess of a deep, large bay, under the shelter of a hill. When we came up to the village we had to inquire for the inn, there being no signboard. It was a well-sized white house, the best in the place. We were conducted up-stairs into a sitting-room that might make any good-humoured travellers happy—a square room, with windows on each side, looking, one way, towards the mountains, and across the lake to Ben Lomond, the other.

There was a pretty stone house before (*i.e.* towards the lake) some huts, scattered trees, two or three green fields with hedgerows, and a little brook making its way towards the lake; the fields are almost flat, and screened on that side nearest the head of the lake by a hill, which, pushing itself out, forms the bay of Tarbet, and, towards the foot, by a gentle slope and trees. The lake is narrow, and Ben Lomond shuts up the prospect, rising directly from the water. We could have believed ourselves to be by the side of Ulswater, at Glenridden, or in some other of the inhabited retirements of that lake. We were in a sheltered place among mountains; it was not an open joyous bay, with a cheerful populous village, like Luss; but a pastoral and retired spot, with a few single dwellings. The people of the inn stared at us when we spoke, without giving us an answer immediately, which we were at first disposed to attribute to coarseness of manners, but found afterwards that they did not understand us at once, Erse being the language spoken in the family.[2] Nothing but salt meat and eggs for dinner—no potatoes; the house smelt strongly of herrings, which were hung to dry over the kitchen fire.

1. The mountain is also called Ben Arthur. Coleridge "Knew it instantly, from recollection of Mr Wilkinson's Drawing" (*Notebooks*, I p. 1468 7.21).
2. The language was Scottish Gaelic. "Erse" is a Scottish variant of Irish.

Walked in the evening towards the head of the lake; the road was steep over the hill, and when we had reached the top of it we had long views up and down the water. Passed a troop of women who were resting themselves by the roadside, as if returning from their day's labour. Amongst them was a man, who had walked with us a considerable way in the morning, and told us he was just come from America, where he had been for some years,—was going to his own home, and should return to America. He spoke of emigration as a glorious thing for them who had money. Poor fellow! I do not think that he had brought much back with him, for he had worked his passage over: I much suspected that a bundle, which he carried upon a stick, tied in a pocket-handkerchief, contained his all. He was almost blind, he said, as were many of the crew. He intended crossing the lake at the ferry; but it was stormy, and he thought he should not be able to get over that day. I could not help smiling when I saw him lying by the roadside with such a company about him, not like a wayfaring man, but seeming as much at home and at his ease as if he had just stepped out of his hut among them, and they had been neighbours all their lives. Passed one pretty house, a large thatched dwelling with out-houses, but the prospect above and below was solitary.

The sun had long been set before we returned to the inn. As travellers, we were glad to see the moon over the top of one of the hills, but it was a cloudy night, without any peculiar beauty or solemnity. After tea we made inquiries respecting the best way to go to Loch Ketterine; the landlord could give but little information, and nobody seemed to know anything distinctly of the place, though it was but ten miles off. We applied to the maid-servant who waited on us: she was a fine-looking young woman, dressed in a white bed-gown, her hair fastened up by a comb, and without shoes and stockings. When we asked her about the Trossachs she could give us no information, but on our saying, 'Do you know Loch Ketterine?' she answered with a smile, 'I *should* know that loch, for I was bred and born there.' After much difficulty we learned from her that the Trossachs were at the foot of the lake, and that by the way we were to go we should come upon them at the head, should have to travel ten miles to the foot of the water, and that there was no inn by the way. The girl spoke English very distinctly; but she had few words, and found it difficult to understand us. She did not much encourage us to go, because the roads were bad, and it was a long way, 'and there was no putting-up for the like of us.' We determined, however, to venture, and throw ourselves upon the hospitality of some cottager or gentleman. We desired the landlady to roast us a couple of fowls to carry with us. There are always plenty of fowls at the doors of a Scotch inn, and eggs are as regularly brought to table at breakfast as bread and butter.

Friday, August 26th.—We did not set off till between ten and eleven o'clock, much too late for a long day's journey.[1] Our boatman lived at the

---

1. See Appendix 4, and map, p. 31.

pretty white house which we saw from the windows: we called at his door
by the way, and, even when we were near the house, the outside looked
comfortable; but within I never saw anything so miserable from dirt, and dirt
alone: it reminded one of the house of a decayed weaver in the suburbs of
a large town, with a sickly wife and a large family; but William says it was
far worse, that it was quite Hottentotish.[1]

After long waiting, and many clumsy preparations, we got ourselves
seated in the boat; but we had not floated five yards before we perceived
that if any of the party—and there was a little Highland woman who was
going over the water with us, the boatman, his helper, and ourselves—
should stir but a few inches, leaning to one side or the other, the boat would
be full in an instant, and we at the bottom; besides, it was very leaky, and
the woman was employed to lade out the water continually. It appeared that
this crazy vessel was not the man's own, and that *his* was lying in a bay at
a little distance. He said he would take us to it as fast as possible, but I was
so much frightened I would gladly have given up the whole day's journey;
indeed not one of us would have attempted to cross the lake in that boat for
a thousand pounds. We reached the larger boat in safety after coasting a
considerable way near the shore, but just as we were landing, William
dropped the bundle which contained our food into the water. The fowls
were no worse, but some sugar, ground coffee, and pepper-cake seemed to
be entirely spoiled. We gathered together as much of the coffee and sugar
as we could and tied it up, and again trusted ourselves to the lake. The sun
shone, and the air was calm—luckily it had been so while we were in the
crazy boat—we had rocks and woods on each side of us, or bare hills;
seldom a single cottage, and there was no rememberable place till we came
opposite to a waterfall of no inconsiderable size, that appeared to drop
directly into the lake: close to it was a hut, which we were told was the
ferry-house. On the other side of the lake was a pretty farm under the
mountains, beside a river, the cultivated grounds lying all together, and
sloping towards the lake from the mountain hollow down which the river
came. It is not easy to conceive how beautiful these spots appeared after
moving on so long between the solitary steeps.

We went a considerable way further, and landed at Rob Roy's Caves,[2]
which are in fact no caves, but some fine rocks on the brink of the lake, in
the crevices of which a man might hide himself cunningly enough; the
water is very deep below them, and the hills above steep and covered with
wood. The little Highland woman, who was in size about a match for our
guide at Lanerk, accompanied us hither. There was something very gracious
in the manners of this woman; she could scarcely speak five English words,

1. Hottentot is a derogatory term used to refer to the Khoikhoi, a southern African people.
The adjective Wordsworth used meant primitive, uncivilized and culturally inferior.
2. See Appendix 5.

yet she gave me, whenever I spoke to her, as many intelligible smiles as I had needed English words to answer me, and helped me over the rocks in the most obliging manner. She had left the boat out of good-will to us, or for her own amusement. She had never seen these caves before; but no doubt had heard of them, the tales of Rob Roy's exploits being told familiarly round the 'ingles' hereabouts, for this neighbourhood was his home. We landed at Inversneyde,[1] the ferry-house by the waterfall, and were not sorry to part with out boatman, who was a coarse hard-featured man, and, speaking of the French, uttered the basest and most cowardly sentiments. His helper, a youth fresh from the Isle of Skye, was innocent of this fault, and though but a bad rower, was a far better companion; he could not speak a word of English, and sang a plaintive Gaelic air in a low tone while he plied his oar.

The ferry-house stood on the bank a few yards above the landing-place where the boat lies. It is a small hut under a steep wood, and a few yards to the right, looking towards the hut, is the waterfall. The fall is not very high, but the stream is considerable, as we could see by the large black stones that were lying bare, but the rains, if they had reached this place, had had little effect upon the waterfall; its noise was not so great as to form a contrast with the stillness of the bay into which it falls, where the boat, and house, and waterfall itself seemed all sheltered and protected. The Highland woman was to go with us the two first miles of our journey. She led us along a bye foot-path a shorter way up the hill from the ferry-house. There is a considerable settling in the hills that border Loch Lomond, at the passage by which we were to cross to Loch Ketterine; Ben Lomond, terminating near the ferry-house, is on the same side of the water with it, and about three miles above Tarbet.

We had to climb right up the hill, which is very steep, and, when close under it, seemed to be high, but we soon reached the top, and when we were there had lost sight of the lake; and now our road was over a moor, or rather through a wide moorland hollow. Having gone a little way, we saw before us, at the distance of about half a mile, a very large stone building, a singular structure, with a high wall round it, naked hill above, and neither field nor tree near; but the moor was not overgrown with heath merely, but grey grass, such as cattle might pasture upon. We could not conjecture what this building was; it appeared as if it had been built strong to defend it from storms; but for what purpose?[2] William called out to us

1. The landing at Inversnaid, the ferry house which stood on the site of the present Inversnaid Hotel, the waterfall, and the general environs inspired not only William Wordsworth's "To a Highland Girl," but later in the century, Gerard Manley Hopkins' poem "Inversnaid."

2. As the travellers were soon to learn, the building was the Garrison, built soon after the rebellion of 1715. The site was selected because it afforded a prospect over two critical passes, and the work, begun in 1718, was completed in 1719. Rob Roy and his men are said to have

that we should observe that place well, for it was exactly like one of the spittals of the Alps, built for the reception of travellers, and indeed I had thought it must be so before he spoke. This building, from its singular structure and appearance, made the place, which is itself in a country like Scotland nowise remarkable, take a character of unusual wildness and desolation—this when we first came in view of it; and afterwards, when we had passed it and looked back, three pyramidal mountains on the opposite side of Loch Lomond terminated the view, which under certain accidents of weather must be very grand. Our Highland companion had not English enough to give us any information concerning this strange building; we could only get from her that it was a 'large house,' which was plain enough.

We walked about a mile and a half over the moor without seeing any other dwelling but one hut by the burn-side, with a peat-stack and a ten-yards'-square enclosure for potatoes; then we came to several clusters of houses, even hamlets they might be called, but where there is any land belonging to the Highland huts there are so many outbuildings near, which differ in no respect from the dwelling-houses except that they send out no smoke, that one house looks like two or three. Near these houses was a considerable quantity of cultivated ground, potatoes and corn, and the people were busy making hay in the hollow places of the open vale, and all along the sides of the becks. It was a pretty sight altogether— men and women, dogs, the little running streams, with linen bleaching near them, and cheerful sunny hills and rocks on every side. We passed by one patch of potatoes that a florist might have been proud of; no carnation-bed ever looked more gay than this square plot of ground on the waste common. The flowers were in very large bunches, and of an extraordinary size, and of every conceivable shade of colouring from snow-white to deep purple. It was pleasing in that place, where perhaps was never yet a flower cultivated by man for his own pleasure, to see these blossoms grow more gladly than elsewhere, making a summer garden near the mountain dwellings.

At one of the clusters of houses we parted with our companion, who had insisted on bearing my bundle while she stayed with us. I often tried to enter into conversation with her, and seeing a small tarn before us, was reminded of the pleasure of fishing and the manner of living there, and asked her what sort of food was eaten in that place, if they lived much upon fish, or had

abducted some of the quarriers and masons working on the job. According to Mike Trubridge: "The building was quite a substantial affair, comprising two barrack blocks facing each other across a walled courtyard . . . During the second Jacobite rebellion of 1745, the Garrison was partially destroyed by Rob Roy MacGregor's eldest son, James MacGregor" (*Inversnaid Hotel*, p. 23). By the time Dorothy Wordsworth passed, it was no longer in use. Today only the remains of the north wall are visible. The Garrison Farm stands on the site and utilizes some of the structure of the original Garrison.

mutton from the hills; she looked earnestly at me, and shaking her head, replied, 'Oh yes! eat fish—no papistes, eat everything.' The tarn had one small island covered with wood; the stream that runs from it falls into Loch Ketterine, which, after we had gone a little beyond the tarn, we saw at some distance before us.

Pursued the road, a mountain horse-track, till we came to a corner of what seemed the head of the lake,[1] and there sate down completely tired, and hopeless as to the rest of our journey. The road ended at the shore, and no houses were to be seen on the opposite side except a few widely parted huts, and on the near side was a trackless heath. The land at the head of the lake was but a continuation of the common we had come along, and was covered with heather, intersected by a few straggling foot-paths.

Coleridge and I were faint with hunger, and could go no further till we had refreshed ourselves, so we ate up one of our fowls, and drank of the water of Loch Ketterine;[2] but William could not be easy till he had examined the coast, so he left us, and made his way along the moor across the head of the lake. Coleridge and I, as we sate, had what seemed to us but a dreary prospect—a waste of unknown ground which we guessed we must travel over before it was possible for us to find a shelter. We saw a long way down the lake; it was all moor on the near side; on the other the hills were steep from the water, and there were large coppice-woods, but no cheerful green fields, and no road that we could see; we knew, however, that there must be a road from house to house; but the whole lake appeared a solitude—neither boats, islands, nor houses, no grandeur in the hills, nor any loveliness in the shores. When we first came in view of it we had said it was like a barren Ulswater—Ulswater dismantled of its grandeur, and cropped of its lesser beauties. When I had swallowed my dinner I hastened after William, and Coleridge followed me. Walked through the heather with some labour for perhaps half a mile, and found William sitting on the top of a small eminence, whence we saw the real head of the lake, which was pushed up into the vale a considerable way beyond the promontory where we now sate. The view up the lake was very pleasing, resembling Thirlemere below Armath. There were rocky promontories and woody islands, and, what was most cheering to us, a neat white house on the opposite shore; but we could see no boats, so, in order to get to it we should be obliged to go round the head of the lake, a long and weary way.

1. Stronachlachar.
2. A prophetic act, since by the middle of the century Loch Katrine was providing water for Glasgow through a twenty-six-mile-long aqueduct. Subsequent acts of Parliament and further engineering led to the advanced system of aqueducts, the damming of Loch Arklet, and continued raising of the water level of Loch Katrine that characterize the Glasgow water supply today.

After Coleridge came up to us, while we were debating whether we should turn back or go forward, we espied a man on horseback at a little distance, with a boy following him on foot, no doubt a welcome sight, and we hailed him. We should have been glad to have seen either man, woman, or child at this time, but there was something uncommon and interesting in this man's appearance, which would have fixed our attention wherever we had met him. He was a complete Highlander in dress, figure, and face, and a very fine-looking man, hardy and vigorous, though past his prime. While he stood waiting for us in his bonnet and plaid, which never look more graceful than on horseback, I forgot our errand, and only felt glad that we were in the Highlands. William accosted him with, 'Sir, do you speak English?' He replied, 'A little.' He spoke however, sufficiently well for our purpose, and very distinctly, as all the Highlanders do who learn English as a foreign language; but in a long conversation they want words; he informed us that he himself was going beyond the Trossachs, to Callander, that no boats were kept to 'let;' but there were two gentlemen's houses at this end of the lake, one of which we could not yet see, it being hidden from us by a part of the hill on which we stood. The other house was that which we saw opposite to us; both the gentlemen kept boats, and probably might be able to spare one of their servants to go with us. After we had asked many questions, which the Highlander answered with patience and courtesy, he parted from us, going along a sort of horse-track, which a foot-passenger, if he once get into it, need not lose if he be careful.

When he was gone we again debated whether we should go back to Tarbet, or throw ourselves upon the mercy of one of the two gentlemen for a night's lodging. What we had seen of the main body of the lake made us little desire to see more of it; the Highlander upon the naked heath, in his Highland dress, upon his careful-going horse, with the boy following him, was worth it all; but after a little while we resolved to go on, ashamed to shrink from an adventure. Pursued the horse-track, and soon came in sight of the other gentleman's house, which stood on the opposite side of the vale, a little above the lake. It was a white house;[1] no trees near it except a new plantation of firs; but the fields were green, sprinkled over with haycocks, and the brook which comes down the valley and falls into the lake ran through them. It was like a new-made farm in a mountain vale, and yet very pleasing after the depressing prospect which had been before us.

Our road was rough, and not easy to be kept. It was between five and six o'clock when we reached the brook side, where Coleridge and I stopped,

1. This, the only house in Glengyle, has "G. Mac G 1704" on the lintel and is very likely the Macfarlane home Dorothy refers to. Known today as Glengyle House, it is privately owned. This white house stands on the site of the building in which Rob Roy was born in 1671. The first gentleman's house Dorothy mentions ("hidden from us") was no doubt The Dhu (or Dow of Glengyle), long since demolished.

and William went up towards the house, which was in a field, where about half a dozen people were at work. He addressed himself to one who appeared like the master, and all drew near him, staring at William as nobody could have stared but out of sheer rudeness, except in such a lonely place. He told his tale, and inquired about boats; there were no boats, and no lodging nearer than Callander, ten miles beyond the foot of the lake. A laugh was on every face when William said we were come to see the Trossachs; no doubt they thought we had better have stayed at our own homes. William endeavoured to make it appear not so very foolish, by informing them that it was a place much celebrated in England, though perhaps little thought of by them, and that we only differed from many of our countrymen in having come the wrong way in consequence of an erroneous direction.

After a little time the gentleman said we should be accommodated with such beds as they had, and should be welcome to rest in their house if we pleased. William came back for Coleridge and me; the men all stood at the door to receive us, and now their behaviour was perfectly courteous. We were conducted into the house by the same man who had directed us hither on the other side of the lake, and afterwards we learned that he was the father of our hostess. He showed us into a room up-stairs, begged we would sit at our ease, walk out, or do just as we pleased. It was a large square deal wainscoted room, the wainscot black with age, yet had never been painted: it did not look like an English room, and yet I do not know in what it differed, except that in England it is not common to see so large and well-built a room so ill-furnished: there were two or three large tables, and a few old chairs of different sorts, as if they had been picked up one did not know how, at sales, or had belonged to different rooms of the house ever since it was built. We sat perhaps three-quarters of an hour, and I was about to carry down our wet coffee and sugar and ask leave to boil it, when the mistress of the house entered, a tall fine-looking woman, neatly dressed in a dark-coloured gown, with a white handkerchief tied round her head; she spoke to us in a very pleasing manner, begging permission to make tea for us, an offer which we thankfully accepted. Encouraged by the sweetness of her manners, I went down-stairs to dry my feet by the kitchen fire; she lent me a pair of stockings, and behaved to me with the utmost attention and kindness. She carried the tea-things into the room herself, leaving me to make tea, and set before us cheese and butter and barley cakes. These cakes are as thin as our oat-bread, but, instead of being crisp, are soft and leathery, yet we, being hungry, and the butter delicious, ate them with great pleasure, but when the same bread was set before us afterwards we did not like it.

After tea William and I walked out; we amused ourselves with watching the Highlanders at work: they went leisurely about everything, and whatever was to be done, all followed, old men, and young, and little children.

We were driven into the house by a shower, which came on with the evening darkness, and the people leaving their work paused at the same time. I was pleased to see them a while after sitting round a blazing fire in the kitchen, father and son-in-law, master and man, and the mother with her little child on her knee. When I had been there before tea I had observed what a contrast there was between the mistress and her kitchen; she did not differ in appearance from an English country lady; but her kitchen, roof, walls, and floor of mud, was all black alike; yet now, with the light of a bright fire upon so many happy countenances, the whole room made a pretty sight.

We heard the company laughing and talking long after we were in bed; indeed I believe they never work till they are tired. The children could not speak a word of English: they were very shy at first; but after I had caressed the eldest, and given her a red leather purse, with which she was delighted, she took hold of my hand and hung about me, changing her side-long looks for pretty smiles. Her mother lamented they were so far from school, they should be obliged to send the children down into the Lowlands to be taught reading and English. Callander, the nearest town, was twenty miles from them, and it was only a small place: they had their groceries from Glasgow. She said that at Callander was their nearest church, but sometimes 'got a preaching at the Garrison.' In explaining herself she informed us that the large building which had puzzled us in the morning had been built by Government, at the request of one of the Dukes of Montrose, for the defence of his domains against the attacks of Rob Roy. I will not answer for the truth of this; perhaps it might have been built for this purpose, and as a check on the Highlands in general; certain it is, however, that it was a garrison; soldiers used to be constantly stationed there, and have only been withdrawn within the last thirteen or fourteen years. Mrs. Macfarlane attended me to my room; she said she hoped I should be able to sleep upon blankets, and said they were 'fresh from the fauld.'

Saturday, August 27th.—Before I rose, Mrs. Macfarlane came into my room to see if I wanted anything, and told me she should send the servant up with a basin of whey, saying, 'We make very good whey in this country;' indeed, I thought it the best I had ever tasted; but I cannot tell how this should be, for they only make skimmed-milk cheeses. I asked her for a little bread and milk for our breakfast, but she said it would be no trouble to make tea, as she must make it for the family; so we all breakfasted together. The cheese was set out, as before, with plenty of butter and barley-cakes, and fresh baked oaten cakes, which, no doubt, were made for us: they had been kneaded with cream, and were excellent. All the party pressed us to eat, and were very jocose about the necessity of helping out their coarse bread with butter, and they themselves ate almost as much butter as bread.

In talking of the French and the present times, their language was what most people would call Jacobinical.[1] They spoke much of the oppressions endured by the Highlanders further up, of the absolute impossibility of their living in any comfort, and of the cruelty of laying so many restraints on emigration. Then they spoke with animation of the attachment of the clans to their lairds: 'The laird of this place, Glengyle, where we live, could have commanded so many men who would have followed him to the death; and now there are none left.' It appeared that Mr. Macfarlane, and his wife's brother, Mr. Macalpine, farmed the place, inclusive of the whole vale upwards to the mountains, and the mountains themselves, under the lady of Glengyle, the mother of the young laird, a minor. It was a sheep-farm.

Speaking of another neighbouring laird, they said he had gone, like the rest of them, to Edinburgh, left his lands and his own people, spending his money where it brought him not any esteem, so that he was of no value either at home or abroad. We mentioned Rob Roy, and the eyes of all glistened; even the lady of the house, who was very diffident, and no great talker, exclaimed, 'He was a good man, Rob Roy! he had been dead only about eighty years, had lived in the next farm, which belonged to him, and there his bones were laid.'[2] He was a famous swordsman. Having an arm much longer than other men, he had a greater command with his sword. As a proof of the length of his arm, they told us that he could garter his tartan stockings below the knee without stooping, and added a dozen different stories of single combats, which he had fought, all in perfect good-humour, merely to prove his prowess. I daresay they had stories of this kind which would hardly have been exhausted in the long evenings of a whole December week, Rob Roy being as famous here as ever Robin Hood was in the Forest of Sherwood; *he* also robbed from the rich, giving to the poor, and defending them from oppression. They tell of his confining the factor of the Duke of Montrose in one of the islands of Loch Ketterine, after having taken his money from him—the Duke's rents—in open day, while they were sitting at table. He was a formidable enemy of the Duke, but being a small laird against a greater, was overcome at last, and forced to resign all his lands on the Braes of Loch Lomond, including the caves which we visited, on account of the money he had taken from the Duke and could not repay.

1. Their language expressed politically radical views and sympathy for the revolutionary democrats active in the French Revolution of 1789. The term "Jacobinical" comes from the meeting place of the activists, which was in the convent of Dominican friars in the Church of St. Jacques in Paris.
2. The information was incorrect. Rob Roy was buried in a graveyard in Balquhidder, near where he spent the last active years of his long (sixty-three-year) life.
   The first of the Clan Gregor burial grounds is in Glengyle. A second burial ground is now at the end of a causeway below Portnellan. It was here Wordsworth took his cue for "Rob Roy's Grave," based on the information given at the Macfarlane house in Glengyle. He later realized his mistake. See note on Rob Roy's grave p. 187.

When breakfast was ended the mistress desired the person whom we took to be her husband to 'return thanks.' He said a short grace, and in a few minutes they all went off to their work. We saw them about the door following one another like a flock of sheep, with the children after, whatever job they were engaged in. Mrs. Macfarlane told me she would show me the burying-place of the lairds of Glengyle, and took me to a square enclosure like a pinfold, with a stone ball at every corner; we had noticed it the evening before, and wondered what it could be.[1] It was in the middle of a 'planting,' as they call plantations, which was enclosed for the preservation of the trees, therefore we had to climb over a high wall: it was a dismal spot, containing four or five graves overgrown with long grass, nettles, and brambles. Against the wall was a marble monument to the memory of one of the lairds, of whom they spoke with veneration: some English verses were inscribed upon the marble, purporting that he had been the father of his clan, a brave and good man. When we returned to the house she said she would show me what curious feathers they had in their country, and brought out a bunch carefully wrapped up in paper. On my asking her what bird they came from, 'Oh!' she replied, 'it is a great beast.' We conjectured it was an eagle, and from her description of its ways, and the manner of destroying it, we knew it was so. She begged me to accept of some of the feathers, telling me that some ladies wore them in their heads. I was much pleased with the gift, which I shall preserve in memory of her kindness and simplicity of manners, and the Highland solitude where she lived.

We took leave of the family with regret: they were handsome, healthy, and happy-looking people. It was ten o'clock when we departed. We had learned that there was a ferry-boat kept at three miles' distance, and if the man was at home he would row us down the lake to the Trossachs. Our walk was mostly through coppice-woods, along a horse-road, upon which narrow carts might travel. Passed that white house which had looked at us with such a friendly face when we were on the other side; it stood on the slope of a hill, with green pastures below it, plots of corn and coppice-wood, and behind, a rocky steep covered with wood. It was a very pretty place, but the morning being cold and dull the opposite shore appeared dreary. Near to the white house we passed by another of those little pinfold squares, which we knew to be a burying-place; it was in a sloping green field among woods, and within sound of the beating of the water against the shore, if there were but a gentle breeze to stir it:[2] I thought if I lived in that house, and my ancestors and kindred were buried there, I should sit many an hour

1. Some MacGregor graves are here, including the one of Rob Roy's nephew, "Black Knee" MacGregor, but Rob Roy is buried elsewhere.
2. The burial place today lies at the end of a causeway, in the area of Portnellan. The stones have been moved back from the shore to ensure they would not be flooded when the level of the lake was raised for the waterworks.

under the walls of this plot of earth, where all the household would be gathered together.

We found the ferryman at work in the field above his hut, and he was at liberty to go with us, but, being wet and hungry, we begged that he would let us sit by his fire till we had refreshed ourselves. This was the first genuine Highland hut we had been in. We entered by the cow-house, the house-door being within, at right angles to the outer door. The woman was distressed that she had a bad fire, but she heaped up some dry peats and heather, and, blowing it with her breath, in a short time raised a blaze that scorched us into comfortable feelings. A small part of the smoke found its way out of the hole of the chimney, the rest through the open window-places, one of which was within the recess of the fireplace, and made a frame to a little picture of the restless lake and the opposite shore, seen when the outer door was open. The woman of the house was very kind: whenever we asked her for anything it seemed a fresh pleasure to her that she had it for us; she always answered with a sort of softening down of the Scotch exclamation, 'Hoot!' 'Ho! yes, ye'll get that,' and hied to her cupboard in the spence.[1] We were amused with the phrase 'Ye'll get that' in the Highlands, which appeared to us as if it came from a perpetual feeling of the difficulty with which most things are procured. We got oatmeal, butter, bread and milk, made some porridge, and then departed. It was rainy and cold, with a strong wind.

Coleridge was afraid of the cold in the boat, so he determined to walk down the lake, pursuing the same road we had come along. There was nothing very interesting for the first three or four miles on either side of the water: to the right, uncultivated heath or poor coppice-wood, and to the left, a scattering of meadow ground, patches of corn, coppice-woods, and here and there a cottage. The wind fell, and it began to rain heavily. On this William wrapped himself in the boatman's plaid, and lay at the bottom of the boat till we came to a place where I could not help rousing him.

We were rowing down that side of the lake which had hitherto been little else than a moorish ridge. After turning a rocky point we came to a bay closed in by rocks and steep woods, chiefly of full-grown birch. The lake was elsewhere ruffled, but at the entrance of this bay the breezes sunk, and it was calm: a small island was near, and the opposite shore, covered with wood, looked soft through the misty rain. William, rubbing his eyes, for he had been asleep, called out that he hoped I had not let him pass by anything that was so beautiful as this; and I was glad to tell him that it was but the beginning of a new land. After we had left this bay we saw before us a long reach of woods and rocks and rocky points, that promised other bays more beautiful than what we had passed. The ferryman was a good-natured fellow, and rowed very industriously, following the ins and outs of the shore; he was delighted with the pleasure we expressed, continually

1. The pantry.

repeating how pleasant it would have been on a fine day. I believe he was attached to the lake by some sentiment of pride, as his own domain—his being almost the only boat upon it—which made him, seeing we were willing gazers, take far more pains than an ordinary boatman; he would often say, after he had compassed the turning of a point, 'This is a bonny part,' and he always chose the bonniest, with greater skill than our prospect-hunters and 'picturesque travellers;' places screened from the winds—that was the first point; the rest followed of course,—richer growing trees, rocks and banks, and curves which the eye delights in.

The second bay we came to differed from the rest; the hills retired a short space from the lake, leaving a few level fields between, on which was a cottage embosomed in trees: the bay was defended by rocks at each end, and the hills behind made a shelter for the cottage, the only dwelling, I believe, except one, on this side of Loch Ketterine. We now came to steeps that rose directly from the lake, and passed by a place called in the Gaelic the Den of the Ghosts, which reminded us of Lodore; it is a rock, or mass of rock, with a stream of large black stones like the naked or dried-up bed of a torrent down the side of it; birch-trees start out of the rock in every direction, and cover the hill above, further than we could see. The water of the lake below was very deep, black, and calm. Our delight increased as we advanced, till we came in view of the termination of the lake, seeing where the river issues out of it through a narrow chasm between the hills.

Here I ought to rest, as we rested, and attempt to give utterance to our pleasure: but indeed I can impart but little of what we felt. We were still on the same side of the water, and, being immediately under the hill, within a considerable bending of the shore, we were enclosed by hills all round, as if we had been upon a smaller lake of which the whole was visible. It was an entire solitude; and all that we beheld was the perfection of loveliness and beauty.

We had been through many solitary places since we came into Scotland, but this place differed as much from any we had seen before, as if there had been nothing in common between them; no thought of dreariness or desolation found entrance here; yet nothing was to be seen but water, wood, rocks, and heather, and bare mountains above. We saw the mountains by glimpses as the clouds passed by them, and were not disposed to regret, with our boatman, that it was not a fine day, for the near objects were not concealed from us, but softened by being seen through the mists. The lake is not very wide here, but appeared to be much narrower than it really is, owing to the many promontories, which are pushed so far into it that they are much more like islands than promontories. We had a longing desire to row to the outlet and look up into the narrow passage through which the river went; but the point where we were to land was on the other side, so we bent our course right across, and just as we came in sight of two huts,

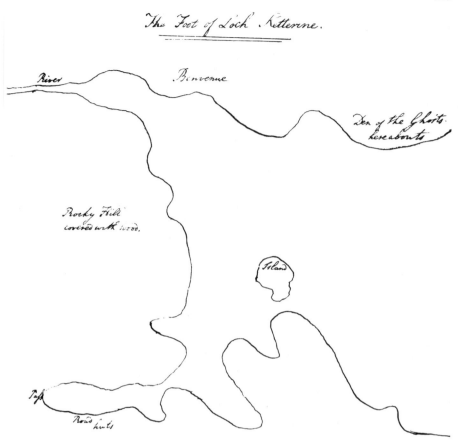

The Foot of Loch Ketterine.

which have been built by Lady Perth as a shelter for those who visit the Trossachs, Coleridge hailed us with a shout of triumph from the door of one of them, exulting in the glory of Scotland. The huts stand at a small distance from each other, on a high and perpendicular rock, that rises from the bed of the lake. A road, which has a very wild appearance, has been cut through the rock; yet even here, among these bold precipices, the feeling of excessive beautifulness overcomes every other. While we were upon the lake, on every side of us were bays within bays, often more like tiny lakes or pools than bays, and these not in long succession only, but all round, some almost on the broad breast of the water, the promontories shot out so far.

After we had landed we walked along the road to the uppermost of the huts, where Coleridge was standing. From the door of this hut we saw Benvenue opposite to us—a high mountain, but clouds concealed its top; its side, rising directly from the lake, is covered with birch-trees to a great height, and seamed with innumerable channels of torrents; but now there was no water in them, nothing to break in upon the stillness and repose of the scene; nor do I recollect hearing the sound of water from any side, the wind being fallen and the lake perfectly still; the place was all eye, and completely satisfied the sense and the heart. Above and below us, to the right and to the left, were rocks, knolls, and hills, which, wherever anything could grow—and that was everywhere between the rocks—were covered with trees and heather; the trees did not in any place grow so thick as an ordinary wood; yet I think there was never a bare space of twenty yards: it was more like a natural forest where the trees grow in groups or singly, not hiding the surface of the ground, which, instead of being green and mossy, was of the richest purple. The heather was indeed the most luxuriant I ever saw; it was so tall that a child of ten years old struggling through it would often have been buried head and shoulders, and the exquisite beauty of the colour, near or at a distance, seen under the trees, is not to be conceived. But if I were to go on describing for evermore, I should give but a faint, and very often a false, idea of the different objects and the various combinations of them in this most intricate and delicious place; besides, I tired myself out with describing at Loch Lomond, so I will hasten to the end of my tale. This reminds me of a sentence in a little pamphlet written by the minister of Callander, descriptive of the environs of that place. After having taken up at least six closely-printed pages with the Trossachs, he concludes thus, 'In a word, the Trossachs beggar all description,'—a conclusion in which every-body who has been there will agree with him. I believe the word Trossachs signifies 'many hills:' it is a name given to all the eminences at the foot of Loch Ketterine, and about half a mile beyond.[1]

We left the hut, retracing the few yards of road which we had climbed; our boat lay at anchor under the rock in the last of all the compartments of the lake, a small oblong pool, almost shut up within itself, as several others had appeared to be, by jutting points of rock; the termination of a long out-shooting of the water, pushed up between the steps of the main shore where the huts stand, and a broad promontory which, with its hillocks and points and lesser promontories, occupies the centre of the foot of the lake. A person sailing through the lake up the middle of it, would just as naturally suppose that the outlet was here as on the other side; and so it might have been, with the most trifling change in the disposition of the ground, for at the end of this slip of water the lake is confined only by a gentle rising of a few yards towards an opening between the hills, a narrow pass or valley through which the river might have flowed. The road is carried through this valley, which only differs from the lower part of the vale of the lake in being

1. The word is Gaelic and means "the bristled country," referring, without the connotation of beauty, to the physical features of this wooded glen which extends from Loch Achray to Loch Katrine and slightly up the northeast side of Loch Katrine.

excessively narrow, and without water; it is enclosed by mountains, rocky mounds, hills and hillocks scattered over with birch-trees, and covered with Dutch myrtle[1] and heather, even surpassing what we had seen before. Our mother Eve had no fairer, though a more diversified garden, to tend, than we found within this little close valley. It rained all the time, but the mists and calm air made us ample amends for a wetting.

At the opening of the pass we climbed up a low eminence, and had an unexpected prospect suddenly before us—another lake, small compared with Loch Ketterine, though perhaps four miles long, but the misty air concealed the end of it. The transition from the solitary wildness of Loch Ketterine and the narrow valley or pass to this scene was very delightful: it was a gentle place, with lovely open bays, one small island, corn fields, woods, and a group of cottages. This vale seemed to have been made to be tributary to the comforts of man, Loch Ketterine for the lonely delight of Nature, and kind spirits delighting in beauty. The sky was grey and heavy,—floating mists on the hill-sides, which softened the objects, and where we lost sight of the lake it appeared so near to the sky that they almost touched one another, giving a visionary beauty to the prospect. While we overlooked this quiet scene we could hear the stream rumbling among the rocks between the lakes, but the mists concealed any glimpse of it which we might have had. This small lake is called Loch Achray.

We returned, of course, by the same road. Our guide repeated over and over again his lamentations that the day was so bad, though we had often told him—not indeed with much hope that he would believe us—that we were glad of it. As we walked along he pulled a leafy twig from a birch-tree, and, after smelling it, gave it to me, saying, how 'sweet and halesome' it was, and that it was pleasant and very halesome on a fine summer's morning to sail under the banks where the birks are growing. This reminded me of the old Scotch songs, in which you continually hear of the 'pu'ing the birks.' Common as birches are in the north of England, I believe their sweet smell is a thing unnoticed among the peasants. We returned again to the huts to take a farewell look. We had shared our food with the ferryman and a traveller whom we had met here, who was going up the lake, and wished to lodge at the ferry-house, so we offered him a place in the boat. Coleridge chose to walk. We took the same side of the lake as before, and had much delight in visiting the bays over again; but the evening began to darken, and it rained so heavily before we had gone two miles that we were completely wet. It was dark when we landed, and on entering the house I was sick with cold.

The good woman had provided, according to her promise, a better fire than we had found in the morning; and indeed when I sate down in the

---

1. Known also as sweet gale, sweet willow, bog myrtle, and, to scientists, Myrica gale, it is a twiggy shrub-like plant that grows well in the bogs and moors and gives off a sweet fragrance.

chimney-corner of her smoky biggin' I thought I had never been more comfortable in my life. Coleridge had been there long enough to have a pan of coffee boiling for us, and having put our clothes in the way of drying, we all sate down, thankful for a shelter. We could not prevail upon the man of the house to draw near the fire, though he was cold and wet, or to suffer his wife to get him dry clothes till she had served us, which she did, though most willingly, not very expeditiously. A Cumberland man of the same rank would not have had such a notion of what was fit and right in his own house, or if he had, one would have accused him of servility; but in the Highlander it only seemed like politeness, however erroneous and painful to us, naturally growing out of the dependence of the inferiors of the clan upon their laird; he did not, however, refuse to let his wife bring out the whisky-bottle at our request: 'She keeps a dram,' as the phrase is; indeed, I believe there is scarcely a lonely house by the wayside in Scotland where travellers may not be accommodated with a dram. We asked for sugar, butter, barley-bread, and milk, and with a smile and a stare more of kindness than wonder, she replied, 'Ye'll get that,' bringing each article separately.

We caroused our cups of coffee, laughing like children at the strange atmosphere in which we were: the smoke came in gusts, and spread along the walls and above our heads in the chimney, where the hens were roosting like light clouds in the sky. We laughed and laughed again, in spite of the smarting of our eyes, yet had a quieter pleasure in observing the beauty of the beams and rafters gleaming between the clouds of smoke. They had been crusted over and varnished by many winters, till, where the firelight fell upon them, they were as glossy as black rocks on a sunny day cased in ice. When we had eaten our supper we sate about half an hour, and I think I had never felt so deeply the blessing of a hospitable welcome and a warm fire. The man of the house repeated from time to time that we should often tell of this night when we got to our homes, and interposed praises of this, his own lake, which he had more than once, when we were returning in the boat, ventured to say was 'bonnier than Loch Lomond.'

Our companion from the Trossachs, who it appeared was an Edinburgh drawing-master going during the vacation on a pedestrian tour to John o' Groat's House,[1] was to sleep in the barn with William and Coleridge, where the man said he had plenty of dry hay. I do not believe that the hay of the Highlands is often very dry, but this year it had a better chance than usual: wet or dry, however, the next morning they said they had slept comfortably. When I went to bed, the mistress, desiring me to 'go ben,' attended me with a candle, and assured me that the bed was dry, though not 'sic as I had been

---

1. At the northern extremity of Scotland. This was the destination of Keats and Brown on their 1818 pedestrian tour, though Keats himself did not make it all the way, for the severe sore throat he acquired on the Isle of Mull forced him to leave Brown just above Inverness and return to London by boat.

used to.' It was of chaff; there were two others in the room, a cupboard and two chests, on one of which stood the milk in wooden vessels covered over; I should have thought that milk so kept could not have been sweet, but the cheese and butter were good. The walls of the whole house were of stone unplastered. It consisted of three apartments,—the cow-house at one end, the kitchen or house in the middle, and the spence at the other end. The rooms were divided, not up to the rigging, but only to the beginning of the roof, so that there was a free passage for light and smoke from one end of the house to the other.

I went to bed some time before the family. The door was shut between us, and they had a bright fire, which I could not see; but the light it sent up among the varnished rafters and beams, which crossed each other in almost as intricate and fantastic a manner as I have seen the under-boughs of a large beech-tree withered by the depth of the shade above, produced the most beautiful effect that can be conceived. It was like what I should suppose an underground cave or temple to be, with a dripping or moist roof, and the moonlight entering in upon it by some means or other, and yet the colours were more like melted gems. I lay looking up till the light of the fire faded away, and the man and his wife and child had crept into their bed at the other end of the room. I did not sleep much, but passed a comfortable night, for my bed, though hard, was warm and clean: the unusualness of my situation prevented me from sleeping. I could hear the waves beat against the shore of the lake; a little 'syke' close to the door made a much louder noise; and when I sate up in my bed I could see the lake through an open window-place at the bed's head. Add to this, it rained all night. I was less occupied by remembrance of the Trossachs, beautiful as they were, than the vision of the Highland hut, which I could not get out of my head. I thought of the Fairyland of Spenser, and what I had read in romance at other times, and then, what a feast would it be for a London pantomime-maker, could he but transplant it to Drury Lane, with all its beautiful colours!

THIRD WEEK

Sunday, August 28th.—We were desirous to have crossed the mountains above Glengyle to Glenfalloch, at the head of Loch Lomond, but it rained so heavily that it was impossible, so the ferryman engaged to row us to the point where Coleridge and I had rested, while William was going on our doubtful adventure. The hostess provided us with tea and sugar for our breakfast; the water was boiled in an iron pan, and dealt out to us in a jug, a proof that she does not often drink tea, though she said she had always tea and sugar in the house. She and the rest of the family breakfasted on curds and whey, as taken out of the pot in which she was making cheese; she insisted upon my taking some also; and her husband joined in with the old story, that it was 'varra halesome.' I thought it exceedingly good, and said to myself that they lived nicely with their cow: she was meat, drink, and company. Before breakfast the housewife was milking behind the chimney, and I thought I had seldom heard a sweeter fire-side sound; in an evening, sitting over a sleepy, low-burnt fire, it would lull one like the purring of a cat.

When we departed, the good woman shook me cordially by the hand, saying she hoped that if ever we came into Scotland again, we would come and see her. The lake was calm, but it rained so heavily that we could see little. Landed at about ten o'clock, almost wet to the skin, and, with no prospect but of streaming rains, faced the mountain-road to Loch Lomond. We recognised the same objects passed before,—the tarn, the potato-bed, and the cottages with their burnies, which were no longer, as one might say, household streams, but made us only think of the mountains and rocks they came from. Indeed, it is not easy to imagine how different everything appeared; the mountains with mists and torrents alive and always changing: but the low grounds where the inhabitants had been at work the day before were melancholy, with here and there a few haycocks and hay scattered about.

Wet as we were, William and I turned out of our path to the Garrison house. A few rooms of it seemed to be inhabited by some wretchedly poor families, and it had all the desolation of a large decayed mansion in the suburbs of a town, abandoned of its proper inhabitants, and become the abode of paupers. In spite of its outside bravery, it was but a poor protection against 'the sword of winter, keen and cold.' We looked at the building through the arch of a broken gateway of the courtyard, in the middle of which it stands. Upon that stormy day it appeared more than desolate; there was something about it even frightful.

When beginning to descend the hill towards Loch Lomond, we overtook two girls, who told us we could not cross the ferry till evening, for the boat was gone with a number of people to church. One of the girls was exceedingly beautiful; and the figures of both of them, in grey plaids falling to their feet, their faces only being uncovered, excited our attention before we spoke to them; but they answered us so sweetly that we were quite delighted, at the same time that they stared at us with an innocent look of wonder. I think I never heard the English language sound more sweetly than from the mouth of the elder of these girls, while she stood at the gate answering our inquiries, her face flushed with the rain; her pronunciation was clear and distinct: without difficulty, yet slow, like that of a foreign speech. They told us we might sit in the ferry-house till the return of the boat, went in with us, and made a good fire as fast as possible to dry our wet clothes. We learnt that the taller was the sister of the ferryman, and had been left in charge with the house for the day, that the other was his wife's sister, and was come with her mother on a visit,—an old woman, who sate in a corner beside the cradle, nursing her little grandchild. We were glad to be housed, with our feet upon a warm hearth-stone; and our attendants were so active and good-humoured that it was pleasant to have to desire them to do anything. The younger was a delicate and unhealthy-looking girl; but there was an uncommon meekness in her countenance, with an air of premature intelligence, which is often seen in sickly young persons. The other made me think of Peter Bell's 'Highland Girl:'

> As light and beauteous as a squirrel,
> As beauteous and as wild.[1]

She moved with unusual activity, which was chastened very delicately by a certain hesitation in her looks when she spoke, being able to understand us but imperfectly. They were both exceedingly desirous to get me what I wanted to make me comfortable. I was to have a gown and petticoat of the mistress's; so they turned out her whole wardrobe upon the parlour floor, talking Erse to one another, and laughing all the time. It was long before they could decide which of the gowns I was to have; they chose at last, no doubt thinking that it was the best, a light-coloured sprigged cotton, with long sleeves, and they both laughed while I was putting it on, with the blue linsey petticoat, and one or the other, or both together, helped me to dress,

---

1. From Wordsworth's poem "Peter Bell":

> But, more than all, his heart is stung
> To think of one, almost a child;
> A sweet and playful Highland girl,
> As light and beauteous as a squirrel,
> As beauteous and as wild!
> (Part Third, ll. 886–90)

repeating at least half a dozen times, 'You never had on the like of that before.' They held a consultation of several minutes over a pair of coarse woollen stockings, gabbling Erse as fast as their tongues could move, and looked as if uncertain what to do: at last, with great diffidence, they offered them to me, adding, as before, that I had never worn 'the like of them.' When we entered the house we had been not a little glad to see a fowl stewing in barley-broth; and now when the wettest of our clothes were stripped off, began again to recollect that we were hungry, and asked if we could have dinner. 'Oh yes, ye may get that,' the elder replied, pointing to the pan on the fire.

Conceive what a busy house it was—all our wet clothes to be dried, dinner prepared and set out for us four strangers, and a second cooking for the family; add to this, two rough 'callans,' as they called them, boys about eight years old, were playing beside us; the poor baby was fretful all the while; the old woman sang doleful Erse songs, rocking it in its cradle the more violently the more it cried; then there were a dozen cookings of porridge, and it could never be fed without the assistance of all three. The hut was after the Highland fashion, but without anything beautiful except its situation; the floor was rough, and wet with the rain that came in at the door, so that the lasses' bare feet were as wet as if they had been walking through street puddles, in passing from one room to another; the windows were open, as at the other hut; but the kitchen had a bed in it, and was much smaller, and the shape of the house was like that of a common English cottage, without its comfort; yet there was no appearance of poverty— indeed, quite the contrary. The peep out of the open door-place across the lake made some amends for the want of the long roof and elegant rafters of our boatman's cottage, and all the while the waterfall, which we could not see, was roaring at the end of the hut, which seemed to serve as a sounding-board for its noise, so that it was not unlike sitting in a house where a mill is going. The dashing of the waves against the shore could not be distinguished; yet in spite of my knowledge of this I could not help fancying that the tumult and storm came from the lake, and went out several times to see if it was possible to row over in safety.

After long waiting we grew impatient for our dinner; at last the pan was taken off, and carried into the other room; but we had to wait at least another half hour before the ceremony of dishing up was completed; yet with all this bustle and difficulty, the manner in which they, and particularly the elder of the girls, performed everything, was perfectly graceful. We ate a hearty dinner, and had time to get our clothes quite dry before the arrival of the boat. The girls could not say at what time it would be at home; on our asking them if the church was far off they replied, 'Not very far;' and when we asked how far, they said, 'Perhaps about four or five miles.' I believe a Church of England congregation would hold themselves excused for non-attendance three parts of the year, having but half as far to go; but in the lonely parts of Scotland they make little of a journey of nine or ten miles to a preaching. They have not perhaps an opportunity of going more than once in a quarter of a year, and, setting piety aside, have other motives to attend: they hear the news, public and private, and see their friends and neighbours; for, though the people who meet at these times may be gathered together from a circle of twenty miles' diameter, a sort of neighbourly connexion must be so brought about. There is something exceedingly pleasing to my imagination in this gathering together of the inhabitants of these secluded districts—for instance, the borderers of these two large lakes meeting at the deserted garrison which I have described. The manner of their travelling is on foot, on horseback, and in boats across the waters,—young and old, rich and poor, all in their best dress.

If it were not for these Sabbath-day meetings one summer month would be like another summer month, one winter month like another—detached from the goings-on of the world, and solitary throughout; from the time of earliest childhood they will be like landing-places in the memory of a person who has passed his life in these thinly peopled regions; they must generally leave distinct impressions, differing from each other so much as they do in circumstances, in time and place, etc.,—some in the open fields, upon hills, in houses, under large rocks, in storms, and in fine weather.

But I have forgotten the fireside of our hut. After long waiting, the girls, who had been on the look-out, informed us that the boat was coming. I went to the water-side, and saw a cluster of people on the opposite shore; but being yet at a distance, they looked more like soldiers surrounding a carriage than a group of men and women; red and green were the distinguishable colours. We hastened to get ourselves ready as soon as we saw the party approach, but had longer to wait than we expected, the lake being wider than it appears to be. As they drew near we could distinguish men in tartan plaids, women in scarlet cloaks, and green umbrellas by the half-dozen. The landing was as pretty a sight as ever I saw. The bay, which had been so quiet two days before, was all in motion with small waves, while the swoln waterfall roared in our ears. The boat came steadily up, being pressed almost to the water's edge by the weight of its cargo; perhaps twenty people landed, one after another. It did not rain much, but the women held up their umbrellas; they were dressed in all the colours of the rainbow, and, with their scarlet cardinals, the tartan plaids of the men, and Scotch bonnets, made a gay appearance. There was a joyous bustle surrounding the boat, which even imparted something of the same character to the waterfall in its tumult, and the restless grey waves; the young men laughed and shouted, the lasses laughed, and the elder folks seemed to be in a bustle to be away. I remember well with what haste the mistress of the house where we were ran up to seek after her child, and seeing us, how anxiously and kindly she inquired how we had fared, if we had had a good fire, had been well waited upon, etc. etc. All this in three minutes—for the boatman had another party to bring from the other side and hurried us off.

The hospitality we had met with at the two cottages and Mr. Macfarlane's gave us very favourable impressions on this our first entrance into the Highlands, and at this day the innocent merriment of the girls, with their kindness to us, and the beautiful figure and face of the elder, come to my mind whenever I think of the ferry-house and waterfall of Loch Lomond, and I never think of the two girls but the whole image of that romantic spot is before me, a living image, as it will be to my dying day. The following poem[1] was written by William not long after our return from Scotland:—

> Sweet Highland Girl, a very shower
> Of beauty is thy earthly dower!
> Twice seven consenting years have shed
> Their utmost bounty on thy head:
> And these grey rocks; this household lawn;
> These trees, a veil just half withdrawn;
> This fall of water, that doth make
> A murmur near the silent Lake;
> This little Bay, a quiet road
> That holds in shelter thy abode;
> In truth together ye do seem
> Like something fashion'd in a dream;
> Such forms as from their covert peep
> When earthly cares are laid asleep!
> Yet, dream and vision as thou art,
> I bless thee with a human heart:
> God shield thee to thy latest years!
> I neither know thee nor thy peers;
> And yet my eyes are filled with tears.
>
> With earnest feeling I shall pray
> For thee when I am far away:
> For never saw I mien or face,
> In which more plainly I could trace
> Benignity and home-bred sense
> Ripening in perfect innocence.

1. "To a Highland Girl, at Inversneyde, upon Loch Lomond." When he was older Wordsworth reflected: "This delightful creature & her demeanour are particularly described in my Sister's Journal. The sort of prophecy with which the verses conclude has through God's goodness been realized, and now, approaching the close of my 73rd year I have a most vivid remembrance of her and the beautiful objects with which she was surrounded" (*Fenwick Notes*, p. 26).

Here, scattered like a random seed,
Remote from men, thou dost not need
Th' embarrass'd look of shy distress
And maidenly shamefacedness;
Thou wear'st upon thy forehead clear
The freedom of a mountaineer:
A face with gladness overspread!
Sweet smiles, by human-kindness bred!
And seemliness complete, that sways
Thy courtesies, about thee plays;
With no restraint but such as springs
From quick and eager visitings
Of thoughts that lie beyond the reach
Of thy few words of English speech:
A bondage sweetly brook'd, a strife
That gives thy gestures grace and life!
So have I, not unmoved in mind,
Seen birds of tempest-loving kind,
Thus beating up against the wind.

What hand but would a garland cull
For thee, who art so beautiful?
O happy pleasure! here to dwell
Beside thee in some heathy dell;
Adopt your homely ways and dress,
A Shepherd, thou a Shepherdess!
But I could frame a wish for thee
More like a grave reality:
Thou art to me but as a wave
Of the wild sea: and I would have
Some claim upon thee, if I could,
Though but of common neighbourhood.
What joy to hear thee and to see!
Thy elder brother I would be,
Thy father—anything to thee.

Now thanks to Heaven! that of its grace
Hath led me to this lonely place!
Joy have I had; and going hence
I bear away my recompence.
In spots like these it is we prize
Our memory, feel that she hath eyes:
Then why should I be loth to stir?
I feel this place is made for her;

> To give new pleasure like the past
> Continued long as life shall last.
> Nor am I loth, though pleased at heart,
> Sweet Highland Girl, from thee to part;
> For I, methinks, till I grow old,
> As fair before me shall behold
> As I do now, the Cabin small,
> The Lake, the Bay, the Waterfall,
> And thee, the Spirit of them all.

We were rowed over speedily by the assistance of two youths, who went backwards and forwards for their own amusement, helping at the oars, and pulled as if they had strength and spirits to spare for a year to come. We noticed that they had uncommonly fine teeth, and that they and the boatman were very handsome people. Another merry crew took our place in the boat.

We had three miles to walk to Tarbet. It rained, but not heavily; the mountains were not concealed from us by the mists, but appeared larger and more grand; twilight was coming on, and the obscurity under which we saw the objects, with the sounding of the torrents, kept our minds alive and wakeful; all was solitary and huge—sky, water, and mountains mingled together. While we were walking forward, the road leading us over the top of a brow, we stopped suddenly at the sound of a half-articulate Gaelic hooting from the field close to us. It came from a little boy, whom we could see on the hill between us and the lake, wrapped up in a grey plaid. He was probably calling home the cattle for the night. His appearance was in the highest degree moving to the imagination: mists were on the hillsides, darkness shutting in upon the huge avenue of mountains, torrents roaring, no house in sight to which the child might belong; his dress, cry, and appearance all different from anything we had been accustomed to. It was a text, as William has since observed to me, containing in itself the whole history of the Highlander's life—his melancholy, his simplicity, his poverty, his superstition, and above all, that visionariness which results from a communion with the unworldliness of nature.

When we reached Tarbet the people of the house were anxious to know how we had fared, particularly the girl who had waited upon us. Our praises of Loch Ketterine made her exceedingly happy, and she ventured to say, of which we had heard not a word before, that it was 'bonnier to *her* fancy than Loch Lomond.'[1] The landlord, who was not at home when we had set off,

---

1. Which lake was "bonnier," was in fact an interesting aesthetic point. Loch Lomond had been considered, from the time of Pennant, the late eighteenth century, to be the most beautiful and significant of the Scottish lakes. Its northern end was in the Highlands; its neighboring mountains—Ben Lomond to the east and Ben Vorlich to the west—thrilled

told us that if he had known of our going he would have recommended us to Mr. Macfarlane's or the other farm-house, adding that they were hospitable people in that vale. Coleridge and I got tea, and William and the drawing-master chose supper; they asked to have a broiled fowl, a dish very common in Scotland, to which the mistress replied, 'Would not a "boiled" one do as well?' They consented, supposing that it would be more easily cooked; but when the fowl made its appearance, to their great disappointment it proved a cold one that had been stewed in the broth at dinner.

Monday, August 29th.—It rained heavily this morning, and, having heard so much of the long rains since we came into Scotland, as well as before, we had no hope that it would be over in less than three weeks at the least, so poor Coleridge, being very unwell, determined to send his clothes to Edinburgh and make the best of his way thither, being afraid to face much wet weather in an open carriage. William and I were unwilling to be confined at Tarbet, so we resolved to go to Arrochar, a mile and a half on the road to Inverary, where there is an inn celebrated as a place of good accommodation for travellers. Coleridge and I set off on foot, and William was to follow with the car, but a heavy shower coming on, Coleridge left me to shelter in a hut and wait for William, while he went on before. This hut was unplastered, and without windows, crowded with beds, uncomfortable, and not in the simplicity of the ferryman's house. A number of good clothes were hanging against the walls, and a green silk umbrella was set up in a corner. I should have been surprised to see an umbrella in such a place before we came into the Highlands; but umbrellas are not so common anywhere as there—a plain proof of the wetness of the climate; even five minutes after this a girl passed us without shoes and stockings, whose gown and petticoat were not worth half a crown, holding an umbrella over her bare head.

We turned at a guide-post, 'To the New Inn,' and, after descending a little, and winding round the bottom of a hill, saw, at a small distance, a

tourists with experiences of the sublime. Travellers were fascinated by the many islands with their Gaelic names and lore, and made their way out to them in boats if possible. Dorothy's drawing of Loch Lomond and her extended written account both reflect her awareness of its importance.

In praising Loch Katrine Dorothy predicted the upstaging that would come after Scott's "Lady of the Lake" was published in 1810. Shairp offers an anecdote that captures the local sentiment at the practical level after tourism shifted away from Loch Lomond. The story concerns an editor named Jamieson who while visiting the Highlands in 1814 "met a savage-looking fellow on the top of Ben Lomond, the image of 'Red Murdoch,' who told him that he had been a guide to the mountain for more than forty years, but now 'a Walter Scott' had spoiled his trade. 'I wish,' said he, 'I had him a ferry over Loch Lomond; I should be after sinking the boat, if I drowned myself into the bargain, for ever since he wrote his "Lady of the Lake," as they call it, everybody goes to see that filthy hole, Loch Ketterine. The devil confound his ladies and his lakes!'" (Annotations to *Recollections* p. 314).

white house half hidden by tall trees upon a lawn that slopes down to the side of Loch Long, a sea-loch, which is here very narrow. Right before us, across the lake, was The Cobbler, which appeared to rise directly from the water; but, in fact, it overtopped another hill, being a considerable way behind. The inn looked so much like a gentleman's house that we could hardly believe it was an inn. We drove down the broad gravel walk, and, making a sweep, stopped at the front door, were shown into a large parlour with a fire, and my first thought was, How comfortable we should be! but Coleridge, who had arrived before us, checked my pleasure: the waiter had shown himself disposed to look coolly upon us, and there had been a hint that we could not have beds;—a party was expected, who had engaged all the beds. We conjectured this might be but a pretence, and ordered dinner in the hope that matters would clear up a little, and we thought they could not have the heart to turn us out in so heavy a rain if it were possible to lodge us. We had a nice dinner, yet would have gladly changed our roasted lamb and pickles, and the gentleman-waiter with his napkin in his pocket, for the more homely fare of the smoky hut at Loch Ketterine, and the good woman's busy attentions, with the certainty of a hospitable shelter at night. After dinner I spoke to the landlord himself, but he was not to be moved: he could not even provide one bed for me, so nothing was to be done but either to return to Tarbet with Coleridge, or that William and I should push on the next stage, to Cairndow. We had an interesting close view from the windows of the room where we sate, looking across the lake, which did not differ in appearance, as we saw it here, from a fresh-water lake. The sloping lawn on which the house stood was prettily scattered over with trees; but we had seen the place to great advantage at our first approach, owing to the mists upon the mountains, which had made them seem exceedingly high, while the strange figures on The Cobbler appeared and disappeared, like living things; but, as the day cleared we were disappointed in what was more like the permanent effect of the scene: the mountains were not so lofty as we had supposed, and the low grounds not so fertile; yet still it is a very interesting, I may say beautiful, place.

The rain ceased entirely, so we resolved to go on to Cairndow, and had the satisfaction of seeing that our landlord had not told us an untruth concerning the expected company; for just before our departure we saw, on the opposite side of the vale, a coach with four horses, another carriage, and two or three men on horseback—a striking procession, as it moved along between the bare mountain and the lake. Twenty years ago, perhaps, such a sight had not been seen here except when the Duke of Argyle, or some other Highland chieftain, might chance to be going with his family to London or Edinburgh. They had to cross a bridge at the head of the lake, which we could not see, so, after disappearing about ten minutes, they drove up to the door—three old ladies, two waiting-women, and store of men-servants. The old ladies were as gaily dressed as bullfinches in spring-time. We heard the next day that they were the renowned Miss Waughs of Carlisle, and that they enjoyed themselves over a game at cards in the evening.

Left Arrochar at about four o'clock in the afternoon. Coleridge accompanied us a little way; we portioned out the contents of our purse before our parting; and, after we had lost sight of him, drove heavily along. Crossed the bridge, and looked to the right, up the vale, which is soon terminated by mountains: it was of a yellow green, with but few trees and few houses; sea-gulls were flying above it. Our road—the same along which the carriages had come—was directly under the mountains on our right hand, and the lake was close to us on our left, the waves breaking among stones overgrown with yellow sea-weed; fishermen's boats, and other larger vessels than are seen on fresh-water lakes were lying at anchor near the opposite shore; sea-birds flying overhead; the noise of torrents mingled with the beating of the waves, and misty mountains enclosed the vale;—a melancholy but not a dreary scene. Often have I, in looking over a map of Scotland, followed the intricate windings of one of these sea-lochs, till, pleasing myself with my own imaginations, I have felt a longing, almost painful, to travel among them by land or by water.

This was the first sea-loch we had seen. We came prepared for a new and great delight, and the first impression which William and I received, as we drove rapidly through the rain down the lawn of Arrochar, the objects dancing before us, was even more delightful than we had expected. But, as I have said, when we looked through the window, as the mists disappeared and the objects were seen more distinctly, there was less of sheltered valley-comfort than we had fancied to ourselves, and the mountains were not so grand; and now that we were near to the shore of the lake,[1] and could see that it was not of fresh water, the wreck, the broken sea-shells, and scattered sea-weed gave somewhat of a dull and uncleanly look to the whole lake, and yet the water was clear, and might have appeared as beautiful as that of Loch Lomond, if with the same pure pebbly shore. Perhaps, had we been in a more cheerful mood of mind we might have seen everything with a different eye. The stillness of the mountains, the motion of the waves, the streaming torrents, the sea-birds, the fishing-boats were all melancholy; yet still, occupied as my mind was with other things, I thought of the long windings through which the waters of the sea had come to this inland retreat, visiting the inner solitudes of the mountains, and I could have wished to have mused out a summer's day on the shores of the lake. From the foot of these mountains whither might not a little barque carry one away? Though so far inland, it is but a slip of the great ocean: seamen,

1. Loch Long, opening into the Firth of Clyde.

fishermen, and shepherds here find a natural home. We did not travel far down the lake, but, turning to the right through an opening of the mountains, entered a glen called Glen Croe.[1]

Our thoughts were full of Coleridge, and when we were enclosed in the narrow dale, with a length of winding road before us, a road that seemed to have insinuated itself into the very heart of the mountains—the brook, the road, bare hills, floating mists, scattered stones, rocks, and herds of black cattle being all that we could see,—I shivered at the thought of his being sickly and alone, travelling from place to place.

The Cobbler, on our right, was pre-eminent above the other hills; the singular rocks on its summit, seen so near, were like ruins—castles or watchtowers. After we had passed one reach of the glen, another opened out, long, narrow, deep, and houseless, with herds of cattle and large stones; but the third reach was softer and more beautiful, as if the mountains had there made a warmer shelter, and there were a more gentle climate. The rocks by the riverside had dwindled away, the mountains were smooth and green, and towards the end, where the glen sloped upwards, it was a cradle-like hollow, and at that point where the slope became a hill, at the very bottom of the curve of the cradle, stood one cottage, with a few fields and beds of potatoes. There was also another house near the roadside, which appeared to be a herdsman's hut. The dwelling in the middle of the vale was a very pleasing object. I said within myself, How quietly might a family live in this pensive solitude, cultivating and loving their own fields! but the herdsman's hut, being the only one in the vale, had a melancholy face; not being attached to any particular plot of land, one could not help considering it as just kept alive and above ground by some dreary connexion with the long barren tract we had travelled through.

The afternoon had been exceedingly pleasant after we had left the vale of Arrochar; the sky was often threatening, but the rain blew off, and the evening was uncommonly fine. The sun had set a short time before we had dismounted from the car to walk up the steep hill at the end of the glen. Clouds were moving all over the sky—some of a brilliant yellow hue, which shed a light like bright moonlight upon the mountains. We could not have seen the head of the valley under more favourable circumstances.

The passing away of a storm is always a time of life and cheerfulness, especially in a mountainous country; but that afternoon and evening the sky was in an extraordinary degree vivid and beautiful. We often stopped in ascending the hill to look down the long reach of the glen. The road,

1. A particularly gloomy, deep glen, always remarked by early travellers for its gothic character, and certainly likely to reinforce the melancholy thoughts of "poor Coleridge." The Scottish traveller John Leyden called it "the most desolate place under heaven" when he visited in 1800 (*Journal of a Tour in the Highlands and Western Islands of Scotland in 1800.* Ed. James Sinton. Edinburgh and London: William Blackwood and Sons, 1903, p. 22).

81. The "Garrison house."
"Wet as we were, William and I turned out of our path to the Garrison house." (p. 108)

82. The Garrison.
". . . it had all the desolation of a large decayed mansion in the suburbs of a town . . ." (p. 108)

83. Highland cattle behind the Garrison Farm. (p. 108)

84. Arrochar. Arrochar Hotel. (The "New Inn.")
"We turned at a guide-post, 'To the New Inn,' and, after descending a little, and winding round the bottom of a hill, saw, at a small distance, a white house half hidden by tall trees upon a lawn that slopes down to the side of Loch Long..." (pp. 115–16)

85. The Cobbler. Reflected in water of Loch Long.
"Right before us, across the lake, was The Cobbler, which appeared to rise directly from the water; but, in fact, it overtopped another hill, being a considerable way behind." (p. 116)

86. Glen Croe.
"We did not travel far down the lake, but, turning to the right through an opening of the mountains,
entered a glen called Glen Croe.
Our thoughts were full of Coleridge, and when we were enclosed in the narrow dale,
with a length of winding road before us, a road that seemed to have insinuated itself into the very heart of
the mountains—the brook, the road, bare hills . . . I shivered at the thought of his being
sickly and alone, travelling from place to place." (p. 118)

87. Rest and Be Thankful.
"At the top of the hill we came to a seat with the well-known inscription, 'Rest and be thankful.' On the same stone it was recorded that the road had been made by Col. Wade's regiment. The seat is placed so as to command a full view of the valley . . ." (p. 119)

88. Glen Kinglas.
"Soon after we had climbed the hill we began to descend into another glen, called Glen Kinglas." (p. 119)
"We descended rapidly into the glen . . ." (p. 120)

89. Cairndow. Cairndow Inn.
"Cairndow is a single house by the side of the loch, I believe resorted to by gentlemen in the fishing season . . ." (p. 120)

90. Inveraray. Winding into town.
"When we had travelled about seven miles from Cairndow, winding round the bottom of a hill, we came in view of a great basin or elbow of the lake. Completely out of sight of the long track of water we had coasted, we seemed now to be on the edge of a very large, almost circular, lake, the town of Inverary before us, a line of white buildings on a low promontory right opposite, and close to the water's edge; the whole landscape a showy scene, and bursting upon us at once." (p. 121)

91. Inveraray. The Duke of Argyll's Castle.
"A few steps more brought us in view of the Castle, a stately turreted mansion, but with a modern air, standing on a lawn, retired from the water, and screened behind by woods covering the sides of high hills to the top, and still beyond, by bare mountains." (p. 121)

92. Inveraray. The Great Inn.
"The range bordering on the water consisted of little else than the inn, being a large house, with very large stables . . ." (p. 121)

93. Inveraray. Duke of Argyll's grounds.
". . . we went towards the Castle, and entered the Duke's grounds by a porter's lodge,
following the carriage-road through the park, which is prettily scattered over with trees, and
slopes gently towards the lake." (p. 122)

94. Inveraray. "Duniquoich Hill."
". . . to the left appears a very steep rocky hill, called Duniquoich Hill, on top of which is a building like a
watch-tower . . ." (pp. 122–23)

95. Cladich. Dashing water under bridge.
"After walking down the hill a long way we came to a bridge, under which the water dashed through a dark channel of rocks among trees . . ." (p. 126)

96. Cladich. Bridge Cottage.
"Close upon the bridge was a small hamlet, a few houses near together, and huddled up in trees—a very sweet spot . . ." (p. 126)

97. Kilchurn Castle, on Loch Awe.

". . . I took a nearer footpath, and at the top came in view of a most impressive scene, a ruined castle on an island almost in the middle of the last compartment of the lake, backed by a mountain cove . . ." (pp. 129–30)

98. Dalmally. Chapel.

"Crossed a bridge to look more nearly at the parsonage-house and the chapel . . ." (p. 131)

99. Ben Cruachan and the Pass of Brander.
"Travelled under the foot of the mountain Cruachan, along an excellent road . . ." (p. 132)

100. Taynuilt. Bunawe Iron Furnace.
". . . the iron-foundry at Bunawe . . ." (p. 134)

101. Loch Etive.
"The Loch is of a considerable width, but the mountains are so very high that, whether we were close under them or looked from one shore to the other, they maintained their dignity." (p. 135)

102. Dunstaffnage Castle, viewed from near Connel.
"On a bold promontory, on the same side of the loch where we were, stood an old castle,
an irregular tall building, not without majesty; and beyond, with leagues of water between,
our eyes settled upon the island of Mull, a high mountain, green in the sunshine, and
overcast with clouds . . ." (p. 139)

103. Connel. Ferry crossing.
"Soon after, we came to the ferry. The boat being on the other shore, we had to wait a
considerable time, though the water was not wide, and our call was heard immediately."
(p. 139)

104. Connel. Lochnell Arms Hotel, formerly the ferry house.
"We had intended breakfasting at this house . . ." (p. 140)

105. Loch Creran.
". . . reached Loch Creran, a large irregular sea loch . . . mountains at a distance." (p. 141)

106. Portnacroish. Former inn.
". . . we inquired concerning the road, and the distance to Portnacroish, our
baiting-place." (p. 142) *See also* p. 143.

107. Strath of Appin. Scene with fence, "wildness in its aspect."
". . . we hardly ever saw a thoroughly pleasing place in Scotland, which had not something of wildness in its aspect of one sort or another." (p. 143)

108. Strath of Appin. Farm buildings.

"... the unenclosed hills on each side of the vale, with black cattle feeding on them, the simplicity of the scattered huts ..." (p. 143)

109. Area of Port Appin and Portnacroish. Castle Stalker.

"Immediately below us, on an island a few yards from the shore, stood an old keep or fortress ..." (p. 144)

110. Ballachulish. Ballachulish Hotel, where the old ferry Inn stood.

"I walked on to the inn, ordered tea, and was conducted into a lodging room." (p. 146)

"This inn is the ferry-house on the main road up into the Highlands by Fort-William, and here Coleridge, though unknown to us, had slept three nights before." (p. 147)

111. Shy horse.
"The horse had taken fright . . ." (p. 146)

112. Glen Coe. Mountains.
"I cannot attempt to describe the mountains. I can only say that I thought those on our right . . . were the grandest I had ever seen." (pp. 151–52)

113. Glen Coe. River.
"The river is, for a short space, hidden between steep rocks: we left the road, and, going to the top of one of the rocks, saw it foaming over stones, or lodged in dark black dens . . ." (p. 152)

114. Glen Coe. Kingshouse. Kings House Hotel.
"Our guide pointed out King's House to us, our resting-place for the night . . ."
"The house looked respectable at a distance—a large square building, cased in blue slates
to defend it from storms,—but when we came close to it the outside forewarned us of
the poverty and misery within." (pp. 152–53)

following the course of the river as far as we could see, the farm and cottage hills, smooth towards the base and rocky higher up, were the sole objects before us. This part of Glen Croe reminded us of some of the dales of the north of England—Grisdale above Ulswater, for instance; but the length of it, and the broad highway, which is always to be seen at a great distance, a sort of centre of the vale, a point of reference, gives to the whole of the glen, and each division of it, a very different character.

At the top of the hill we came to a seat with the well-known inscription, 'Rest and be thankful.'[1] On the same stone it was recorded that the road had been made by Col. Wade's regiment. The seat is placed so as to command a full view of the valley, and the long, long road, which, with the fact recorded, and the exhortation, makes it an affecting resting-place. We called to mind with pleasure a seat under the braes of Loch Lomond on which I had rested, where the traveller is informed by an inscription upon a stone that the road was made by Col. Lascelles' regiment. There, the spot had not been chosen merely as a resting-place, for there was no steep ascent in the highway, but it might be for the sake of a spring of water and a beautiful rock, or, more probably, because at that point the labour had been more than usually toilsome in hewing through the rock. Soon after we had climbed the hill we began to descend into another glen, called Glen Kinglas. We now saw the western sky, which had hitherto been hidden from us by the hill—a glorious mass of clouds uprising from a sea of distant mountains, stretched out in length before us, towards the west—and close by us was a small lake or tarn. From the reflection of the crimson clouds the water appeared of a deep red, like melted rubies, yet with a mixture of a grey or blackish hue: the gorgeous light of the sky, with the singular colour of the lake, made the scene exceedingly romantic; yet it was more melancholy than cheerful. With all the power of light from the clouds, there was an overcasting of the gloom of evening, a twilight upon the hills.

1. Dorothy uses "seat" and "stone" interchangeably, but Stoddart (1801) identified "a green seat, near the twenty-ninth milestone" (*Remarks*, I p. 250). The stone at the top of the pass today resembles a milestone and reads:

REST & BE THANKFUL
MILITARY ROAD REP[D]
BY 93RD REG[T] 1768
TRANSFERRED TO
COMMR: FOR H.R.H.[?] H
IN THE YEAR 1814
A.D.

Keats in 1818 was not thankful to rest in this place! He and his friend Charles Brown had hoped to have breakfast at the top of the pass after trudging through Glen Croe. "We were up at 4 this morning and have walked to breakfast 15 Miles through two tremendous Glens— at the end of the first there is a place called rest and be thankful which we took for an Inn— it was nothing but a Stone" (Carol Kyros Walker, *Walking North with Keats*. New Haven and London: Yale University Press, 1994, p. 184; see note on same page for other travellers' references to a stone and/or bench at the top of the pass).

We descended rapidly into the glen, which resembles the lower part of Glen Croe, though it seemed to be inferior in beauty; but before we had passed through one reach it was quite dark, and I only know that the steeps were high, and that we had the company of a foaming stream; and many a vagrant torrent crossed us, dashing down the hills. The road was bad, and, uncertain how we should fare, we were eager and somewhat uneasy to get forward; but when we were out of the close glen, and near to Cairndow, as a traveller had told us, the moon showed her clear face in the sky, revealing a spacious vale, with a broad loch and sloping corn fields; the hills not very high. This cheerful sight put us into spirits, and we thought it was at least no dismal place to sit up all night in, if they had no beds, and they could not refuse us a shelter. We were, however, well received, and sate down in a neat parlour with a good fire.

Tuesday, August 30th.—Breakfasted before our departure, and ate a herring, fresh from the water, at our landlord's earnest recommendation—much superior to the herrings we get in the north of England. Though we rose at seven, could not set off before nine o'clock; the servants were in bed; the kettle did not boil—indeed, we were completely out of patience; but it had always been so, and we resolved to go off in future without breakfast. Cairndow is a single house by the side of the loch, I believe resorted to by gentlemen in the fishing season:[1] it is a pleasant place for such a purpose; but the vale did not look so beautiful as by moonlight—it had a sort of sea-coldness without mountain grandeur. There is a ferry for footpassengers from Cairndow to the other side of the water, and the road along which all carriages go is carried round the head of the lake, perhaps a distance of three miles.

After we had passed the landing-place of the ferry opposite to Cairndow we saw the lake spread out to a great width, more like an arm of the sea or a great river than one of our lakes; it reminded us of the Severn at the Chepstow passage; but the shores were less rich and the hills higher. The sun shone, which made the morning cheerful, though there was a cold wind. Our road never carried us far from the lake, and with the beating of the waves, the sparkling sunshiny water, boats, the opposite hills, and, on the side on which we travelled, the chance cottages, the coppice woods, and common business of the fields, the ride could not but be amusing. But what most excited our attention was, at one particular place, a cluster of fishing-boats at anchor in a still corner of the lake, a small bay or harbour by the wayside. They were overshadowed by fishermen's nets hung out to dry,

1. The Cairndow Inn, on Loch Fyne, still caters to tourists and fishermen. Keats visited in 1818, ate herring, and got bitten by gadflies after swimming in Loch Fyne which resulted in a bawdy poem, "All gentle folks who owe a grudge."

which formed a dark awning that covered them like a tent, overhanging the water on each side, and falling in the most exquisitely graceful folds. There was a monastic pensiveness, a funereal gloom in the appearance of this little company of vessels, which was the more interesting from the general liveliness and glancing motions of the water, they being perfectly still and silent in their sheltered nook.

When we had travelled about seven miles from Cairndow, winding round the bottom of a hill, we came in view of a great basin or elbow of the lake. Completely out of sight of the long track of water we had coasted, we seemed now to be on the edge of a very large, almost circular, lake, the town of Inverary before us, a line of white buildings on a low promontory right opposite, and close to the water's edge; the whole landscape a showy scene, and bursting upon us at once. A traveller who was riding by our side called out, 'Can that be the Castle?' Recollecting the prints which we had seen, we knew it could not; but the mistake is a natural one at that distance: it is so little like an ordinary town, from the mixture of regularity and irregularity in the buildings. With the expanse of water and pleasant mountains, the scattered boats and sloops, and those gathered together, it had a truly festive appearance. A few steps more brought us in view of the Castle, a stately turreted mansion, but with a modern air, standing on a lawn, retired from the water, and screened behind by woods covering the sides of high hills to the top, and still beyond, by bare mountains. Our road wound round the semicircular shore, crossing two bridges of lordly architecture. The town looked pretty when we drew near to it in connexion with its situation, different from any place I had ever seen, yet exceedingly like what I imaged to myself from representations in raree-shows, or pictures of foreign places— Venice, for example—painted on the scene of a play-house, which one is apt to fancy are as cleanly and gay as they look through the magnifying-glass of the raree-show or in the candle-light dazzle of a theatre. At the door of the inn, though certainly the buildings had not that delightful outside which they appeared to have at a distance, yet they looked very pleasant. The range bordering on the water consisted of little else than the inn, being a large house, with very large stables, the county gaol, the opening into the main street into the town, and an arched gateway, the entrance into the Duke of Argyle's private domain.

We were decently well received at the inn, but it was over-rich in waiters and large rooms to be exactly to our taste, though quite in harmony with the neighbourhood. Before dinner we went into the Duke's pleasure-grounds, which are extensive, and of course command a variety of lively and interesting views. Walked through avenues of tall beech-trees, and observed some that we thought even the tallest we had ever seen; but they were all scantily covered with leaves, and the leaves exceedingly small—indeed, some of them, in the most exposed situations, were almost bare, as if it had been winter. Travellers who wish to view the inside of the Castle send in their names, and the Duke appoints the time of their going; but we did not think that what we should see would repay us for the trouble, there being no pictures, and the house, which I believe has not been built above half a century, is fitted up in the modern style. If there had been any reliques of the ancient costume of the castle of a Highland chieftain, we should have been sorry to have passed it.

Sate after dinner by the fireside till near sunset, for it was very cold, though the sun shone all day. At the beginning of this our second walk we passed through the town, which is but a doleful example of Scotch filth. The houses are plastered or rough-cast, and washed yellow—well built, well sized, and sash-windowed, bespeaking a connexion with the Duke, such a dependence as may be expected in a small town so near to his mansion; and indeed he seems to have done his utmost to make them comfortable, according to our English notions of comfort: they are fit for the houses of people living decently upon a decent trade; but the windows and door-steads were as dirty as in a dirty by-street of a large town, making a most unpleasant contrast with the comely face of the buildings towards the water, and the ducal grandeur and natural festivity of the scene. Smoke and blackness are the wild growth of a Highland hut: the mud floors cannot be washed, the door-steads are trampled by cattle, and if the inhabitants be not very cleanly it gives one little pain; but dirty people living in two-storied stone houses, with dirty sash windows, are a melancholy spectacle anywhere, giving the notion either of vice or the extreme of wretchedness.

Returning through the town, we went towards the Castle, and entered the Duke's grounds by a porter's lodge, following the carriage-road through the park, which is prettily scattered over with trees, and slopes gently towards the lake. A great number of lime-trees were growing singly, not beautiful in their shape, but I mention them for the resemblance to one of the same kind we had seen in the morning, which formed a shade as impenetrable as the roof of any house. The branches did not spread far, nor any one branch much further than another; on the outside it was like a green bush shorn with shears, but when we sate upon a bench under it, looking upwards, in the middle of the tree we could not perceive any green at all; it was like a hundred thousand magpies' nests clustered and matted together, the twigs and boughs being so intertwined that neither the light of the mid-day sun nor showers of hail or rain could pierce through them. The lime-trees on the lawn resembled this tree both in shape and in the manner of intertwisting their twigs, but they were much smaller, and not an impenetrable shade.

The views from the Castle are delightful. Opposite is the lake, girt with mountains, or rather smooth high hills; to the left appears a very steep rocky hill, called Duniquoich Hill, on the top of which is a building like a watch-tower; it rises boldly and almost perpendicular from the plain, at a little distance from the river Arey, that runs through the grounds. To the right is the town, overtopped by a sort of spire or pinnacle of the church,[1] a thing unusual in Scotland, except in the large towns, and which would often give an elegant appearance to the villages, which, from the uniformity of the huts, and the frequent want of tall trees, they seldom exhibit.

In looking at an extensive prospect, or travelling through a large vale, the Trough of the Clyde for instance, I could not help thinking that in England there would have been somewhere a tower or spire to warn us of a village lurking under the covert of a wood or bank, or to point out some particular spot on the distant hills which we might look at with kindly feelings. I well remember how we used to love the little nest of trees out of which Ganton[2] spire rose on the distant Wolds opposite to the windows at Gallow Hill. The spire of Inverary is not of so beautiful a shape as those of the English churches, and, not being one of a class of buildings which is understood at once, seen near or at a distance, is a less interesting object; but it suits well with the outlandish trimness of the buildings bordering on the water; indeed, there is no one thing of the many gathered together in the extensive circuit of the basin or vale of Inverary, that is not in harmony with the effect of the whole place. The Castle is built of a beautiful hewn stone, in colour resembling our blue slates. The author-tourists have quarrelled with the architecture of it, but we did not find much that we were disposed to blame. A castle in a deep glen, overlooking a roaring stream, and defended by precipitous rocks, is, no doubt, an object far more interesting; but, dropping all ideas of danger or insecurity, the natural retinue in our minds of an ancient Highland chieftain,—take a Duke of Argyle at the end of the eighteenth century, let him have his house in Grosvenor Square, his London liveries, and daughters glittering at St. James's, and I think you will be satisfied with his present mansion in the Highlands, which seems to suit with the present times and its situation, and that is indeed a noble one for a modern Duke of the mountainous district of Argyleshire, with its bare valleys, its rocky coasts, and sea lochs.

There is in the natural endowments of Inverary something akin to every feature of the general character of the county; yet even the very mountains and the lake itself have a kind of princely festivity in their appearance. I do not know how to communicate the feeling, but it seemed as if it were no insult to the hills to look on them as the shield and enclosure of the ducal domain, to which the water might delight in bearing its tribute. The hills near the lake are smooth, so smooth that they might have been shaven or

1. The spire of the church has been missing since World War Two, when it was taken down and stored. Efforts to raise money to put it up again have not been successful.
2. In the Yorkshire Wolds, roughly ten miles from Scarborough.

swept; the shores, too, had somewhat of the same effect, being bare, and having no roughness, no woody points; yet the whole circuit being very large, and the hills so extensive, the scene was not the less cheerful and festive, rejoicing in the light of heaven. Behind the Castle the hills are planted to a great height, and the pleasure-grounds extend far up the valley of Arey. We continued our walk a short way along the river, and were sorry to see it stripped of its natural ornaments, after the fashion of Mr. Brown,[1] and left to tell its tale—for it would not be silent like the river at Blenheim—to naked fields and the planted trees on the hills. We were disgusted with the stables, outhouses, or farm-houses in different parts of the grounds behind the Castle: they were broad, out-spreading, fantastic, and unintelligible buildings.

Sate in the park till the moonlight was perceived more than the light of day. We then walked near the town by the water-side. I observed that the children who were playing did not speak Erse, but a much worse English than is spoken by those Highlanders whose common language is the Erse. I went into the town to purchase tea and sugar to carry with us on our journey. We were tired when we returned to the inn, and went to bed directly after tea. My room was at the very top of the house—one flight of steps after another!—but when I drew back the curtains of my window I was repaid for the trouble of panting up-stairs by one of the most splendid moonlight prospects that can be conceived: the whole circuit of the hills, the Castle, the two bridges, the tower on Duniquoich Hill, and the lake with many boats—fit scene for summer midnight festivities! I should have liked to have seen a bevy of Scottish ladies sailing, with music, in a gay barge. William, to whom I have read this, tells me that I have used the very words of Browne of Ottery, Coleridge's fellowtownsman:—

> As I have seen when on the breast of Thames
> A heavenly bevy of sweet English dames,
> In some calm evening of delightful May,

1. "Capability" Brown (1715–83), whose actual name was Lancelot Brown, was a landscape architect widely known in the eighteenth century for his designs of parks on the estates of English gentry. He was later in his career appointed Master Gardener to George III. Dorothy Wordsworth alludes to Capability Brown's famous grand-scale landscape work for Blenheim Park, a job he undertook for the fourth Duke of Marlborough and worked on from 1764–74. Here the River Glyme ("the river at Blenheim") was dammed to create an artificial lake. Dorothy is comparing the Blenheim landscape to the Duke of Argyll's park. Though the River Aray obviously had not been dammed and Loch Fyne was a natural lake, the natural growth along the river had been cleared and the environment manipulated so that there was no baffling for the sound of the river. Such effort to alter the natural appearance of the landscape seemed to her comparable to Brown's effort to create Blenheim.

Ironically, Capability Brown was best known for his taking landscape architecture away from the knot gardens and contrived designs of the Age of Reason and for producing instead a natural look. Dorothy's expression "after the fashion of Mr. Brown" might have more to do with Brown himself (as someone fashionable to employ) than his aesthetics.

> With music give a farewell to the day,
> Or as they would (with an admired tone)
> Greet night's ascension to her ebon throne.[1]
> > Browne's *Britannia's Pastorals.*

Wednesday, August 31st.—We had a long day's journey before us, without a regular baiting-place on the road, so we breakfasted at Inverary, and did not set off till nine o'clock, having, as usual, to complain of the laziness of the servants. Our road was up the valley behind the Castle, the same we had gone along the evening before. Further up, though the plantations on the hills are noble, the valley was cold and naked, wanting hedgerows and comfortable houses. We travelled several miles under the plantations, the vale all along seeming to belong almost exclusively to the Castle. It might have been better distinguished and adorned, as we thought, by neater farm-houses and cottages than are common in Scotland, and snugger fields with warm hedgerows, at the same time testifying as boldly its adherence to the chief.

At that point of the valley where the pleasure-grounds appear to end, we left our horse at a cottage door, and turned a few steps out of the road to see a waterfall, which roared so loud that we could not have gone by without looking about for it, even if we had not known that there was one near Inverary. The waterfall is not remarkable for anything but the good taste with which it has been left to itself, though there is a pleasure-road from the Castle to it. As we went further up the valley the roads died away, and it became an ordinary Scotch glen, the poor pasturage of the hills creeping down into the valley, where it was little better for the shelter, I mean little greener than on the hill-sides; but a man must be of a churlish nature if, with a mind free to look about, he should not find such a glen a pleasing place to travel through, though seeing little but the busy brook, with here and there a bush or tree, and cattle pasturing near the thinly-scattered dwellings. But we came to one spot which I cannot forget, a single green field at the junction of another brook with the Arey, a peninsula surrounded with a close row of trees, which overhung the streams, and under their branches we could just see a neat white house that stood in the middle of the field enclosed by the trees. Before us was nothing but bare hills, and the road through the bare glen. A person who has not travelled in Scotland can scarcely imagine the pleasure we have had from a stone house, though fresh from the workmen's hands, square and sharp; there is generally

---

1. William Browne (*c.*1590–*c.*1645) was born in Devonshire. While Dorothy may consider Ottery St. Mary, which is Coleridge's birthplace, close enough (because it too is in Devonshire) to call Browne Coleridge's "fellow-townsman," she is mistaken in calling him "Browne of Ottery." He would correctly be referred to as Browne of Tavistock.
   The lines she quotes are 231–32 of Song 2, Book 2 of *Britannia's Pastorals.*

such an appearance of equality in poverty through the long glens of Scotland, giving the notion of savage ignorance—no house better than another, and barns and houses all alike. This house had, however, other recommendations of its own; even in the fertile parts of Somersetshire it would have been a delicious spot; here, ''Mid mountain wild set like a little nest,' it was a resting-place for the fancy, and to this day I often think of it, the cottage and its green covert, as an image of romance, a place of which I have the same sort of knowledge as of some of the retirements, the little valleys, described so livelily by Spenser in his Fairy Queen.

We travelled on, the glen now becoming entirely bare. Passed a miserable hut on a naked hill-side, not far from the road, where we were told by a man who came out of it that we might refresh ourselves with a dram of whisky. Went over the hill, and saw nothing remarkable till we came in view of Loch Awe, a large lake far below us, among high mountains—one very large mountain right opposite, which we afterwards found was called Cruachan. The day was pleasant—sunny gleams and a fresh breeze; the lake—we looked across it—as bright as silver, which made the islands, three or four in number, appear very green. We descended gladly, invited by the prospect before us, travelling downwards, along the side of the hill, above a deep glen, woody towards the lower part near the brook; the hills on all sides were high and bare, and not very stony: it made us think of the descent from Newlands into Buttermere, though on a wider scale, and much inferior in simple majesty.

After walking down the hill a long way we came to a bridge, under which the water dashed through a dark channel of rocks among trees, the lake being at a considerable distance below, with cultivated lands between. Close upon the bridge was a small hamlet,[1] a few houses near together, and huddled up in trees—a very sweet spot, the only retired village we had yet seen which was characterized by 'beautiful' wildness with sheltering warmth. We had been told at Inverary that we should come to a place where we might give our horse a feed of corn, and found on inquiry that there was a little public-house here, or rather a hut 'where they kept a dram.' It was a cottage, like all the rest, without a sign-board. The woman of the house helped to take the horse out of harness, and, being hungry, we asked her if she could make us some porridge, to which she replied that 'we should get that,' and I followed her into the house, and sate over her hearth while she was making it. As to fire, there was little sign of it, save the smoke, for a long time, she having no fuel but green wood, and no bellows but her breath. My eyes smarted exceedingly, but the woman seemed so kind and cheerful that I was willing to endure it for the sake of warming my feet in the ashes and talking to her. The fire was in the middle of the room, a crook

1. Cladich.

being suspended from a cross-beam, and a hole left at the top for the smoke to find its way out by: it was a rude Highland hut, unadulterated by Lowland fashions, but it had not the elegant shape of the ferry-house at Loch Ketterine, and the fire, being in the middle of the room, could not be such a snug place to draw to on a winter's night.

We had a long afternoon before us, with only eight miles to travel to Dalmally, and, having been told that a ferry-boat was kept at one of the islands, we resolved to call for it, and row to the island, so we went to the top of an eminence, and the man who was with us set some children to work to gather sticks and withered leaves to make a smoky fire—a signal for the boatman, whose hut is on a flat green island, like a sheep pasture, without trees, and of a considerable size: the man told us it was a rabbit-warren. There were other small islands, on one of which was a ruined house, fortification, or small castle: we could not learn anything of its history, only a girl told us that formerly gentlemen lived in such places. Immediately from the water's edge rose the mountain Cruachan on the opposite side of the lake; it is weedy near the water and craggy above, with deep hollows on the surface. We thought it the grandest mountain we had seen, and on saying to the man who was with us that it was a fine mountain, 'Yes,' he replied, 'it is an excellent mountain,' adding that it was higher than Ben Lomond, and then told us some wild stories of the enormous profits it brought to Lord Breadalbane, its lawful owner. The shape of Loch Awe is very remarkable, its outlet being at one side, and only about eight miles from the head, and the whole lake twenty-four miles in length. We looked with longing after that branch of it opposite to us out of which the water issues: it seemed almost like a river gliding under steep precipices. What we saw of the larger branch, or what might be called the body of the lake, was less promising, the banks being merely gentle slopes, with not very high mountains behind, and the ground moorish and cold.

The children, after having collected fuel for our fire, began to play on the green hill where we stood, as heedless as if we had been trees or stones, and amused us exceedingly with their activity: they wrestled, rolled down the hill, pushing one another over and over again, laughing, screaming, and chattering Erse: they were all without shoes and stockings, which, making them fearless of hurting or being hurt, gave a freedom to the action of their limbs which I never saw in English children: they stood upon one another, body, breast, or face, or any other part; sometimes one was uppermost, sometimes another, and sometimes they rolled all together, so that we could not know to which body this leg or that arm belonged. We waited, watching them, till we were assured that the boatman had noticed our signal.—By the bye, if we had received proper directions at Loch Lomond, on our journey to Loch Ketterine, we should have made our way down the lake till we had come opposite to the ferryman's house, where there is a hut, and the people who live there are accustomed to call him by the same signal as here. Luckily for us we were not so well instructed, for we should have missed the pleasure of receiving the kindness of Mr. and Mrs. Macfarlane and their family.

A young woman who wanted to go to the island accompanied us to the water-side. The walk was pleasant, through fields with hedgerows, the greenest fields we had seen in Scotland; but we were obliged to return without going to the island. The poor man had taken his boat to another

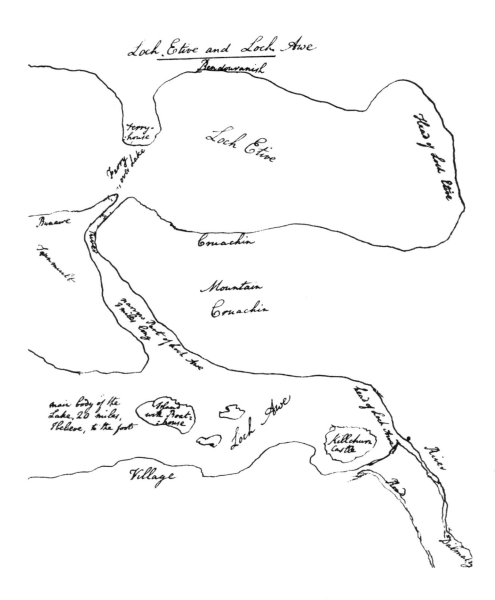

place, and the waters were swollen so that we could not go close to the shore, and show ourselves to him, nor could we make him hear by shouting. On our return to the public–house we asked the woman what we should pay her, and were not a little surprised when she answered, 'Three shillings.' Our horse had had a sixpenny feed of miserable corn, not worth threepence; the rest of the charge was for skimmed milk, oat-bread, porridge, and blue milk cheese: we told her it was far too much; and, giving her half-a-crown, departed. I was sorry she had made this unreasonable demand, because we had liked the woman, and we had before been so well treated in the Highland cottages; but, on thinking more about it, I satisfied myself that it was no scheme to impose upon us, for she was contented with the half-crown, and would, I daresay, have been so with two shillings, if we had offered it her at first. Not being accustomed to fix a price upon porridge and milk, to such as we, at least, when we asked her she did not know what to say; but, seeing that we were travelling for pleasure, no doubt she concluded we were rich, and that what was a small gain to her could be no great loss to us.

When we had gone a little way we saw before us a young man with a bundle over his shoulder, hung on a stick, bearing a great boy on his back: seeing that they were travellers, we offered to take the boy on the car, to which the man replied that he should be more than thankful, and set him up beside me. They had walked from Glasgow, and that morning from Inverary; the boy was only six years old, 'But,' said his father, 'he is a stout walker,' and a fine fellow he was, smartly dressed in tight clean clothes and a nice round hat: he was going to stay with his grandmother at Dalmally. I found him good company; though I could not draw a single word out of him, it was a pleasure to see his happiness gleaming through the shy glances of his healthy countenance. Passed a pretty chapel by the lake-side, and an island with a farm-house upon it, and corn and pasture fields; but, as we went along, we had frequent reason to regret the want of English hedgerows and English culture; for the ground was often swampy or moorish near the lake where comfortable dwellings among green fields might have been. When we came near to the end of the lake we had a steep hill to climb, so William and I walked; and we had such confidence in our horse that we were not afraid to leave the car to his guidance with the child in it; we were soon, however, alarmed at seeing him trot up the hill a long way before us; the child, having raised himself up upon the seat, was beating him as hard as he could with a little stick which he carried in his hand; and when he saw our eyes were on him he sate down, I believe very sorry to resign his office: the horse slackened his pace, and no accident happened.

When we had ascended half-way up the hill, directed by the man, I took a nearer footpath, and at the top came in view of a most impressive scene, a ruined castle on an island almost in the middle of the last compartment of the lake, backed by a mountain cove, down which came a roaring stream. The castle occupied every foot of the island that was visible to us, appearing to rise out of the water; mists rested upon the mountain side, with spots of sunshine between; there was a mild desolation in the low grounds, a solemn grandeur in the mountains, and the castle was wild, yet stately, not dismantled of its turrets, nor the walls broken down, though completely in ruin. After having stood some minutes I joined William on the high road, and both wishing to stay longer near this place, we requested the man to drive his little boy on to Dalmally, about two miles further, and leave the car at the inn. He told us that the ruin was called Kilchurn Castle, that it belonged to Lord Breadalbane, and had been built by one of the ladies of that family for her defence during her Lord's absence at the Crusades, for which purpose she levied a tax of seven years' rent upon her tenants;★ he said that from that side of the lake it did not appear, in very dry weather, to stand upon an island; but that it was possible to go over to it without being wet-shod. We were very lucky in seeing it after a great flood; for its enchanting effect was chiefly owing to its situation in the lake, a decayed palace rising out of the plain of waters! I have called it a palace, for such feeling it gave to me, though having been built as a place of defence, a castle or fortress. We turned again and reascended the hill, and sate a long time in the middle of it looking on the castle and the huge mountain cove opposite, and William, addressing himself to the ruin, poured out there verses:—

> Child of loud-throated War! the mountain stream
> Roars in thy hearing; but thy hour of rest
> Is come, and thou art silent in thy age.[2]

We walked up the hill again, and, looking down the vale, had a fine view of the lake and islands, resembling the views down Windermere, though much less rich. Our walk to Dalmally was pleasant: the vale makes a turn to the right, beyond the head of the lake, and the village of Dalmally, which is, in fact, only a few huts, the manse or minister's house, the chapel, and the inn, stands near the river, which flows into the head of the lake. The whole vale is very pleasing, the lower part of the hill-sides being sprinkled with thatched cottages, cultivated ground in small patches near them, which evidently belonged to the cottages.

We were overtaken by a gentleman who rode on a beautiful white pony, like Lilly,[1] and was followed by his servant, a Highland boy, on another

★ Not very probable. [D.W.]

1. The correspondence of Sara Hutchinson in August 1813 reveals that Henry Hutchinson's pony, named Lilly, had been injured. Possibly this pony was part of the Grasmere scene at the time of Dorothy's writing.
2. From William Wordsworth's "Address to Kilchurn Castle, Upon Loch Awe," ll. 1–3.

pony, a little creature, not much bigger than a large mastiff, on which were slung a pair of crutches and a tartan plaid. The gentleman entered into conversation with us, and on our telling him that we were going to Glen Coe, he advised us, instead of proceeding directly to Tyndrum, the next stage, to go round by the outlet of Loch Awe to Loch Etive, and thence to Glen Coe. We were glad to change our plan, for we wanted much to see more of Loch Awe, and he told us that the whole of the way by Loch Etive was pleasant, and the road to Tyndrum as dreary as possible; indeed, we could see it at that time several miles before us upon the side of a bleak mountain; and he said that there was nothing but moors and mountains all the way. We reached the inn a little before sunset, ordered supper, and I walked out. Crossed a bridge to look more nearly at the parsonage-house and the chapel, which stands upon a bank close to the river, a pretty stream overhung in some parts by trees. The vale is very pleasing; but, like all the other Scotch vales we had yet seen, it told of its kinship with the mountains and of poverty or some neglect on the part of man.

Thursday, September 1st.—We had been attended at supper by a civil boy, whom we engaged to rouse us at six o'clock, and to provide us each a basin of milk and bread, and have the car ready; all which he did punctually, and we were off in good time. The morning was not unpleasant, though rather cold, and we had some fear of rain. Crossed the bridge, and passed by the manse and chapel, our road carrying us back again in the direction we had come; but on the opposite side of the river. Passed close to many of the houses we had seen on the hill-side, which the lame gentleman had told us belonged to Lord Breadalbane, and were attached to little farms, or 'crofts,' as he called them. Lord Breadalbane had lately laid out a part of his estates in this way as an experiment, in the hope of preventing discontent and emigration. We were sorry we had not an opportunity of seeing into these cottages, and of learning how far the people were happy or otherwise. The dwellings certainly did not look so comfortable when we were near to them as from a distance; but this might be chiefly owing to what the inhabitants did not feel as an evil—the dirt about the doors. We saw, however—a sight always painful to me—two or three women, each creeping after her single cow, while it was feeding on the slips of grass between the corn-grounds. Went round the head of the lake, and onwards close to the lake-side. Kilchurn Castle was always interesting, though not so grand as seen from the other side, with its own mountain cove and roaring stream. It combined with the vale of Dalmally and the distant hills—a beautiful scene, yet overspread with a gentle desolation. As we went further down we lost sight of the vale of Dalmally. The castle, which we often stopped to look back upon, was very beautiful seen in combination with the opposite shore of the lake—perhaps a little bay, a tuft of trees, or a slope of the hill. Travelled under the foot of the mountain Cruachan, along an excellent road, having the lake close to us on our left, woods overhead, and frequent torrents tumbling down the hills. The distant views across the lake were not peculiarly interesting after we were out of sight of Kilchurn Castle, the lake being wide, and the opposite shore not rich, and those mountains which we could see were not high.

Came opposite to the village where we had dined the day before, and, losing sight of the body of the lake, pursued the narrow channel or pass,[1] which is, I believe, three miles long, out of which issues the river that flows into Loch Etive. We were now enclosed between steep hills, on the opposite side entirely bare, on our side bare or woody; the branch of the lake generally filling the whole area of the vale. It was a pleasing, solitary scene; the long reach of naked precipices on the other side rose directly out of the water, exceedingly steep, not rugged or rocky, but with scanty sheep pasturage and large beds of small stones, purple, dove-coloured, or red, such as are called Screes in Cumberland and Westmoreland. These beds, or rather streams of stones, appeared as smooth as the turf itself, nay, I might say, as soft as the feathers of birds, which they resembled in colour. There was no building on either side of the water; in many parts only just room for the road, and on the other shore no footing, as it might seem, for any creature larger than the mountain sheep, and they, in treading amongst the shelving stones, must often send them down into the lake below.

After we had wound for some time through the valley, having met neither foot-traveller, horse, nor cart, we started at the sight of a single vessel, just as it turned round the point of a hill, coming into the reach of the valley where we were. She floated steadily through the middle of the water, with one large sail spread out, full swollen by the breeze, that blew her right towards us. I cannot express what romantic images this vessel brought along with her—how much more beautiful the mountains appeared, the lake how much more graceful. There was one man on board, who state at the helm, and he, having no companion, made the boat look more silent than if we could not have seen him. I had almost said the ship, for on that narrow water it appeared as large as the ships which I have watched sailing out of a harbour of the sea. A little further on we passed a stone hut by the lake-side, near which were many charcoal sacks, and we conjectured that the vessel had been depositing charcoal brought from other parts of Loch Awe to be carried to the iron-works at Loch Etive. A little further on we came to the end of the lake, but where exactly it ended was not easy to determine, for the river was as broad as the lake, and we could only say when it became positively a river by the rushing of the water. It is, indeed, a grand stream, the quantity of water being very large, frequently

1. The Pass of Brander.

forming rapids, and always flowing very quickly; but its greatness is short-lived, for, after a course of three miles, it is lost in the great waters of Loch Etive, a sea loch.

Crossed a bridge, and climbing a hill towards Taynuilt, our baiting-place, we saw a hollow to the right below us, through which the river continued its course between rocks and steep banks of wood. William turned aside to look into the dell, but I was too much tired. We had left it, two or three hundred yards behind, an open river, the hills, enclosing the branch of the lake, having settled down into irregular slopes. We were glad when we reached Taynuilt, a village of huts, with a chapel and one stone house, which was the inn. It had begun to rain, and I was almost benumbed with the cold, besides having a bad headache; so it rejoiced me to see kind looks on the landlady's face, and that she was willing to put herself in a bustle for our comfort; we had a good fire presently, and breakfast was set out—eggs, preserved gooseberries, excellent cream, cheese, and butter, but no wheat bread, and the oaten cakes were so hard I could not chew them. We wished to go upon Loch Etive; so, having desired the landlady to prepare a fowl for supper, and engaged beds, which she promised us willingly—a proof that we were not in the great road—we determined to find our way to the lake and endeavour to procure a boat. It rained heavily, but we went on, hoping the sky would clear up.

Walked through unenclosed fields, a sort of half-desolate country; but when we came to the mouth of the river which issues out of Loch Awe, and which we had to cross by a ferry, looking up that river we saw that the vale down which it flowed was richly wooded and beautiful.

We were now among familiar fireside names. We could see the town of Bunawe,[1] a place of which the old woman with whom William lodged ten years at Hawkshead used to tell tales half as long as an ancient romance. It is a small village or port on the same side of Loch Etive on which we stood, and at a little distance is a house built by a Mr. Knott of Coniston Water-head, a partner in the iron-foundry at Bunawe, in the service of whose family the old woman had spent her youth. It was an ugly yellow-daubed building, staring this way and that, but William looked at it with pleasure for poor Ann Tyson's sake.[2] We hailed the ferry-boat, and a little boy came to fetch us; he rowed up against the stream with all his might for a considerable way, and then yielding to it, the boat was shot towards the shore almost like an arrow from a bow. It was pleasing to observe the dexterity with which the lad managed his oars, glorying in the appearance of danger—for he observed us watching him, and afterwards, while he conveyed us over, his

1. Today Bunawe, as a designated place on a map, is on the opposite side of Loch Etive. However, the Bunawe Iron Furnace, a restoration of the complex of buildings that made up the ironworks, remains in the village of Taynuilt, bearing testimony to the existence on that side of Loch Etive of the "town of Bunawe," where indeed early maps place it. Established here in 1752–53, the ironworks was an offshoot of a parent company in the Furness district of Lancashire, now in Cumbria, and many of the workers were immigrants from England.
2. Ann Tyson was the woman in whose cottage William lived, with other boys she had taken in as boarders, while he attended grammar school in Hawkshead. When she was younger she worked as a domestic servant for the family of George Knott, of Rydal. When Knott moved his ironmongering business from Furness to the foundry in Bunawe, Ann Tyson moved with the family. It was here she garnered the tales of Scottish history and lore with which she entertained the schoolboys living under affectionate care. She was beloved by William, for whom she filled a needed maternal role.

pride redoubled; for my part, I was completely dizzy with the swiftness of the motion.

We could not have a boat from the ferry, but were told that if we would walk to a house half a mile up the river, we had a chance of getting one. I went a part of the way with William, and then sate down under the umbrella near some houses. A woman came out to talk with me, and pressed me to take shelter in her house, which I refused, afraid of missing William. She eyed me with extreme curiosity, asking fifty questions respecting the object of our journey. She told me that it rained most parts of the year there, and that there was no chance of fine weather that day; and I believe when William came to tell me that we could have a boat, she thought I was half crazed. We went down to the shore of the lake, and, after having sate some time under a wall, the boatman came to us, and we went upon the water. At first it did not rain heavily, and the air was not cold, and before we had gone far we rejoiced that we had not been faint-hearted. The loch is of a considerable width, but the mountains are so very high that, whether we were close under them or looked from one shore to the other, they maintained their dignity. I speak of the higher part of the loch, above the town of Bunawe and the large river, for downwards they are but hills, and the water spreads out wide towards undetermined shores. On our right was the mountain Cruachan, rising directly from the lake, and on the opposite side another mountain, called Ben Durinish, craggy, and exceedingly steep, with wild wood growing among the rocks and stones.

We crossed the water, which was very rough in the middle, but calmer near the shores, and some of the rocky basins and little creeks among the rocks were as still as a mirror, and they were so beautiful with the reflection of the orange-coloured seaweed growing on the stones or rocks, that a child, with a child's delight in gay colours, might have danced with joy at the sight of them. It never ceased raining, and the tops of the mountains were concealed by mists, but as long as we could see across the water we were contented; for though little could be seen of the true shapes and permanent appearances of the mountains, we saw enough to give us the most exquisite delight: the powerful lake which filled the large vale, roaring torrents, clouds floating on the mountain sides, sheep that pastured there, sea-birds and land birds. We sailed a considerable way without coming to any houses or cultivated fields. There was no horse-road on either side of the loch, but a person on foot, as the boatman told us, might make his way at the foot of Ben Durinish, namely on that side of the loch on which we were; there was, however, not the least track to be seen, and it must be very difficult and laborious.

We happened to say that we were going to Glen Coe, which would be the journey of a long day and a half, when one of the men, pointing to the head of the loch, replied that if we were there we should be but an hour's walk from Glen Coe. Though it continued raining, and there was no hope that the rain would cease, we could not help wishing to go by that way: it was an adventure; we were not afraid of trusting ourselves to the hospitality of the Highlanders, and we wanted to give our horse a day's rest, his back having been galled by the saddle. The owner of the boat, who understood English much better than the other man, his helper, said he would make inquiries about the road at a farm-house a little further on. He was very ready to talk with us, and was rather an interesting companion; he spoke after a slow and solemn manner, in book and sermon language and phrases:

A stately speech, such as grave livers do in Scotland use.[1]

When we came to the farm-house of which the man had spoken, William and he landed to make the necessary inquiries. It was a thatched house at the foot of the high mountain Ben Durinish—a few patches or little beds of corn belonging to it; but the spot was pastoral, the green grass growing to the walls of the house. The dwelling-house was distinguished from the outer buildings, which were numerous, making it look like two or three houses, as is common in Scotland, by a chimney and one small window with sash-panes; on one side was a little woody glen, with a precipitous stream that fell into the bay, which was perfectly still, and bordered with the rich orange-colour reflected from the sea-weed. Cruachan, on the other side of the lake, was exceedingly grand, and appeared of an enormous height, spreading out two large arms that made a cove down which fell many streams swoln by the rain, and in the hollow of the cove were some huts which looked like a village. The top of the mountain was concealed from us by clouds, and the mists floated high and low upon the sides of it.

William came back to the boat highly pleased with the cheerful hospitality and kindness of the woman of the house, who would scarcely permit him and his guide to go away without taking some refreshment. She was the only person at home, so they could not obtain the desired information; but William had been well repaid for the trouble of landing; indeed, rainy as it was, I regretted that I had not landed also, for I should have wished to bear away in my memory a perfect image of this place,—the view from the doors, as well as the simple Highland comforts and contrivances which were near it. I think I never saw a retirement that would have so completely satisfied me, if I had wanted to be altogether shut out from the world, and at the same time among the grandest of the works of God; but it must be remembered that mountains are often so much dignified by clouds, mists, and other accidents of weather, that one could not know them again in the full sunshine of a summer's noon. But, whatever the mountains

1. The lines are from William's "Resolution and Independence," xiv ll. 5–6.

may be in their own shapes, the farm-house with its pastoral grounds and corn fields won from the mountain, its warm out-houses in irregular stages one above another on the side of the hill, the rocks, the stream, and sheltering bay, must at all times be interesting objects. The household boat lay at anchor, chained to a rock, which like the whole border of the lake, was edged with sea-weed, and some fishing-nets were hung upon poles,— affecting images, which led our thoughts out to the wide ocean, yet made these solitudes of the mountains bear the impression of greater safety and more deep seclusion.

The rain became so heavy that we should certainly have turned back if we had not felt more than usual courage from the pleasure we had enjoyed, which raised hope where none was. There were some houses a little higher up, and we determined to go thither and make further inquiries. We could now hardly see to the other side of the lake, yet continued to go on, and presently heard some people pushing through a thicket close to us, on which the boatman called out, 'There's one that can tell us something about the road to Glen Coe, for he was born there.' We looked up and saw a ragged, lame fellow, followed by some others, with a fishing-rod over his shoulder; and he was making such good speed through the boughs that one might have half believed he was the better for his lame leg. He was the head of a company of tinkers, who, as the men told us, travel with their fishing-rods as duly as their hammers. On being hailed by us the whole company stopped; and their lame leader and our boatmen shouted to each other in Erse—a savage cry to our ears, in that lonely and romantic place. We could not learn from the tinker all we wished to know, therefore when we came near to the houses William landed again with the owner of the boat. The rain was now so heavy that we could see nothing at all—not even the houses whither William was going.

We had given up all thought of proceeding further at that time, but were desirous to know how far that road to Glen Coe was practicable for us. They met with an intelligent man, who was at work with others in a hay field, thought it rained so heavily; he gave them the information they desired, and said that there was an acquaintance of his between that place and Glen Coe, who, he had no doubt, would gladly accommodate us with lodging and anything else we might need. When William returned to the boat we shaped our course back again down the water, leaving the head of Loch Etive not only unvisited, but unseen—to our great regret. The rain was very heavy; the wind had risen, and both wind and tide were against us, so that it was hard labour for the boatmen to push us on. They kept as close to the shore as they could, to be under the wind; but at the doubling of many of the rocky points the tide was so strong that it was difficult to get on at all, and I was sometimes afraid that we should be dashed against the rocks, though I believe, indeed, there was not much danger.

Came down the same side of the lake under Ben Durinish, and landed at a ferry-house opposite to Bunawe, where we gave the men a glass of whisky; but our chief motive for landing was to look about the place, which had a most wild aspect at that time. It was a low promontory, pushed far into the water, narrowing the lake exceedingly; in the obscurity occasioned by the mist and rain it appeared to be an island; it was stained and weatherbeaten, a rocky place, seeming to bear no produce but such as might be cherished by cold and storms, lichens or the incrustations of sea rocks. We rowed right across the water to the mouth of the river of Loch Awe, our boat following the ferry-boat which was conveying the tinker crew to the other side, whither they were going to lodge, as the men told us, in some kiln, which they considered as their right and privilege—a lodging always to be found where there was any arable land—for every farm has its kiln to dry the corn in: another proof of the wetness of the climate. The kilns are built of stone, covered in, and probably as good a shelter as the huts in which these Highland vagrants were born. They gather sticks or heather for their fire, and, as they are obstinate beggars, for the men said they would not be denied, they probably have plenty of food with little other trouble than that of wandering in search of it, for their smutty faces and tinker equipage serve chiefly for a passport to a free and careless life. It rained very heavily, and the wind blew when we crossed the lake, and their boat and ours went tilting over the high waves. They made a romantic appearance; three women were of the party; two men rowed them over; the lame fellow sate at one end of the boat, and his companion at the other, each with an enormous fishing-rod, which looked very graceful, something like masts to the boat. When we had landed at the other side we saw them, after having begged at the ferry-house, strike merrily through the fields, no doubt betaking themselves to their shelter for the night.

We were completely wet when we reached the inn; the landlady wanted to make a fire for me up-stairs, but I went into her own parlour to undress, and her daughter, a pretty little girl, who could speak a few words of English, waited on me; I rewarded her with one of the penny books bought at Dumfries for Johnny,[1] with which she was greatly delighted. We had an excellent supper—fresh salmon, a fowl, gooseberries and cream, and potatoes; good beds; and the next morning boiled milk and bread, and were only charged seven shillings and sixpence for the whole—horse, liquor, supper, and the two breakfasts. We thought they had made a mistake, and told them so—for it was only just half as much as we had paid the day before at Dalmally, the case being that Dalmally is in the main road of the tourists. The landlady insisted on my bringing away a little cup instead of our tin can,

---

1. Dorothy's nephew, William and Mary's first child, born 18 June 1803, not yet three months old.

which she told me had been taken from the car by some children: we set no little value on this cup as a memorial of the good woman's honesty and kindness, and hoped to have brought it home. . . .

Friday, September 2d.—Departed at about seven o'clock this morning, having to travel eight miles down Loch Etive, and then to cross a ferry. Our road was at first at a considerable distance from the lake, and out of sight of it, among undulating hills covered with coppice woods, resembling the country between Coniston and Windermere, but it afterwards carried us close to the water's edge; and in this part of our ride we were disappointed. We knew that the high mountains were all at the head of the lake, therefore had not expected the same awful grandeur which we beheld the day before, and perceived by glimpses; but the gentleman whom we met with at Dalmally had told us that there were many fine situations for gentlemen's seats on this part of the lake, which had made us expect greater loveliness near the shores, and better cultivation. It is true there are pleasant bays, with grounds prettily sloping to the water, and coppice woods, where houses would stand in shelter and sun, looking on the lake; but much is yet wanting—waste lands to be ploughed, peat-mosses drained, hedgerows reared; and the woods demand a grant of longer life than is now their privilege.

But after we had journeyed about six miles a beautiful scene opened upon us. The morning had been gloomy, and at this time the sun shone out, scattering the clouds. We looked right down the lake, that was covered with streams of dazzling sunshine, which revealed the indentings of the dark shores. On a bold promontory, on the same side of the loch where we were, stood an old castle,[1] an irregular tall building, not without majesty; and beyond, with leagues of water between, our eyes settled upon the island of Mull, a high mountain, green in the sunshine, and overcast with clouds,— an object as inviting to the fancy as the evening sky in the west, and though of a terrestrial green, almost as visionary. We saw that it was an island of the sea, but were unacquainted with its name; it was of a gem-like colour, and as soft as the sky. The shores of Loch Etive, in their moorish, rocky wildness, their earthly bareness, as they lay in length before us, produced a contrast which, with the pure sea, the brilliant sunshine, the long distance, contributed to the aërial and romantic power with which the mountain island was invested.

Soon after, we came to the ferry. The boat being on the other shore, we had to wait a considerable time, though the water was not wide, and our call was heard immediately. The boatmen moved with surly tardiness, as if glad to make us know that they were our masters. At this point the lake was

1. Dunstaffnage Castle.

narrowed to the breadth of not a very wide river by a round ear or
promontory on the side on which we were, and a low ridge of peat-mossy
ground on the other. It was a dreary place, shut out from the beautiful
prospect of the Isle of Mull, and Dunstaffnage Castle—so the fortress was
called. Four or five men came over with the boat; the horse was unyoked,
and being harshly driven over rough stones, which were as slippery as ice,
with slimy seaweed, he was in terror before he reached the boat, and they
completed the work by beating and pushing him by main force over the
ridge of the boat, for there was no open end, or plank, or any other
convenience for shipping either horse or carriage. I was very uneasy when
we were launched on the water. A blackguard-looking fellow, blind of one
eye, which I could not but think had been put out in some strife or other,
held him by force like a horse-breaker, while the poor creature fretted, and
stamped with his feet against the bare boards, frightening himself more and
more with every stroke; and when we were in the middle of the water I
would have given a thousand pounds to have been sure that we should reach
the other side in safety. The tide was rushing violently in, making a strong
eddy with the stream of the loch, so that the motion of the boat and the
noise and foam of the waves terrified him still more, and we thought it
would be impossible to keep him in the boat, and when we were just far
enough from the shore to have been all drowned he became furious, and,
plunging desperately, his hind-legs were in the water, then, recovering
himself, he beat with such force against the boat-side that we were afraid he
should send his feet through. All the while the men were swearing terrible
oaths, and cursing the poor beast, redoubling their curses when we reached
the landing-place, and whipping him ashore in brutal triumph.

We had only room for half a heartful of joy when we set foot on dry
land, for another ferry was to be crossed five miles further. We had intended
breakfasting at this house if it had been a decent place; but after this affair we
were glad to pay the men off and depart, though I was not well and needed
refreshment. The people made us more easy by assuring us that we might
easily swim the horse over the next ferry. The first mile or two of our road
was over a peat-moss; we then came near to the seashore, and had beautiful
views backwards towards the Island of Mull and Dunstaffnage Castle, and
forward where the sea ran up between the hills. In this part, on the opposite
side of the small bay or elbow of the sea, was a gentleman's house on a
hillside, and a building on the hill-top which we took for a lighthouse, but
were told that it belonged to the mansion, and was only lighted up on
rejoicing days—the laird's birthday, for instance.

Before we had left the peat-moss to travel close to the sea-shore we
delighted ourselves with looking on a range of green hills, in shape like those
bordering immediately upon the sea, abrupt but not high; they were, in fact,
a continuation of the same; but retiring backwards, and rising from the black

peat-moss. These hills were of a delicate green, uncommon in Scotland; a foaming rivulet ran down one part, and near it lay two herdsmen full in the sun, with their dogs, among a troop of black cattle which were feeding near, and sprinkled over the whole range of hills—a pastoral scene, to our eyes the more beautiful from knowing what a delightful prospect it must overlook. We now came under the steeps by the sea-side, which were bold rocks, mouldering scars, or fresh with green grass. Under the brow of one of these rocks was a burying-ground, with many upright grave-stones and hay-cocks between, and fenced round by a wall neatly sodded. Near it were one or two houses, with out-houses under a group of trees, but no chapel. The neatness of the burying-ground would in itself have been noticeable in any part of Scotland where we have been; but it was more interesting from its situation than for its own sake—within the sound of the gentlest waves of the sea, and near so many quiet and beautiful objects. There was a range of hills opposite, which we were here first told were the hills of Morven, so much sung of by Ossian.[1] We consulted with some men respecting the ferry, who advised us by all means to send our horse round the loch, and go ourselves over in the boat: they were very civil, and seemed to be intelligent men, yet all disagreed about the length of the loch, though we were not two miles from it: one said it was only six miles long, another ten or fifteen, and afterwards a man whom we met told us it was twenty.

We lost sight of the sea for some time, crossing a half-cultivated space, then reached Loch Creran, a large irregular sea loch, with low sloping banks, coppice woods, and uncultivated grounds, with a scattering of corn fields; as it appeared to us, very thinly inhabited: mountains at a distance. We found only women at home at the ferry-house. I was faint and cold, and went to sit by the fire, but, though very much needing refreshment, I had not heart to eat anything there—the house was so dirty, and there were so many wretchedly dirty women and children; yet perhaps I might have got over the dirt, though I believe there are few ladies who would not have been turned sick by it, if there had not been a most disgusting combination of laziness and coarseness in the countenances and manners of the women, though two of them were very handsome. It was a small hut, and four women were living in it: one, the mother of the children and mistress of the house; the others I supposed to be lodgers, or perhaps servants; but there was no work amongst them. They had just taken from the fire a great pan full of potatoes, which they mixed up with milk, all helping themselves out of the same

1. If one accepts the prevalent Scottish tradition, Ossian was the third-century Gaelic bard, son of Fingal, whose works had been "translated" by the Scottish Highland schoolmaster and poet James Macpherson (1736–96). The Wordsworths did not engage in the Ossian-bashing stirred up by Dr. Johnson, who attacked the authenticity of Macpherson's work. Rather, they embraced Scottish literary tradition and the Romantic mystery of an ancient folk hero endowed with bardic vision. Morvern was the setting of some of the tales of Ossian.

vessel, and the little children put in their dirty hands to dig out of the mess at their pleasure. I though to myself, How light the labour of such a house as this! Little sweeping, no washing of floors, and as to scouring the table, I believe it was a thing never thought of.

After a long time the ferryman came home; but we had to wait yet another hour for the tide. In the meanwhile our horse took fright in consequence of his terror at the last ferry, ran away with the car, and dashed out umbrellas, greatcoats, etc.; but luckily he was stopped before any serious mischief was done. We had determined, whatever it cost, not to trust ourselves with him again in the boat; but sending him round the lake seemed almost out of the question, there being no road, and probably much difficulty in going round with a horse; so after some deliberation with the ferryman it was agreed that he should swim over. The usual place of ferrying was very broad, but he was led to the point of a peninsula at a little distance. It being an unusual affair,—indeed, the people of the house said that he was the first horse that had ever swum over,—we had several men on board, and the mistress of the house offered herself as an assistant: we supposed for the sake of a share in eighteen-pennyworth of whisky which her husband called for without ceremony, and of which she and the young lasses, who had helped to push the boat into the water, partook as freely as the men. At first I feared for the horse: he was frightened, and strove to push himself under the boat; but I was soon tolerably easy, for he went on regularly and well, and after from six to ten minutes swimming landed in safety on the other side. Poor creature! he stretched out his nostrils and stared wildly while the man was trotting him about to warm him, and when he put him into the car he was afraid of the sound of the wheels. For some time our road was up a glen, the banks chiefly covered with coppice woods, an unpeopled, but, though without grandeur, not a dreary tract.

Came to a moor and descended into a broad vale, which opened to Loch Linnhe, an arm of the sea, the prospect being shut in by high mountains, on which the sun was shining among mists and resting clouds. A village and chapel stood on the opposite hill; the hills sloped prettily down to the bed of the vale, a large level area—the grounds in general cultivated, but not rich. We went perhaps half a mile down the vale, when out road struck right across it towards the village on the hill-side. We overtook a tall, well-looking man, seemingly about thirty years of age, driving a cart, of whom we inquired concerning the road, and the distance to Portnacroish, our baiting-place.[1] We made further inquiries respecting our future journey, which he answered in an intelligent manner, being perfectly acquainted with the geography of Scotland. He told us that the village which we saw before us and the whole tract of country was called Appin. William said that it was a pretty wild place, to which the man replied, 'Sir, it is a very bonny place

1. The inn where the Wordsworths stayed is now a private residence.

if you did but see it on a fine day,' mistaking William's praise for a half-censure; I must say, however, that we hardly ever saw a thoroughly pleasing place in Scotland, which had not something of wildness in its aspect of one sort or other. It come from many causes here: the sea, or sea-loch, of which we only saw as it were a glimpse crossing the vale at the foot of it, the high mountains on the opposite shore, the unenclosed hills on each side of the vale, with black cattle feeding on them, the simplicity of the scattered huts, the half-sheltered, half-exposed situation of the village, the imperfect culture of the fields, the distance from any city or large town, and the very names of Morven and Appin, particularly at such a time, when old Ossian's old friends, sunbeams and mists, as like ghosts as any in the mid-afternoon could be, were keeping company with them. William did all he could to efface the unpleasant impression he had made on the Highlander, and not without success, for he was kind and communicative when we walked up the hill towards the village. He had been a great traveller, in Ireland and elsewhere; but I believe that he had visited no place so beautiful to his eyes as his native home, the strath of Appin under the heathy hills.

We arrived at Portnacroish soon after parting from this man. It is a small village—a few huts and an indifferent inn by the side of the loch. Ordered a fowl for dinner, had a fire lighted, and went a few steps from the door up the road, and turning aside into a field stood at the top of a low eminence, from which, looking down the loch to the sea through a long vista of hills and mountains, we beheld one of the most delightful prospects that, even when we dream of fairer worlds than this, it is possible for us to conceive in our hearts. A covering of clouds rested on the long range of the hills of Morven, mists floated very near to the water on their sides, and were slowly shifting about: yet the sky was clear, and the sea, from the reflection of the sky, of an ethereal or sapphire blue, which was intermingled in many places, and mostly by gentle gradations, with beds of bright dazzling sunshine; green islands lay on the calm water, islands far greener, for so it seemed, than the grass of other places; and from their excessive beauty, their unearthly softness, and the great distance of many of them, they made us think of the islands of the blessed in the Vision of Mirza—a resemblance more striking from the long tract of mist which rested on the top of the steeps of Morven.[1] The view was endless, and though not so wide, had something of the

---

1. Joseph Addison (1672–1719), essayist and critic (as an anonymous narrator) in *The Spectator* No. 159, alleges that he picked up some manuscripts entitled *The Visions of Mizrah* when he was at Grand Cairo. He claims to have translated the first vision "word for word." The tale he recounts concerns a meditative hero named Mizrah who, in the hills of Baghdad, is guided by a "genius" to have two contrasting visions. The first is of a vale of misery, into which bad men fall after death. But the second, which Mizrah sees after penetrating a thick mist, is of "a vast ocean planted with innumerable islands." The latter is where good men went after death—"the island of the blessed"—as Dorothy puts it. There are interesting parallels here between the hills of Morvern and the hills of Baghdad, and the two visionary experiences.

intricacy of the islands and water of Loch Lomond as we saw them from Inch-ta-vanach; and yet how different! At Loch Lomond we could never forget that it was an inland lake of fresh water, nor here that it was the sea itself, though among multitudes of hills. Immediately below us, on an island a few yards from the shore, stood an old keep or fortress;[1] the vale of Appin opened to the water-side, with cultivated fields and cottages. If there were trees near the shore they contributed little to the delightful effect of the scene: it was the immeasurable water, the lofty mist-covered steeps of Morven to the right, the emerald islands without a bush or tree, the celestial colour and brightness of the calm sea, and the innumerable creeks and bays, the communion of land and water as far as the eye could travel. My description must needs be languid; for the sight itself was too fair to be remembered. We sate a long time upon the hill, and pursued our journey at about four o'clock. Had an indifferent dinner, but the cheese was so excellent that William wished to buy the remainder; but the woman would not consent to sell it, and forced us to accept a large portion of it.

We had to travel up the loch, leaving behind us the beautiful scene which we had viewed with such delight before dinner. Often, while we were climbing the hill, did we stop to look back, and when we had gone twenty or thirty yards beyond the point where we had the last view of it, we left the car to the care of some children who were coming from school, and went to take another farewell, always in the hope of bearing away a more substantial remembrance. Travelled for some miles along a road which was so smooth it was more like a gravel walk in a gentleman's grounds than a public highway. Probably the country is indebted for this excellent road to Lord Tweeddale, now a prisoner in France. His house stands upon an eminence within a mile of Portnacroish, commanding the same prospect which I have spoken of, except that it must lose something in not having the old fortress at the foot of it—indeed, it is not to be seen at all from the house or grounds.

We travelled under steep hills, stony or smooth, with coppice-woods and patches of cultivated land, and houses here and there; and at every hundred yards, I may almost venture to say, a streamlet, narrow as a ribbon, came tumbling down, and, crossing our road, fell into the lake below. On the opposite shore, the hills—namely, the continuation of the hills of Morven— were stern and severe, rising like upright walls from the water's edge, and in colour more resembling rocks than hills, as they appeared to us. We did not see any house, or any place where it was likely a house could stand, for many miles; but as the loch was broad we could not perhaps distinguish the objects thoroughly. A little after sunset our road led us from the vale of the

1. Castle Stalker.

loch. We came to a small river, a bridge, a mill, and some cottages at the foot of a hill, and close to the loch.

Did not cross the bridge, but went up the brook, having it on our left, and soon found ourselves in a retired valley, scattered over with many grey huts, and surrounded on every side by green hills. The hay grounds in the middle of the vale were unenclosed, which was enough to keep alive the Scottish wildness, here blended with exceeding beauty; for there were trees growing irregularly or in clumps all through the valley, rocks or stones here and there, which, with the people at work, hay-cocks sprinkled over the fields, made the vale look full and populous. It was a sweet time of the evening: the moon was up; but there was yet so much of day that her light was not perceived. Our road was through open fields; the people suspended their work as we passed along, and leaning on their pitchforks or rakes, with their arms at their sides, or hanging down, some in one way, some in another, and no two alike, they formed most beautiful groups, the outlines of their figures being much more distinct than by day, and all that might have been harsh or unlovely softened down. The dogs were, as usual, attendant on their masters, and, watching after us, they barked aloud; yet even their barking hardly disturbed the quiet of the place.

I cannot say how long this vale was; it made the larger half of a circle, or a curve deeper than that of half a circle, before it opened again upon the loch. It was less thoroughly cultivated and woody after the last turning—the hills steep and lofty. We met a very tall stout man, a fine figure, in a Highland bonnet, with a little girl, driving home their cow: he accosted us, saying that we were late travellers, and that we had yet four miles to go before we should reach Ballachulish—a long way, uncertain as we were respecting our accommodations. He told us that the vale was called the Strath of Duror, and when we said it was a pretty place, he answered, Indeed it was, and that they lived very comfortably there, for they had a good master, Lord Tweeddale, whose imprisonment he lamented, speaking earnestly of his excellent qualities. At the end of vale we came close upon a large bay of the loch, formed by a rocky hill, a continuation of the ridge of high hills on the left side of the strath, making a very grand promontory, under which was a hamlet, cluster of huts, at the water's edge, with their little fleet of fishing-boats at anchor, and behind, among the rocks, a hundred slips of corn, slips and patches, often no bigger than a garden such as a child, eight years old, would make for sport: it might have been the work of a small colony from China. There was something touching to the heart in this appearance of scrupulous industry, and excessive labour of the soil, in a country where hills and mountains, and even valleys, are left to the care of nature and the pleasure of the cattle that feed among them. It was, indeed, a very interesting place, the more so being in perfect contrast with the few houses at the entrance of the strath—a sea hamlet, without trees, under a naked stony mountain, yet perfectly sheltered, standing in the middle of a large bay which half the winds that travel over the lake can never visit. The other, a little bowery spot, with its river, bridge, and mill, might have been a hundred miles from the sea-side.

The moon was now shining, and though it reminded us how far the evening was advanced, we stopped for many minutes before we could resolve to go on; we saw nothing stirring, neither men, women, nor cattle; but the linen was still bleaching by the stony rivulet, which ran near the houses in water-breaks and tiny cataracts. For the first half mile after we had left this scene there was nothing remarkable; and afterwards we could only see the hills, the sky, the moon, and moonlight water. When we came within, it might be, half a mile of Ballachulish, the place where we were to lodge, the loch narrowed very much, the hills still continuing high. I speak inaccurately, for it split into two divisions, the one along which we went being called Loch Leven.[1]

The road grew very bad, and we had an anxious journey till we saw a light before us, which with great joy we assured ourselves was from the inn; but what was our distress when, on going a few steps further, we came to a bridge half broken down, with bushes laid across to prevent travellers from going over. After some perplexity we determined that I should walk on to the house before us—for we could see that the bridge was safe for foot-passengers—and ask for assistance. By great good luck, at this very moment four or five men came along the road towards us and offered to help William in driving the car through the water, which was not very deep at that time, though, only a few days before, the damage had been done to the bridge by a flood.

I walked on to the inn, ordered tea, and was conducted into a lodging room. I desired to have a fire, and was answered with the old scruple about 'giving fire,'—with, at the same time, an excuse 'that it was so late,'—the girl, however, would ask the landlady, who was lying-in; the fire was brought immediately, and from that time the girl was very civil. I was not, however, quite at ease, for William stayed long, and I was going to leave my fire to seek after him, when I heard him at the door with the horse and car. The horse had taken fright with the roughness of the river-bed and the rattling of the wheels—the second fright in consequence of the ferry—and the men had been obliged to unyoke him and drag the car through, a troublesome affair for William; but he talked less of the trouble and alarm than of the pleasure he had felt in having met with such true good-will and ready kindness in the Highlanders. They drank their glass of whisky at the door, wishing William twenty good wishes, and asking him twice as many

---

1. See William Wordsworth's "The Blind Highland Boy, a Tale Told by the Fire-side, after returning to the Vale of Grasmere," the events of which take place on Loch Leven.

questions,—if he was married, if he had an estate, where he lived, etc. etc. This inn is the ferry-house on the main road up into the Highlands by Fort-William,[1] and here Coleridge, though unknown to us, had slept three nights before.

Saturday, September 3d.—When we have arrived at an unknown place by moonlight, it is never a moment of indifference when I quit it again with the morning light, especially if the objects have appeared beautiful, or in any other way impressive or interesting. I have kept back, unwilling to go to the window, that I might not lose the picture taken to my pillow at night. So it was at Ballachulish: and instantly I felt that the passing away of my own fancies was a loss. The place had appeared exceedingly wild by moonlight; I had mistaken corn-fields for naked rocks, and the lake had appeared narrower and the hills more steep and lofty than they really were.

We rose at six o'clock, and took a basin of milk before we set forward on our journey to Glen Coe. It was a delightful morning, the road excellent, and we were in good spirits, happy that we had no more ferries to cross, and pleased with the thought that we were going among the grand mountains which we saw before us at the head of the loch. We travelled close to the water's edge, and were rolling along a smooth road, when the horse suddenly backed, frightened by the upright shafts of a roller rising from behind the wall of a field adjoining the road. William pulled, whipped, and struggled in vain; we both leapt upon the ground, and the horse dragged the car after him, he going backwards down the bank of the loch, and it was turned over, half in the water, the horse lying on his back, struggling in the harness, a frightful sight! I gave up everything; thought that the horse would be lamed, and the car broken to pieces. Luckily a man came up in the same moment, and assisted William in extricating the horse, and, after an hour's delay, with the help of strings and pocket-handkerchiefs, we mended the harness and set forward again, William leading the poor animal all the way, for the regular beating of the waves frightened him, and any little gushing stream that crossed the road would have sent him off. The village where the blacksmith lived was before us—a few huts under the mountains, and, as it seemed, at the head of the loch; but it runs further up to the left, being narrowed by a hill above the village, near which, at the edge of the water, was a slate quarry, and many large boats with masts, on the water below, high mountains shutting in the prospect, which stood in single, distinguishable shapes, yet clustered together—simple and bold in their forms, and their surfaces of all characters and all colours—some that looked as if scarified by fire, others green; and there was one that might have been blasted by an eternal frost, its summit and sides for a considerable way down

---

1. The present-day hotel is situated where the old ferry inn stood.

being as white as hoar-frost at eight o'clock on a winter's morning. No clouds were on the hills; the sun shone bright, but the wind blew fresh and cold.

When we reached the blacksmith's shop, I left William to help to take care of the horse, and went into the house. The mistress, with a child in her arms and two or three running about, received me very kindly, making many apologies for the dirty house, which she partly attributed to its being Saturday; but I could plainly see that it was dirt of all days. I sate in the midst of it with great delight, for the woman's benevolent, happy countenance almost converted her slovenly and lazy way of leaving all things to take care of themselves into a comfort and a blessing.

It was not a Highland hut, but a slated house built by the master of the quarry for the accommodation of his blacksmith,—the shell of an English cottage, as if left unfinished by the workmen, without plaster, and with floor of mud. Two beds, with not over-clean bedclothes, were in the room. Luckily for me, there was a good fire and a boiling kettle. The woman was very sorry she had no butter; none was to be had in the village: she gave me oaten and barley bread. We talked over the fire; I answered her hundred questions, and in my turn put some to her. She asked me, as usual, if I was married, how many brothers I had, etc. etc. I told her that William was married, and had a fine boy; to which she replied, 'And the man's a decent man too.' Her next-door neighbour came in with a baby on her arm, to request that I would accept of some fish, which I broiled in the ashes. She joined in our conversation, but with more shyness than her neighbour, being a very young woman. She happened to say that she was a stranger in that place, and had been bred and born a long way off. On my asking her where, she replied, 'At Leadhills;' and when I told her that I had been there, a joy lighted up her countenance which I shall never forget, and when she heard that it was only a fortnight before, her eyes filled with tears. I was exceedingly affected with the simplicity of her manners; her tongue was now let loose, and she would have talked for ever of Leadhills, of her mother, of the quietness of the people in general, and the goodness of Mrs. Otto, who, she told me, was a 'varra discreet woman.' She was sure we should be 'well put up' at Mrs. Otto's, and praised her house and furniture; indeed, it seemed she thought all earthly comforts were gathered together under the bleak heights that surround the villages of Wanlockhead and Leadhills: and afterwards, when I said it was a wild country thereabouts, she even seemed surprised, and said it was not half so wild as where she lived now. One circumstance which she mentioned of Mrs. Otto I must record, both in proof of her 'discretion,' and the sobriety of the people at Leadhills, namely, that no liquor was ever drunk in her house after a certain hour of the night—I have forgotten what hour; but it was an early one, I am sure not later than ten.

The blacksmith, who had come in to his breakfast, was impatient to finish our job, that he might go out into the hay-field, for, it being a fine day, every plot of hay-ground was scattered over with hay-makers. On my saying that I guessed much of their hay must be spoiled, he told me no, for that they had high winds, which dried it quickly,—the people understood the climate, 'were clever at the work, and got it in with a blink.' He hastily swallowed his breakfast, dry bread and a basin of weak tea without sugar, and held his baby on his knee till he had done.

The women and I were again left to the fireside, and there were no limits to their joy in me, for they discovered another bond of connexion. I lived in the same part of England from which Mr. Rose, the superintendent of the slate-quarries, and his wife, had come. 'Oh!' said Mrs. Stuart—so her neighbour called her, they not giving each other their Christian names, as is common in Cumberland and Westmoreland,—'Oh!' said she, 'what would not I give to see anybody that came from within four or five miles of Leadhills?' They both exclaimed that I must see Mrs. Rose; she would make much of me—she would have given me tea and bread and butter and a good breakfast. I learned from the two women, Mrs. Stuart and Mrs. Duncan— so the other was called—that Stuart had come from Leadhills for the sake of better wages, to take the place of Duncan, who had resigned his office of blacksmith to the quarries, as far as I could learn, in a pet, intending to go to America, that his wife was averse to go, and that the scheme, for this cause and through other difficulties, had been given up. He appeared to be a good-tempered man, and made us a most reasonable charge for mending the car. His wife told me that they must give up the house in a short time to the other blacksmith; she did not know whither they should go, but her husband, being a good workman, could find employment anywhere. She hurried me out to introduce me to Mrs. Rose, who was at work in the hay-field; she was exceedingly glad to see one of her country-women, and entreated that I would go up to her house. It was a substantial plain house, that would have held half-a-dozen of the common huts. She conducted me into a sitting-room up-stairs, and set before me red and white wine, with the remnant of a loaf of wheaten bread, which she took out of a cupboard in the sitting-room, and some delicious butter. She was a healthy and cheerful-looking woman, dressed like one of our country lasses, and had certainly had no better education than Aggy Ashburner,[1] but she was as a chief in this secluded place, a Madam of the village, and seemed to be treated with the utmost respect.

In our way to and from the house we met several people who interchanged friendly greetings with her, but always as with one greatly superior.

1. Aggy was one of the daughters of Thomas and Peggy Ashburner, whose cottage was just across the road, a little north of Dove Cottage.

She attended me back to the blacksmith's, and would not leave me till she had seen us set forward again on our journey. Mrs. Duncan and Mrs. Stuart shook me cordially, nay, affectionately, by the hand. I tried to prevail upon the former, who had been my hostess, to accept of some money, but in vain; she would not take a farthing, and though I told her it was only to buy something for her little daughter, even seemed grieved that I should think it possible. I forgot to mention that while the blacksmith was repairing the car, we walked to the slate-quarry, where we saw again some of the kind creatures who had helped us in our difficulties the night before. The hovel under which they split their slates stood upon an out-jutting rock, a part of the quarry rising immediately out of the water, and commanded a fine prospect down the loch below Ballachulish, and upwards towards the grand mountains, and the other horn of the vale where the lake was concealed. The blacksmith drove our car about a mile of the road; we then hired a man and horse to take me and the car to the top of Glen Coe, being afraid that if the horse backed or took fright we might be thrown down some precipice.

But before we departed we could not resist our inclination to climb up the hill which I have mentioned as appearing to terminate the loch. The mountains, though inferior to those of Glen Coe, on the other side are very majestic; and the solitude in which we knew the unseen lake was bedded at their feet was enough to excite our longings. We climbed steep after steep, far higher than they appeared to us, and I was going to give up the accomplishment of our aim, when a glorious sight on the mountain before us made me forget my fatigue. A slight shower had come on, its skirts falling upon us, and half the opposite side of the mountain was wrapped up in rainbow light, covered as by a veil with one dilated rainbow: so it continued for some minutes; and the shower and rainy clouds passed away as suddenly as they had come, and the sun shone again upon the tops of all the hills. In the meantime we reached the wished-for point, and saw to the head of the loch. Perhaps it might not be so beautiful as we had imaged it in our thoughts, but it was beautiful enough not to disappoint us,—a narrow deep valley, a perfect solitude, without house or hut. One of the hills was thinly sprinkled with Scotch firs, which appeared to be the survivors of a large forest: they were the first natural wild Scotch firs we had seen. Though thinned of their numbers, and left, comparatively, to a helpless struggle with the elements, we were much struck with the gloom, and even grandeur, of the trees.

Hastened back again to join the car, but were tempted to go a little out of our way to look at a nice white house belonging to the laird of Glen Coe, which stood sweetly in a green field under the hill near some tall trees and coppice woods. At this house the horrible massacre of Glen Coe began, which we did not know when we were there; but the house must have been rebuilt since that time. We had a delightful walk through fields, among copses, and by a river-side: we could have fancied ourselves in some part of the north of England unseen before, it was so much like it, and yet so different. I must not forget one place on the opposite side of the water, where we longed to live—a snug white house on the mountain-side, surrounded by its own green fields and woods, the high mountain above, the loch below, and inaccessible but by means of boats. A beautiful spot indeed it was; but in the retired parts of Scotland a comfortable white house is itself such a pleasant sight, that I believe, without our knowing how or why, it makes us look with a more loving eye on the fields and trees than for their own sakes they deserve.

At about one o'clock we set off, William on our own horse, and I with my Highland driver. He was perfectly acquainted with the country, being a sort of carrier or carrier-merchant or shopkeeper, going frequently to Glasgow with his horse and cart to fetch and carry goods and merchandise. He knew the name of every hill, almost every rock; and I made good use of his knowledge; but partly from laziness, and still more because it was inconvenient, I took no notes, and now I am little better for what he told me. He spoke English tolerably; but seldom understood what was said to him without a 'What's your wull?' We turned up to the right, and were at the foot of the glen—the laird's house cannot be said to be *in* the glen. The afternoon was delightful,—the sun shone, the mountain-tops were clear, the lake glittered in the great vale behind us, and the stream of Glen Coe flowed down to it glittering among alder-trees. The meadows of the glen were of the freshest green; one new-built stone house in the first reach, some huts, hillocks covered with wood, alder-trees scattered all over. Looking backward, we were reminded of Patterdale and the head of Ulswater, but forward the greatness of the mountains overcame every other idea.

The impression was, as we advanced up to the head of this first reach, as if the glen were nothing, its loneliness and retirement—as if it made up no part of my feeling: the mountains were all in all. That which fronted us— I have forgotten its name—was exceedingly lofty, the surface stony, nay, the whole mountain was one mass of stone, wrinkled and puckered up together. At the second and last reach—for it is not a winding vale—it makes a quick turning almost at right angles to the first; and now we are in the depths of the mountains; no trees in the glen, only green pasturage for sheep, and here and there a plot of hay-ground, and something that tells of former cultivation. I observed this to the guide, who said that formerly the glen had had many inhabitants, and that there, as elsewhere in the Highlands, there had been a great deal of corn where now the lands were left waste, and nothing fed upon them but cattle. I cannot attempt to describe the mountains. I can only say that I thought those on our right—for the other side was only a continued high ridge or craggy barrier, broken along the top into petty spiral forms—were the grandest I had ever seen. It seldom happens that mountains in a very clear air look exceedingly high, but these, though we could see the whole of them to their very summits, appeared to me more majestic in their own nakedness than our imaginations could have conceived them to be, had they been half hidden by clouds, yet showing some of their highest pinnacles. They were such forms as Milton might be supposed to have had in his mind when he applied to Satan that sublime expression—

His stature reached the sky.

The first division of the glen, as I have said, was scattered over with rocks, trees, and woody hillocks, and cottages were to be seen here and there. The second division is bare and stony, huge mountains on all sides, with a slender pasturage in the bottom of the valley; and towards the head of it is a small lake or tarn, and near the tarn a single inhabited dwelling, and some unfenced hay-ground—a simple impressive scene! Our road frequently crossed large streams of stones, left by the mountain-torrents, losing all appearance of a road. After we had passed the tarn the glen became less interesting, or rather the mountains, from the manner in which they are looked at; but again, a little higher up, they resume their grandeur. The river is, for a short space, hidden between steep rocks: we left the road, and, going to the top of one of the rocks, saw it foaming over stones, or lodged in dark black dens; birch-trees grew on the inaccessible banks, and a few old Scotch firs towered above them. At the entrance of the glen the mountains had been all without trees, but here the birches climb very far up the side of one of them opposite to us, half concealing a rivulet, which came tumbling down as white as snow from the very top of the mountain. Leaving the rock, we ascended a hill which terminated the glen. We often stopped to look behind at the majestic company of mountains we had left. Before us was no single paramount eminence, but a mountain waste, mountain beyond mountain, and a barren hollow or basin into which we were descending.

We parted from our companion at the door of a whisky hovel, a building which, when it came out of the workmen's hands with its unglassed windows, would, in that forlorn region, have been little better than a howling place for the winds, and was now half unroofed. On seeing a smoke, I exclaimed, 'Is it possible any people can live there?' when at least half a dozen, men, women, and children, came to the door. They were about to rebuild the hut, and I suppose that they, or some other poor creatures, would dwell there through the winter, dealing out whisky to the starved travellers. The sun was now setting, the air very cold, the sky clear; I could have fancied that it was winter-time, with hard frost. Our guide pointed out King's House to us, our resting-place for the night.[1] We could just distinguish the house at the bottom of the moorish hollow or basin— I call it so, for it was nearly as broad as long—lying before us, with three miles of naked road winding through it, every foot of which we could see. The road was perfectly white, making a dreary contrast with the ground, which was of a dull earthy brown. Long as the line of road appeared before us, we could scarcely believe it to be three miles—I suppose owing to its being unbroken by any one object, and the moor naked as the road itself, but we found it the longest three miles we had yet travelled, for the surface was so stony we had to walk most of the way.

The house looked respectable at a distance—a large square building, cased in blue slates to defend it from storms,—but when we came close to it the outside forewarned us of the poverty and misery within. Scarce a blade of grass could be seen growing upon the open ground; the heath-plant itself found no nourishment there, appearing as if it had but sprung up to be blighted. There was no enclosure for a cow, no appropriated ground but a small plot like a churchyard, in which were a few starveling dwarfish potatoes, which had, no doubt, been raised by means of the dung left by travellers' horses: they had not come to blossoming, and whether they would either yield fruit or blossom I know not. The first thing we saw on entering the door was two sheep hung up, as if just killed from the barren moor, their bones hardly sheathed in flesh. After we had waited a few minutes, looking about for a guide to lead us into some corner of the house, a woman, seemingly about forty years old, came to us in a great bustle, screaming in Erse, with the most horrible guinea-hen or peacock voice I ever heard, first to one person, then another. She could hardly spare time to show us up-stairs, for crowds of men were in the house—drovers, carriers, horsemen, travellers, all of whom she had to provide with supper, and she was, as she told us, the only woman there.

Never did I see such a miserable, such a wretched place,—long rooms with ranges of beds, no other furniture except benches, or perhaps one or two crazy chairs, the floors far dirtier than an ordinary house could be if it were never washed,—as dirty as a house after a sale on a rainy day, and the rooms being large, and the walls naked, they looked as if more than half the goods had been sold out. We sate shivering in one of the large rooms for three quarters of an hour before the woman could find time to speak to us again; she then promised a fire in another room, after two travellers, who were going a stage further, had finished their whisky, and said we should have supper as soon as possible. She had no eggs, no milk, no potatoes, no loaf-bread, or we should have preferred tea. With length of time the fire was

1. After the battle of Culloden (1746) the building was used as a barracks for the troops of King George III, which perhaps explains the "long rooms with ranges of beds" Dorothy complains of below.

kindled, and, after another hour's waiting, supper came,—a shoulder of mutton so hard that it was impossible to chew the little flesh that might be scraped off the bones, and some sorry soup made of barley and water, for it had no other taste.

After supper, the woman, having first asked if we slept on blankets, brought in two pair of sheets, which she begged that I would air by the fire, for they would be dirtied below-stairs. I was very willing, but behold! the sheets were so wet, that it would have been at least a two-hours' job before a far better fire than could be mustered at King's House,—for, that nothing might be wanting to make it a place of complete starvation, the peats were not dry, and if they had not been helped out by decayed wood dug out of the earth along with them, we should have had no fire at all. The woman was civil, in her fierce, wild way. She and the house, upon that desolate and extensive Wild, and everything we saw, made us think of one of those places of rendezvous which we read of in novels—Ferdinand Count Fathom, or Gil Blas,[1]—where there is one woman to receive the booty, and prepare the supper at night. She told us that she was only a servant, but that she had now lived there five years, and that, when but a 'young lassie,' she had lived there also. We asked her if she had always served the same master, 'Nay, nay, many masters, for they were always changing.' I verily believe that the woman was attached to the place like a cat to the empty house when the family who brought her up are gone to live elsewhere. The sheets were so long in drying that it was very late before we went to bed. We talked over our day's adventures by the fireside, and often looked out of the window towards a huge pyramidal mountain at the entrance of Glen Coe. All between, the dreary waste was clear, almost, as sky, the moon shining full upon it. A rivulet ran amongst stones near the house, and sparkled with light: I could have fancied that there was nothing else, in that extensive circuit over which we looked, that had the power of motion.

In comparing the impressions we had received at Glen Coe, we found that though the expectations of both had been far surpassed by the grandeur of the mountains, we had upon the whole both been disappointed, and from the same cause: we had been prepared for images of terror, had expected a deep, den-like valley with overhanging rocks, such as William has described in these lines, speaking of the Alps:[2]—

> Brook and road
> Were fellow-travellers in this gloomy Pass,
> And with them did we journey several hours

---

1. *The Adventures of Ferdinand Count Fathom* (1753) was a melodramatic novel by Tobias Smollett; *Gil Blas* (1715–35), by René Le Sage, was a picaresque novel, translated by Smollett in 1749.
2. From *The Prelude* (1805) Book Sixth, ll. 621–40.

At a slow step. The immeasurable height
Of woods decaying, never to be decayed!
The stationary blasts of waterfalls;
And everywhere along the hollow rent
Winds thwarting winds, bewilder'd and forlorn;
The torrents shooting from the clear blue sky,
The rocks that mutter'd close upon our ears,
Black drizzling crags that spake by the way-side
As if a voice were in them; the sick sight
And giddy prospect of the raving stream;
The unfetter'd clouds, and region of the heavens,
Tumult and peace, the darkness and the light,
Were all like workings of one mind, the features
Of the same face, blossoms upon one tree,
Characters of the great Apocalypse,
The Types and Symbols of Eternity,
Of first, and last, and midst, and without end.

The place had nothing of this character, the glen being open to the eye of day, the mountains retiring in independent majesty. Even in the upper part of it, where the stream rushed through the rocky chasm, it was but a deep trench in the vale, not the vale itself, and could only be seen when we were close to it.

FOURTH WEEK

Sunday, September 4th.—We had desired to be called at six o'clock, and rose at the first summons. Our beds had proved better than we expected, and we had not slept ill; but poor Coleridge had passed a wretched night here four days before. This we did not know; but since, when he told us of it, the notion of what he must have suffered, with the noise of drunken people about his ears all night, himself sick and tired, has made our discomfort cling to my memory, and given these recollections a twofold interest. I asked if it was possible to have a couple of eggs boiled before our departure: the woman hesitated; she thought I might, and sent a boy into the out-houses to look about, who brought in one egg after long searching. Early as we had risen it was not very early when we set off, for everything at King's House was in unison—equally uncomfortable. As the woman had told us the night before, 'They had no hay, and that was a loss.' There were neither stalls nor bedding in the stable, so that William was obliged to watch the horse while it was feeding, for there were several others in the stable, all standing like wild beasts, ready to devour each other's portion of corn: this, with the slowness of the servant and other hindrances, took up much time, and we were completely starved, for the morning was very cold, as I believe all the mornings in that desolate place are.

When we had gone about a quarter of a mile I recollected that I had left the little cup given me by the kind landlady at Taynuilt, which I had intended that John should hereafter drink out of, in memory of our wanderings. I would have turned back for it, but William pushed me on, unwilling that we should lose so much time, though indeed he was as sorry to part with it as myself.

Our road was over a hill called the Black Mount. For the first mile, or perhaps more, after we left King's House, we ascended on foot; then came upon a new road, one of the finest that was ever trod; and, as we went downwards almost all the way afterwards, we travelled very quickly. The motion was pleasant, the different reaches and windings of the road were amusing; the sun shone, the mountain-tops were clear and cheerful, and we in good spirits, in a bustle of enjoyment, though there never was a more desolate region: mountains behind, before, and on every side; I do not remember to have seen either patch of grass, flower, or flowering heather within three or four miles of King's House. The low ground was not rocky, but black, and full of white frost-bleached stones, the prospect only varied by pools, seen everywhere both near and at a distance, as far as the ground stretched out below us: these were interesting spots, round which the mind assembled living objects, and they shone as bright as mirrors in the forlorn waste. We passed neither tree nor shrub for miles—I include the whole space from Glen Coe—yet we saw perpetually traces of a long decayed forest, pieces of black mouldering wood.

Through such a country as this we had travelled perhaps seven and a half miles this morning, when, after descending a hill, we turned to the right, and saw an unexpected sight in the moorland hollow into which we were entering, a small lake bounded on the opposite side by a grove of Scotch firs, two or three cottages at the head of it, and a lot of cultivated ground with scattered hay-cocks. The road along which we were going, after having made a curve considerably above the tarn, was seen winding through the trees on the other side, a beautiful object, and, luckily for us, a drove of cattle happened to be passing there at the very time, a stream coursing the road, with off-stragglers to the borders of the lake, and under the trees on the sloping ground.

In conning over our many wanderings I shall never forget the gentle pleasure with which we greeted the lake of Inveroran and its few grey cottages: we suffered our horse to slacken his pace, having now no need of the comfort of quick motion, though we were glad to think that one of those cottages might be the public-house where we were to breakfast. A forest—now, as it appeared, dwindled into the small grove bordering the lake—had, not many years ago, spread to that side of the vale where we were: large stumps of trees which had been cut down were yet remaining undecayed, and there were some single trees left alive, as if by their battered black boughs to tell us of the storms that visit the valley which looked now so sober and peaceful. When we arrived at the huts, one of them proved to be the inn, a thatched house without a sign-board. We were kindly received, had a fire lighted in the parlour, and were in such good humour that we seemed to have a thousand comforts about us; but we had need of a little patience in addition to this good humour before breakfast was brought, and at last it proved a disappointment: the butter not eatable, the barley-cakes fusty, the oat-bread so hard I could not chew it, and there were only four eggs in the house, which they had boiled as hard as stones.

Before we had finished breakfast two foot-travellers came in, and seated themselves at our table; one of them was returning, after a long absence, to Fort-William, his native home; he had come from Egypt, and, many years ago, had been on a recruiting party at Penrith, and knew many people there. He seemed to think his own country but a dismal land.

There being no bell in the parlour, I had occasion to go several times and ask for what we wanted in the kitchen, and I would willingly have given twenty pounds to have been able to take a lively picture of it. About seven or eight travellers, probably drovers, with as many dogs, were sitting in a complete circle round a large peat-fire in the middle of the floor, each with a mess of porridge, in a wooden vessel, upon his knee; a pot, suspended from one of the black beams, was boiling on the fire; two or three women pursuing their household business on the outside of the circle, children playing on the floor. There was nothing uncomfortable in this confusion: happy, busy, or vacant faces, all looked pleasant; and even the smoky air, being a sort of natural indoor atmosphere of Scotland, served only to give a softening, I may say harmony, to the whole.

We departed immediately after breakfast; our road leading us, as I have said, near the lake-side and through the grove of firs, which extended backward much further than we had imagined. After we had left it we came again among bare moorish wastes, as before, under the mountains, so that Inveroran still lives in our recollection as a favoured place, a flower in the desert.

Descended upon the whole, I believe very considerably, in our way to Tyndrum; but it was a road of long ups and downs, over hills and through hollows of uncultivated ground; a chance farm perhaps once in three miles, a glittering rivulet bordered with greener grass than grew on the broad waste, or a broken fringe of alders or birches, partly concealing and partly pointing out its course.

Arrived at Tyndrum at about two o'clock. It is a cold spot. Though, as I should suppose, situated lower than Inveroran, and though we saw it in the hottest time of the afternoon sun, it had a far colder aspect from the want of trees. We were here informed that Coleridge, who, we supposed, was gone to Edinburgh, had dined at this very house a few days before, in his road to Fort-William. By the help of the cook, who was called in, the landlady made out the very day: it was the day after we parted from him; as she expressed it, the day after the 'great speet,' namely, the great rain. We had a moorfowl and mutton-chops for dinner, well cooked, and a reasonable charge. The house was clean for a Scotch inn, and the people about the doors were well dressed. In one of the parlours we saw a company of nine or ten, with the landlady, seated round a plentiful table,—a sight which made us think of the fatted calf in the alehouse pictures of the Prodigal Son. There seemed to be a whole harvest of meats and drinks, and there was something of festivity and picture-like gaiety even in the fresh-coloured dresses of the people and their Sunday faces. The white table-cloth, glasses, English dishes, etc., were all in contrast with what we had seen at Inveroran: the places were but about nine miles asunder, both among hills; the rank of the people little different, and each house appeared to be a house of plenty.

We were I think better pleased with our treatment at this inn than any of the lonely houses on the road, except Taynuilt; but Coleridge had not fared so well, and was dissatisfied, as he has since told us, and the two travellers who breakfasted with us at Inveroran had given a bad account of the house.

Left Tyndrum at about five o'clock; a gladsome afternoon; the road excellent, and we bowled downwards through a pleasant vale, though not populous, or well cultivated, or woody, but enlivened by a river that glittered as it flowed. On the side of a sunny hill a knot of men and women were gathered together at a preaching. We passed by many droves of cattle and Shetland ponies, which accident stamped a character upon places, else unrememberable—not an individual character, but the soul, the spirit, and solitary simplicity of many a Highland region.

We had about eleven miles to travel before we came to our lodging, and had gone five or six, almost always descending, and still in the same vale, when we saw a small lake before us after the vale had made a bending to the left; it was about sunset when we came up to the lake; the afternoon breezes had died away, and the water was in perfect stillness. One grove-like island, with a ruin that stood upon it overshadowed by the trees, was reflected on the water. This building, which, on that beautiful evening, seemed to be wrapped up in religious quiet, we were informed had been raised for defence by some Highland chieftain. All traces of strength, or war, or danger are passed away, and in the mood in which we were we could only look upon it as a place of retirement and peace. The lake is called Loch Dochart. We passed by two others of inferior beauty, and continued to travel along the side of the same river, the Dochart, through an irregular, undetermined vale,—poor soil and much waste land.

At that time of the evening when, by looking steadily, we could discover a few pale stars in the sky, we saw upon an eminence, the bound of our horizon, though very near to us, and facing the bright yellow clouds of the west, a group of figures that made us feel how much we wanted in not being painters. Two herdsmen, with a dog beside them, were sitting on the hill, overlooking a herd of cattle scattered over a large meadow by the riverside. Their forms, looked at through a fading light, and backed by the bright west, were exceedingly distinct, a beautiful picture in the quiet of a Sabbath evening, exciting thoughts and images of almost patriarchal simplicity and grace. We were much pleased with the situation of our inn, where we arrived between eight and nine o'clock. The river was at the distance of a broad field from the door; we could see it from the upper windows and hear its murmuring; the moon shone, enlivening the large corn fields with cheerful light. We had a bad supper, and the next morning they made us an unreasonable charge; and the servant was uncivil, because, forsooth! we had no wine.

N.B.—The travellers in the morning had spoken highly of this inn.

Monday, September 5th.—After drinking a bason of milk we set off again at a little after six o'clock—a fine morning—eight miles to Killin—the river Dochart always on our left. The face of the country not very interesting, though not unpleasing, reminding us of some of the vales of the north of England, though meagre, nipped-up, or shrivelled compared with them. There were rocks, and rocky knolls, as about Grasmere and Wytheburn, and copses, but of a starveling growth; the cultivated ground poor. Within a mile or two of Killin the land was better cultivated, and, looking down the vale, we had a view of Loch Tay, into which the Dochart falls. Close to the town, the river took up a roaring voice, beating its way over a rocky descent among large black stones: islands in the middle turning the stream this way and that; the whole course of the river very wide. We crossed it by means of three bridges, which make one continued bridge of a great length. On an island below the bridge is a gateway with tall pillars, leading to an old burying-ground belonging to some noble family.[1] It has a singular appearance, and the place is altogether uncommon and romantic— a remnant of ancient grandeur: extreme natural wildness—the sound of roaring water, and withal, the ordinary half-village, half-town bustle of an every-day place.

The inn at Killin is one of the largest on the Scotch road: it stands pleasantly, near the chapel, at some distance from the river Dochart, and out of reach of its tumultuous noise; and another broad, stately, and silent stream, which you cannot look at without remembering its boisterous neighbour, flows close under the windows of the inn, and beside the churchyard, in which are many graves. That river falls into the lake at the distance of nearly a mile from the mouth of the Dochart. It is bordered with tall trees and corn fields, bearing plentiful crops, the richest we had seen in Scotland.

After breakfast we walked onwards, expecting that the stream would lead us into some considerable vale; but it soon became little better than a common rivulet, and the glen appeared to be short; indeed, we wondered how the river had grown so great all at once. Our horse had not been able to eat his corn, and we waited a long time in the hope that he would be better. At eleven o'clock, however we determined to set off, and give him all the ease possible by walking up the hills, and not pushing beyond a slow walk. We had fourteen miles to travel to Kenmore, by the side of Loch Tay. Crossed the same bridge again, and went down the south side of the lake. We had a delightful view of the village of Killin, among rich green fields, corn and wood, and up towards the two horns of the vale of Tay, the valley of the Dochart, and the other valley with its full-grown river, the prospect terminated by mountains. We travelled through lanes, woods, or open fields, never close to the lake, but always near it, for many miles, the road being carried along the side of a hill, which rose in an almost regularly receding steep from the lake. The opposite shore did not much differ from that down which we went, but it seemed more thinly inhabited, and not so well cultivated. The sun shone, the cottages were pleasant, and the goings-on of the harvest—for all the inhabitants were at work in the corn fields—made the way cheerful. But there is an uniformity in the lake which, comparing it with other lakes, made it appear tiresome. It has no windings: I should even imagine, although it is so many miles long, that, from some points not very high on the hills, it may be seen from one end to the other. There are few bays, no lurking-places where the water hides itself in the land, no outjutting points or promontories, no islands; and there are no commanding mountains or precipices. I think that this lake would be the most pleasing in spring-time, or in summer before the corn begins to change colour, the long tracts of hills on each side of the vale having at this season a kind of patchy appearance, for the corn fields in general were very small, mere plots, and of every possible shade of bright yellow. When we came in view of the foot of the lake we perceived that it ended, as it had begun, in pride and loveliness. The village of Kenmore, with its neat church and cleanly houses, stands on a gentle eminence at the end of the water. The view, though not near so beautiful as that of Killin, is exceedingly pleasing. Left our car, and turned out of the road at about the distance of a mile from the town,[1] and after having climbed perhaps a quarter of a mile, we were conducted into a locked-up plantation, and guessed by the sound that we were near the cascade, but could not see it. Our guide opened a door, and we entered a dungeon-like passage, and, after walking some yards in total darkness, found ourselves in a quaint apartment stuck over with moss, hung about with stuffed foxes and other wild animals, and ornamented with a library of wooden books covered with old leather backs, the mock furniture of a hermit's cell. At the end of the room, through a large bow-window, we saw the waterfall, and at the same time, looking down to the left, the village of Kenmore and a part of the lake—a very beautiful prospect.

MEMORANDUM

The transcript of the First Part of this Journal, and the Second as far as page 149, were written before the end of the year 1803. I do not know exactly when I concluded the remainder of the Second Part, but it was resumed on

---

1. Doubling back from Kenmore about a mile, on the south side of Loch Tay, one comes to a circular course arching around the Falls of Acharn—a steep farm road on one side, a wooded path on the other, with views of the Falls along the way. Near the top, on the right side of the Falls (as one ascends) is a Hermit's Cave (so signposted) with two tunnel-like openings about 5–5½ft high. Decending on the other side of the Falls, one looks across a cavern to see the "front" of the Hermit's Cave, which had a viewing balcony. (Without a tip from Dorothy Wordsworth, the average traveller would not seek and find this curiosity!)

the 2d of February 1804. The Third Part was begun at the end of the month of April 1805, and finished on the 31st of May.[1]

April 11th, 1805.—I am setting about a task which, however free and happy the state of my mind, I could not have performed well at this distance of time; but now, I do not know that I shall be able to go on with it at all.[2] I will strive, however, to do the best I can, setting before myself a different object from that hitherto aimed at, which was, to omit no incident, however trifling, and to describe the country so minutely that you should, where the objects were the most interesting, feel as if you had been with us. I shall now only attempt to give you an idea of those scenes which pleased us most, dropping the incidents of the ordinary days, of which many have slipped from my memory, and others which remain it would be difficult, and often painful to me, to endeavour to draw out and disentangle from other thoughts. I the less regret my inability to do more, because, in describing a great part of what we saw from the time we left Kenmore, my work would be little more than a repetition of what I have said before, or, where it was not so, a longer time was necessary to enable us to bear away what was most interesting than we could afford to give.

Monday, September 5th.—We arrived at Kenmore after sunset.

Tuesday, September 6th.—Walked before breakfast in Lord Breadalbane's grounds, which border upon the river Tay. The higher elevations command fine views of the lake; and the walks are led along the river's banks, and shaded with tall trees: but it seemed to us that a bad taste had been at work, the banks being regularly shaven and cut as if by rule and line. One or two of such walks I should well have liked to see; but they are all equally trim, and I could not but regret that the fine trees had not been left to grow out of a turf that cattle were permitted to feed upon. There was one avenue which would well have graced the ruins of an abbey or some stately castle. It was of a very great length, perfectly straight, the trees meeting at the top in a cathedral arch, lessening in perspective,—the boughs the roof, the stems the pillars. I never saw so beautiful an avenue. We were told that some

1. This memorandum comes at the end of Dorothy Wordsworth's manuscript and has been repositioned by Shairp. The page numbers she gives refer to the pagination of her manuscript and do not correspond to the present text.
2. The death of her beloved younger brother John just a month before, on 5 February 1805, made the resumption of her writing difficult. John Wordsworth went down with his ship, the *Earl of Abergavenny*, after it struck a rock in the Shambles off Portland Bill, and sank two miles off Weymouth Beach in the English Channel. The ship had been bound for India and China. Though some passengers survived, John stayed with the ship, which was under his command, to the end, and was last seen clinging to a rope.

improver of pleasure-grounds had advised Lord B. to cut down the trees, and lay the whole open to the lawn, for the avenue is very near his house. His own better taste, or that of some other person, I suppose, had saved them from the axe. Many workmen were employed in building a large mansion something like that of Inverary, close to the old house, which was yet standing; the situation, as we thought, very bad, considering that Lord Breadalbane had the command of all the ground at the foot of the lake, including hills both high and low. It is in a hollow, without prospect either of the lake or river, or anything else—seeing nothing and adorning nothing. After breakfast, left Kenmore, and travelled through the vale of Tay, I believe fifteen or sixteen miles; but in the course of this we turned out of our way to the Falls of Moness, a stream tributary to the Tay, which passes through a narrow glen with very steep banks. A path like a woodman's track has been carried through the glen, which, though the private property of a gentleman, has not been taken out of the hands of Nature, but merely rendered accessible by this path, which ends at the waterfalls. They tumble from a great height, and are indeed very beautiful falls, and we could have sate with pleasure the whole morning beside the cool basin in which the waters rest, surrounded by high rocks and overhanging trees. In one of the most retired parts of the dell, we met a young man coming slowly along the path, intent upon a book which he was reading: he did not seem to be of the rank of a gentleman, though above that of a peasant.

Passed through the village of Aberfeldy, at the foot of the glen of Moness. The birks of Aberfeldy are spoken of in some of the Scotch songs,[1] which no doubt grew in the stream of Moness; but near the village we did not see any trees that were remarkable, except a row of laburnums, growing as a common field hedge; their leaves were of a golden colour, and as lively as the yellow blossoms could have been in the spring. Afterwards we saw many laburnums in the woods, which we were told had been 'planted;' though I remember that Withering[2] speaks of the laburnum as one of the British plants, and growing in Scotland. The twigs and branches being stiff, were not so graceful as those of our garden laburnums, but I do not think I ever before saw any that were of so brilliant colours in their autumnal decay. In our way to and from Moness we crossed the Tay by a bridge of ambitious and ugly architecture. Many of the bridges in Scotland are so, having eye-

1. Robert Burns composed his well known "The Birks of Aberfeldy" on the spot—"standing under the Falls of Moness at or near Aberfeldy," as he tells us in a prefatory note to the poem.
2. A 1796 edition of William Withering's *An Arrangement of British Plants; According to the latest Improvements of the Linnean System.* Birmingham: printed for the author (3rd edn., 4 vols) is in the Dove Cottage Library. Records indicate that William purchased two copies of Withering's *Botany* (part of the 4-volume work) and two microscopes on 7 August 1800. However, in my own perusal of Withering at the Dove Cottage Library, I found no discussion of laburnum.

holes between the arches, not in the battlements but at the outspreading of the pillar of the arch, which destroys its simplicity, and takes from the appearance of strength and security, without adding anything of lightness. We returned, by the same road, to the village of Weem, where we had left our car. The vale of Tay was very wide, having been so from within a short distance of Kenmore: the reaches of the river are long; and the ground is more regularly cultivated than in any vale we had yet seen—chiefly corn, and very large tracts. Afterwards the vale becomes narrow and less cultivated, the reaches shorter—on the whole resembling the vale of Nith, but we thought it inferior in beauty.

One among the cottages in this narrow and wilder part of the vale fixed our attention almost as much as a Chinese or a Turk would do passing through the vale of Grasmere. It was a cottage, I believe, little differing in size and shape from all the rest; but it was like a visitor, a stranger come into the Highlands, or a model set up of what may be seen in other countries. The walls were neatly plastered or rough-cast, the windows of clean bright glass, and the door was painted—before it a flower-garden, fenced with a curiously-clipped hedge, and against the wall was placed the sign of a spinning-wheel. We could not pass this humble dwelling, so distinguished by an appearance of comfort and neatness, without some conjectures respecting the character and manner of life of the person inhabiting it. Leisure he must have had; and we pleased ourselves with thinking that some self-taught mind might there have been nourished by knowledge gathered from books, and the simple duties and pleasures of rural life.

At Logierait, the village where we dined, the vale widens again, and the Tummel joins the Tay and loses its name; but the Tay falls into the channel of the Tummel, continuing its course in the same direction, almost at right angles to the former course of the Tay. We were sorry to find that we had to cross the Tummel by a ferry, and resolved not to venture in the same boat with the horse. Dined at a little public-house, kept by a young widow, very talkative and laboriously civil. She took me out to the back-door, and said she would show me a place which had once been very grand, and, opening a door in a high wall, I entered a ruinous court-yard, in which was a large old mansion, the walls entire and very strong, but the roof broken in. The woman said it has been a palace of one of the kings of Scotland.[1] It was a striking and even an affecting object, coming

1. Two historical settings are confused here. The castle of Robert III (*c.*1340–1406), king of Scotland, once stood on a hill near the village of Logierait, which takes its name from the Gaelic lag-an-rath, meaning "hollow of the castle." In the village itself stood the regality court of the lords of Atholl, with a court house, a jail, and the Tom-na-croiche, or gallow knoll. The court hall, seventy feet long, with galleries at either end, was reputed to be one of the grandest suites of rooms in Perthshire. It was this hall, and not the castle, that Dorothy viewed. Her impressionistic recollection betrays no awareness of the despotic judgments of the lords of Atholl or even of the romantic escape from the prison of Rob Roy in 1717.

upon it, as I did, unawares,—a royal residence shut up and hidden, while yet in its strength, by mean cottages; there was no appearance of violence, but decay from desertion, and I should think that it may remain many years without undergoing further visible change. The woman and her daughter accompanied us to the ferry and crossed the water with us; the woman said, but with not much appearance of honest heart-feeling, that she could not be easy to let us go without being there to know how we sped, so I invited the little girl to accompany her, that she might have a ride in the car. The men were cautious, and the horse got over with less alarm than we could have expected. Our way was now up the vale, along the banks of the Tummel, an impetuous river; the mountains higher than near the Tay, and the vale more wild, and the different reaches more interesting.

When we approached near to Fascally, near the junction of the Garry with the Tummel, the twilight was far advanced, and our horse not being perfectly recovered, we were fearful of taking him on to Blair-Athole—five miles further; besides, the Pass of Killicrankie was within half a mile, and we were unwilling to go through a place so celebrated in the dark; therefore, being joined by a traveller, we inquired if there was any public-house near; he said there was; and that though the accommodations were not good, we might do well enough for one night, the host and his wife being very honest people. It proved to be rather better than a common cottage of the country; we seated ourselves by the fire, William called for a glass of whisky, and asked if they could give us beds. The woman positively refused to lodge us, though we had every reason to believe that she had at least one bed for me; we entreated again and again in behalf of the poor horse, but all in vain; she urged, though in an uncivil way, that she had been sitting up the whole of one or two nights before on account of a fair, and that now she wanted to go to bed and sleep; so we were obliged to remount our car in the dark, and with a tired horse we moved on, and went through the Pass of Killicrankie, hearing only the roaring of the river, and seeing a black chasm with jagged-topped black hills towering above. Afterwards the moon rose, and we should not have had an unpleasant ride if our horse had been in better plight, and we had not been annoyed, as we were almost at every twenty yards, by people coming from a fair held that day near Blair[1]—no pleasant prognostic of what might be our accommodation at the inn, where we arrived between ten and eleven o'clock, and found the house in an uproar; but we were civilly treated, and were glad, after eating a morsel of cold beef, to retire to rest, and I fell asleep in spite of the noisy drunkards below stairs, who had outstayed the fair.

---

1. Now distinguished from Blair Atholl by the designation Old Blair.

Wednesday, September 7th.—Rose early, and went before breakfast to the Duke of Athol's gardens and pleasure-grounds, where we completely tired ourselves with a three-hours' walk. Having been directed to see all the waterfalls, we submitted ourselves to the gardener, who dragged us from place to place, calling our attention to, it might be, half-a-dozen—I cannot say how many—dripping streams, very pretty in themselves, if we had had the pleasure of discovering them; but they were generally robbed of their grace by the obtrusive ornaments which were first seen. The whole neighbourhood, a great country, seems to belong to the Duke of Athol. In his domain are hills and mountains, glens and spacious plains, rivers and innumerable torrents; but near Blair are no old woods, and the plantations, except those at a little distance from the house, appear inconsiderable, being lost to the eye in so extensive a circuit.

The castle stands on low ground, and far from the Garry, commanding a prospect all round of distant mountains, a bare and cold scene, and, from the irregularity and width of it, not so grand as one should expect, knowing the great height of some of the mountains. Within the Duke's park are three glens, the glen of the river Tilt and two others, which, if they had been planted more judiciously, would have been very sweet retirements; but they are choked up, the whole hollow of the glens—I do not speak of the Tilt, for that is rich in natural wood—being closely planted with trees, and those chiefly firs; but many of the old fir-trees are, as single trees, very fine. On each side of the glen is an ell-wide gravel walk, which the gardener told us was swept once a week. It is conducted at the top of the banks, on each side, at nearly equal height, and equal distance from the stream; they lead you up one of these paths, and down the other—very wearisome, as you will believe—mile after mile! We went into the garden, where there was plenty of fruit—gooseberries, hanging as thick as possible upon the trees, ready to drop off; I thought the gardener might have invited us to refresh ourselves with some of his fruit after our long fatigue. One part of the garden was decorated with statues, 'images,' as poor Mr. Gill[1] used to call those at Racedown, dressed in gay-painted clothes; and in a retired corner of the grounds, under some tall trees, appeared the figure of a favourite old gamekeeper of one of the former Dukes, in the attitude of pointing his gun at the game—'reported to be a striking likeness,' said the gardener. Looking at some of the tall larches, with long hairy twigs, very beautiful trees, he told us that they were among the first which had ever been planted in Scotland, that a Duke of Athol had brought a single larch from London in a pot, in his coach, from which had sprung the whole family that had overspread Scotland. This, probably, might not be accurate, for others might afterwards have come, or seed from other trees. He told us many anecdotes of the present Duke, which I wish I could perfectly remember. He is an indefati-

1. Joseph Gill was a caretaker and gardener for the house in which Dorothy and William lived in Racedown.

Fourth Week
4–10 September

115. Inveroran Hotel.
"When we arrived at the huts, one of them proved to be the inn, a thatched house without a sign-board." (p. 157)

116. Loch Dochart. Ruin on island.
"One grove-like island, with a ruin that stood upon it overshadowed by the trees,
was reflected on the water. This building, which, on that beautiful evening, seemed to be
wrapped up in religious quiet, we were informed had been raised for defence by some
Highland chieftain . . . The Lake is called Loch Dochart." (p. 159)

117. Killin. River Dochart and Falls of Dochart.
"Close to the town, the river took up a roaring voice, beating its way over a rocky descent
among large black stones: islands in the middle turning the stream this way and that;
the whole course of the river very wide." (p. 160)

118. Killin. Bridges.
"We crossed it by means of three bridges, which make one continued bridge of a great length." (p. 160)

119. Killin. Clan Macnab Burial Ground.
"On an island below the bridge is a gateway with tall pillars, leading to an old burying-
ground belonging to some noble family. It has a singular appearance,
and the place is altogether uncommon and romantic—a remnant of ancient grandeur:
extreme natural wildness—the sound of roaring water, and withal, the ordinary half-village,
half-town bustle of an every-day place." (p. 160)

120. Killin. Killin Hotel. ("The inn.")

"The inn at Killin is one of the largest on the Scotch road: it stands pleasantly, near the chapel . . ." (p. 160)

121. Killin. Chapel near the inn.

122. Killin. River near the inn.
". . . another broad, stately, and silent stream, which you cannot look at without remembering its boisterous neighbour [the Dochart] flows close under the windows of the inn, and beside the churchyard . . ." (p. 160)

123. Loch Tay. Scene.
"We had fourteen miles to travel to Kenmore, by the side of Loch Tay." (p. 160)

124. Above Falls of Acharn. Entrance to the hermit's cell.

"... we were conducted into a locked-up plantation, and guessed by the sound that we were near the cascade, but could not see it. Our guide opened a door, and we entered a dungeon-like passage ..." (p. 161)

125. Falls of Acharn. "The waterfall."

126. Kenmore. At the end of Loch Tay.
"The village of Kenmore, with its neat church and cleanly houses, stands on a gentle eminence at the end of the water." (p. 161)
"We arrived at Kenmore after sunset." (p. 162)

127. Kenmore. Lord Breadalbane's grounds.
"Walked before breakfast in Lord Breadalbane's grounds, which border upon the river Tay." (p. 162)

128. Kenmore. Lord Breadalbane's estate.
"Many workmen were employed in building a large mansion something like that of Inveraray, close to the old house, which was yet standing . . ." (p. 162)

129. Kenmore. Fall of Moness.
". . . we turned out of our way to the Falls of Moness . . . They tumble from a great height, and are indeed very beautiful falls . . ." (p. 163)

130. General Wade's Bridge over the Tay.
"In our way to and from Moness we crossed the Tay by a bridge of ambitious and ugly architecture."
(p. 163)

131. Weem. The Inn of Weem, home to General Wade in 1773.
"We returned, by the same road, to the village of Weem, where we had left our car." (p. 164)

132. Logierait. Hotel.
"At Logierait, the village where we dined, the vale widens again . . . Dined at a little public-house, kept by a young widow, very talkative and laboriously civil." (p. 164)

133. Blair Atholl. ("Blair.") Blair Castle.
"The castle stands on low ground, and far from the Garry, commanding a prospect all
round of distant mountains, a bare and cold scene . . ." (p. 166)

134. Blair Atholl. ("Blair.") Grounds of Blair Castle.
"Within the Duke's park are three glens . . ." (p. 166)

135. Old Blair. ("Blair.") Former coaching inn (now a private residence).
It is from this coaching inn that they see the following sights (pls. 136–38).

136. Old Blair. ("Blair.") St. Bride's Chapel.
"The most interesting object we saw at Blair was the chapel, shaded by trees . . ." (p. 167)

137. Old Blair. ("Blair.") St. Bride's Chapel. Interior.
". . . in which the body of the impetuous Dundee lies buried. This quiet spot is seen from the windows of
the inn . . ." (p. 167)

138. Old Blair. ("Blair.") Wall, street, cottages.
". . . whence you look, at the same time, upon a high wall and a part of the town—a contrast which, I know not
why, made the chapel and its grove appear more peaceful, as if kept so for some sacred purpose." (p. 167)

139. Falls of Bruar.
"The falls are high, the rocks and stones fretted and gnawed by the water. I do not wonder at the pleasure which Burns received from this stream . . ." (p. 168)

140. Pass of Killiecrankie. ("Pass of Killicrankie.")
"Before breakfast we walked to the Pass of Killicrankie. A very fine scene; the river Garry forcing its way
down a deep chasm between rocks, at the foot of high rugged hills covered with wood, to a great height."
(p. 171)

141. Pass of Killiecrankie. Trooper's Den sign.
"Everybody knows that this Pass is famous in military history." (p. 171)

142. Dunkeld. Very old buildings of the town.
"Reached Dunkeld at about three o'clock. It is a pretty, small town . . ." (p. 173)

143. Dunkeld. Cathedral.
". . . with a respectable and rather large ruined abbey, which is greatly injured by being
made the nest of a modern Scotch kirk, with sash windows . . ." (p. 173)

144. Dunkeld. Street near cathedral, leading to River Tay.

145. Near Dunkeld "Falls of the Bran." Grounds.
". . . we entered into another part of the Duke's pleasure-grounds bordering on the
Bran . . ." (p. 173)

146. Near Dunkeld "Falls of the Bran." The Hermitage folly, or Ossian's Hall. Entrance.
"The waterfall, which we came to see, warned us by a loud roaring that we must expect it;
we were first, however, conducted into a small apartment, where the gardener desired us to
look at a painting of the figure of Ossian, which, while he was telling us the story of the
young artist who performed the work, disappeared, parting in the middle, flying asunder as
if by the touch of magic, and lo! we are at the entrance of a splendid room, which was
almost dizzy and alive with waterfalls, that tumbled in all directions—the great cascade,
which was opposite to the window that faced us, being reflected in innumerable mirrors
upon the ceiling and against the walls." (pp. 173–74)

147. Near Dunkeld "Falls of the Bran." Below Hermitage folly viewing balcony.

148. Birnam wood (remains of). One of the few original trees.
"The hill of Birnam, no longer Birnam 'wood,' was pointed out to us." (p. 174)

149. Rumblin' Brig. ("Rumbling Brig.")
"Left our car, and went about a hundred yards from the road to see the Rumbling Brig, which, though well worth our going out of the way even much further..." (p. 175)

150. Rumblin' Brig. Rocks, water below bridge.
"... disappointed us, as places in general do which we hear much spoken of as savage, tremendous, etc.,—and no wonder, for they are usually described by people to whom rocks are novelties." (p. 175)

151. Glen below Amulree.
"The gardener had told us that we should pass through the most populous glen in Scotland,
the glen of Amulree. It is not populous in the usual way, with scattered dwellings . . ."
(p. 175)

152. Sma' Glen. "Narrow Glen" or "Glen Almain." Ossian's Stone.

In this still place remote from men
Sleeps Ossian, in the Narrow Glen.
(William Wordsworth, p. 176)

153. Loch Lubnaig.
"We next came to a lake, called Loch Lubnaig, a name which signifies 'winding.' . . . The character of this lake is simple and grand." (p. 178)

154. Pass of Leny.
". . . the stream on our right, generally concealed by wood, made a loud roaring; at one place, in particular, it fell down the rocks in a succession of cascades. The scene is much celebrated in Scotland, and is called the Pass of Leny." (p. 179)

155. Callander. At night.
"It was nearly dark when we reached Callander." (p. 179)

gable sportsman, hunts the wild deer on foot, attended by twelve Highlanders in the Highland dress, which he himself formerly used to wear; he will go out at four o'clock in the morning, and not return till night. His fine family, 'Athol's honest men, and Athol's bonny lasses,' to whom Burns, in his bumpers, drank health and long life, are dwindled away: of nine, I believe only four are left: the mother of them is dead in a consumption, and the Duke married again. We rested upon the heather seat which Burns was so loth to quit that moonlight evening when he first went to Blair Castle, and had a pleasure in thinking that he had been under the same shelter, and viewed the little waterfall opposite with some of the happy and pure feelings of his better mind. The castle has been modernized, which has spoiled its appearance. It is a large irregular pile, not handsome, but I think may have been picturesque, and even noble, before it was docked of its battlements and whitewashed.

The most interesting object we saw at Blair was the chapel, shaded by trees, in which the body of the impetuous Dundee lies buried. This quiet spot is seen from the windows of the inn, whence you look, at the same time, upon a high wall and a part of the town—a contrast which, I know not why, made the chapel and its grove appear more peaceful, as if kept so for some sacred purpose. We had a very nice breakfast, which we sauntered over after our weary walk.

Being come to the most northerly point of our destined course, we took out the map, loth to turn our backs upon the Highlands, and, looking about for something which we might yet see, we fixed our eyes upon two or three spots not far distant, and sent for the landlord to consult with him. One of them was Loch Rannoch, a fresh-water lake, which he told us was bordered by a natural pine forest, that its banks were populous, and that the place being very remote, we might there see much of the simplicity of the Highlander's life. The landlord said that we must take a guide for the first nine or ten miles; but afterwards the road was plain before us, and very good, so at about ten o'clock we departed, having engaged a man to go with us. The Falls of Bruar, which we wished to visit for the sake of Burns, are about three miles from Blair, and our road was in the same direction for two miles.

After having gone for some time under a bare hill, we were told to leave the car at some cottages, and pass through a little gate near a brook which crossed the road. We walked upwards at least three quarters of a mile in the hot sun, with the stream on our right, both sides of which to a considerable height were planted with firs and larches intermingled—children of poor Burns's song;[1] for his sake we wished that they had been the natural trees of

1. Soon after visiting the Falls of Bruar in 1787, Burns wrote "The Humble Petition of Bruar Water to the Noble Duke of Athole," a poem in which Bruar Water, personified (and in Burns's voice) begs the Duke of Atholl to plant trees along its banks. At the time Burns visited Bruar Water flowed through an open field. John Murray, 4th Duke of Atholl, began the plantation of firs not long after Burns's visit.

Scotland, birches, ashes, mountain-ashes, etc.; however, sixty or seventy years hence they will be no unworthy monument to his memory. At present, nothing can be uglier than the whole chasm of the hill-side with its formal walks. I do not mean to condemn them, for, for aught I know, they are as well managed as they could be; but it is not easy to see the use of a pleasure-path leading to nothing, up a steep and naked hill in the midst of an unlovely tract of country, though by the side of a tumbling stream of clear water. It does not surely deserve the name of a pleasure-path. It is three miles from the Duke of Athol's house, and I do not believe that one person living within five miles of the place would wish to go twice to it. The falls are high, the rocks and stones fretted and gnawed by the water. I do not wonder at the pleasure which Burns received from this stream; I believe we should have been much pleased if we had come upon it as he did. At the bottom of the hill we took up our car, and, turning back, joined the man who was to be our guide.

Crossed the Garry, and went along a moor without any road but straggling cart-tracks. Soon began to ascend a high hill, and the ground grew so rough—road there was none—that we were obliged to walk most of the way. Ascended to a considerable height, and commanded an extensive prospect bounded by lofty mountains, and having crossed the top of the fell we parted with our guide, being in sight of the vale into which we were to descend, and to pursue upwards till we should come to Loch Rannoch, a lake, as described to us, bedded in a forest of Scotch pines.

When left to ourselves we sate down on the hillside,[1] and looked with delight into the deep vale below, which was exceedingly green, not regularly fenced or cultivated, but the level area scattered over with bushes and trees, and through that level ground glided a glassy river, not in serpentine windings, but in direct turnings backwards and forwards, and then flowed into the head of the Lake of Tummel; but I will copy a rough sketch which I made while we sate upon the hill, which, imperfect as it is, will give a better idea of the course of the river—which I must add is more curious than beautiful—than my description. The ground must be often overflowed in winter, for the water seemed to touch the very edge of its banks. At this time the scene was soft and cheerful, such as invited us downwards, and made us proud of our adventure. Coming near to a cluster of huts, we turned thither, a few steps out of our way, to inquire about the road; these huts were on the hill, placed side by side, in a figure between a square and a circle, as if for the sake of mutual shelter, like haystacks in a farmyard—no trees near them. We called at one of the doors, and three hale, stout men came out, who could speak very little English, and stared at us with an almost savage look of wonder. One of them took much pains to set us forward, and went a con-

1. Probably at Queen's View, a vantage point offering beautiful views, especially down Loch Tummel, and perhaps taking its name from the visit of Mary, Queen of Scots, in 1564.

Windings of the River Tummel.

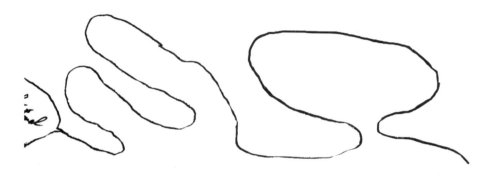

siderable way down the hill till we came in sight of the cart road, which we were to follow; but we had not gone far before we were disheartened. It was with the greatest difficulty William could lead the horse and car over the rough stones, and to sit in it was impossible; the road grew worse and worse, therefore we resolved to turn back, having no reason to expect anything better, for we had been told that after we should leave the untracked ground all would be fair before us. We knew ourselves where we stood to be about eight miles distant from the point where the river Tummel, after having left the lake, joins the Garry at Fascally[1] near the Pass of Killicrankie, therefore we resolved to make our way thither, and endeavour to procure a lodging at the same public-house where it had been refused to us the night before. The road was likely to be very bad; but, knowing the distance, we thought it more prudent than to venture farther with nothing before us but uncertainty. We were forced to unyoke the horse, and turn the car ourselves, owing to the steep banks on either side of the road, and after much trouble we got him in again, and set our faces down the vale towards Loch Tummel, William leading the car and I walking by his side.

For the first two or three miles we looked down upon the lake, our road being along the side of the hill directly above it. On the opposite side another range of hills rose up in the same manner,—farm-houses thinly scattered among the copses near the water, and cultivated ground in patches.

1. A lovely plain to early travellers (but undistinguished today), Faskally was described by Stoddart as: "a triangular piece of ground, surrounded with wood, watered by . . . streams, and within sight of the fall of Tumel. On all sides are hills of every variety of form and size, with their glens opening in different directions" (*Remarks*, II pp. 185–86).

The lake does not wind, nor are the shores much varied by bays,—the mountains not commanding; but the whole a pleasing scene. Our road took us out of sight of the water, and we were obliged to procure a guide across a high moor, where it was impossible that the horse should drag us at all, the ground being exceedingly rough and untracked: of course fatiguing for foot-travellers, and on foot we must travel. After some time, the river Tummel again served us for a guide, when it had left the lake. It was no longer a gentle stream, a mirror to the sky, but we could hear it roaring at a considerable distance between steep banks of rock and wood. We had to cross the Garry by a bridge, a little above the junction of the two rivers; and were now not far from the public-house, to our great joy, for we were very weary with our laborious walk. I do not think that I had walked less than sixteen miles, and William much more, to which add the fatigue of leading the horse, and the rough roads, and you will not wonder that we longed for rest. We stopped at the door of the house, and William entered as before, and again the woman refused to lodge us, in a most inhuman manner, giving no other reason than that she would not do it. We pleaded for the poor horse, entreated, soothed, and flattered, but all in vain, though the night was cloudy and dark. We begged to sit by the fire till morning, and to this she would not consent; indeed, if it had not been for the sake of the horse, I would rather have lain in a barn than on the best of feather-beds in the house of such a cruel woman.

We were now, after our long day's journey, five miles from the inn at Blair, whither we, at first, thought of returning; but finally resolved to go to a public-house which we had seen in a village we passed through, about a mile above the ferry over the Tummel, having come from that point to Blair, for the sake of the Pass of Killicrankie and Blair itself, and had now the same road to measure back again. We were obliged to leave the Pass of Killicrankie unseen; but this disturbed us little at a time when we had seven miles to travel in the dark, with a poor beast almost sinking with fatigue, for he had not rested once all day. We went on spiritless, and at a dreary pace. Passed by one house which we were half inclined to go up to and ask for a night's lodging; and soon after, being greeted by a gentle voice from a poor woman, whom, till she spoke, though we were close to her, we had not seen, we stopped, and asked if she could tell us where we might stay all night, and put up our horse. She mentioned the public-house left behind, and we told our tale, and asked her if she had no house to which she could take us. 'Yes, to be sure she had a house, but it was only a small cottage;' and she had no place for the horse, and how we could lodge in her house she could not tell; but we should be welcome to whatever she had, so we turned the car, and she walked by the side of it, talking to us in a tone of human kindness which made us friends at once.

I remember thinking to myself, as I have often done in a stage-coach, though never with half the reason to pre-judge favourably, What sort of countenance and figure shall we see in this woman when we come into the light? And indeed it was an interesting moment when, after we had entered her house, she blew the embers on the hearth, and lighted a candle to assist us in taking the luggage out of the car. Her husband presently arrived, and he and William took the horse to the public-house. The poor woman hung the kettle over the fire. We had tea and sugar of our own, and she set before us barley cakes, and milk which she had just brought in; I recollect she said she 'had been west to fetch it.' The Highlanders always direct you by east and west, north and south—very confusing to strangers. She told us that it was her business to 'keep the gate' for Mr.———, who lived at ———, just below,—that is, to receive messages, take in letters, etc. Her cottage stood by the side of the road leading to his house, within the gate, having, as we saw in the morning, a dressed-up porter's lodge outside; but within was nothing but the naked walls, unplastered, and floors of mud, as in the common huts. She said that they lived rent-free in return for their services; but spoke of her place and Mr.———with little respect, hinting that he was very proud; and indeed her appearance, and subdued manners, and that soft voice which had prepossessed us so much in her favour, seemed to belong to an injured and oppressed being. We talked a great deal with her, and gathered some interesting facts from her conversation, which I wish I had written down while they were fresh in my memory. They had only one child, yet seemed to be very poor, not discontented but languid, and willing to suffer rather than rouse to any effort. Though it was plain she despised and hated her master, and had no wish to conceal it, she hardly appeared to think it worth while to speak ill of him. We were obliged to sit up very late while our kind hostess was preparing our beds. William lay upon the floor on some hay, without sheets; my bed was of chaff; I had plenty of covering, and a pair of very nice strong clean sheets,—she said with some pride that she had good linen. I believe the sheets had been of her own spinning, perhaps when she was first married, or before, and she probably will keep them to the end of her life of poverty.

Thursday, September 8th.—Before breakfast we walked to the Pass of Killicrankie. A very fine scene; the river Garry forcing its way down a deep chasm between rocks, at the foot of high rugged hills covered with wood, to a great height. The Pass did not, however, impress us with awe, or a sensation of difficulty or danger, according to our expectations; but, the road being at a considerable height on the side of the hill, we at first only looked into the dell or chasm. It is much grander seen from below, near the river's bed. Everybody knows that this Pass is famous in military history.[1] When we

1. The battle of Killiecrankie occurred in July 1689. Under Viscount Dundee (Claverhouse), Jacobite Highlanders charged the English troops, commanded by General Mackay, and defeated them. Half of Mackay's troops were killed. Dundee was fatally wounded.

were travelling in Scotland an invasion was hourly looked for, and one could not but think with some regret of the times when from the now depopulated Highlands forty or fifty thousand men might have been poured down for the defence of the country, under such leaders as the Marquis of Montrose or the brave man who had so distinguished himself upon the ground where we were standing. I will transcribe a sonnet suggested to William[1] by this place, and written in October 1803:—

> Six thousand Veterans practised in War's game,
> Tried men, at Killicrankie were array'd
> Against an equal host that wore the Plaid,
> Shepherds and herdsmen. Like a whirlwind came
> The Highlanders; the slaughter spread like flame,
> And Garry, thundering down his mountain road,
> Was stopp'd, and could not breathe beneath the load
> Of the dead bodies. 'Twas a day of shame
> For them whom precept and the pedantry
> Of cold mechanic battle do enslave.
> Oh! for a single hour of that Dundee
> Who on that day the word of onset gave:
> Like conquest might the men of England see,
> And her Foes find a like inglorious grave.

We turned back again, and going down the hill below the Pass, crossed the same bridge we had come over the night before, and walked through Lady Perth's grounds by the side of the Garry till we came to the Tummel, and then walked up to the cascade of the Tummel. The fall is inconsiderable, scarcely more than an ordinary 'wear;' but it makes a loud roaring over large stones, and the whole scene is grand—hills, mountains, woods, and rocks.——is a very pretty place, all but the house. Stoddart's print gives no notion of it.[2] The house stands upon a small plain[3] at the junction of the two rivers, a close deep spot, surrounded by high hills and woods. After we had breakfasted William fetched the car, and, while we were conveying the luggage to the outside of the gate, where it stood, Mr.——, *mal apropos*, came very near to the door, called the woman out, and railed at her in the most abusive manner for 'harbouring' people in that way. She soon slipped

1. "In the Pass of Killicranky, an Invasion Being Expected, October, 1803."
2. An 1801 edition of Stoddart's *Remarks*, to be found in the University of Glasgow Special Collections library, is illustrated with hand-colored aquatints. (Not all editions of Stoddart contain these illustrations). The print of Faskally to which Dorothy Wordsworth refers here shows a river flowing over gentle rapids, with a sort of bend in the river.
2. Stoddart comments that the house "has little beauty in its exterior; but it is comfortable and convenient within" and identifies its owner as "——Butter, Esq." (*Remarks* II p. 186).

from him, and came back to us: I wished that William should go and speak to her master, for I was afraid that he might turn the poor woman away; but she would not suffer it, for she did not care whether they stayed or not. In the meantime, Mr.——continued scolding her husband; indeed, he appeared to be not only proud, but very ignorant, insolent, and low-bred. The woman told us that she had sometimes lodged poor travellers who were passing along the road, and permitted others to cook their victuals in her house, for which Mr.——had reprimanded her before; but, as she said, she did not value her place, and it was no matter. In sounding forth the dispraise of Mr.——, I ought not to omit mentioning that the poor woman had great delight in talking of the excellent qualities of his mother, with whom she had been a servant, and lived many years. After having interchanged good wishes we parted with our charitable hostess, who, telling us her name, entreated us, if ever we came that way again, to inquire for her.

We travelled down the Tummel till it is lost in the Tay, and then, in the same direction, continued our course along the vale of Tay, which is very wide for a considerable way, but gradually narrows, and the river, always a fine stream, assumes more dignity and importance. Two or three miles before we reached Dunkeld, we observed whole hill-sides, the property of the Duke of Athol, planted with fir-trees till they are lost among the rocks near the tops of the hills. In forty or fifty years these plantations will be very fine, being carried from hill to hill, and not bounded by a visible artificial fence.

Reached Dunkeld at about three o'clock. It is a pretty, small town, with a respectable and rather large ruined abbey, which is greatly injured by being made the nest of a modern Scotch kirk, with sash windows,—very incongruous with the noble antique tower,—a practice which we afterwards found is not uncommon in Scotland. Sent for the Duke's gardener after dinner, and walked with him into the pleasure-grounds, intending to go to the Falls of the Bran, a mountain stream which here joins the Tay. After walking some time on a shaven turf under the shade of old trees, by the side of the Tay, we left the pleasure-grounds, and crossing the river by a ferry, went up a lane on the hill opposite till we came to a locked gate by the road-side, through which we entered into another part of the Duke's pleasure-grounds bordering on the Bran, the glen being for a considerable way—for aught I know, two miles—thridded by gravel walks. The walks are quaintly enough intersected, here and there by a baby garden of fine flowers among the rocks and stones. The waterfall, which we came to see, warned us by a loud roaring that we must expect it; we were first, however, conducted into a small apartment, where the gardener desired us to look at a painting of the figure of Ossian,[1] which, while he was telling us the story

3. See Appendix 6.

of the young artist who performed the work, disappeared, parting in the middle, flying asunder as if by the touch of magic, and lo! we are at the entrance of a splendid room, which was almost dizzy and alive with water-falls, that tumbled in all directions—the great cascade, which was opposite to the window that faced us, being reflected in innumerable mirrors upon the ceiling and against the walls. We both laughed heartily, which, no doubt, the gardener considered as high commendation; for he was very eloquent in pointing out the beauties of the place.

We left the Bran, and pursued our walk through the plantations, where we readily forgave the Duke his little devices for their sakes. They are already no insignificant woods, where the trees happen to be oaks, birches, and others natural to the soil; and under their shade the walks are delightful. From one hill, through different openings under the trees, we looked up the vale of Tay to a great distance, a magnificent prospect at that time of the evening; woody and rich—corn, green fields, and cattle, the winding Tay, and distant mountains. Looked down the river to the town of Dunkeld, which lies low, under irregular hills, covered with wood to their rocky summits, and bounded by higher mountains, which are bare. The hill of Birnam, no longer Birnam 'wood,' was pointed out to us. After a very long walk we parted from our guide when it was almost dark, and he promised to call on us in the morning to conduct us to the gardens.

Friday, September 9th.—According to appointment, the gardener came with his keys in his hand, and we attended him whithersoever he chose to lead, in spite of past experience at Blair. We had, however, no reason to repent, for we were repaid for the trouble of going through the large gardens by the apples and pears of which he gave us liberally, and the walks through the woods on that part of the grounds opposite to where we had been the night before were very delightful. The Duke's house is neither large nor grand, being just an ordinary gentleman's house, upon a green lawn, and whitewashed, I believe. The old abbey faces the house on the east side, and appears to stand upon the same green lawn, which, though close to the town, is entirely excluded from it by high walls and trees.

We had been undetermined respecting our future course when we came to Dunkeld, whether to go on directly to Perth and Edinburgh, or to make a circuit and revisit the Trossachs. We decided upon the latter plan, and accordingly after breakfast set forward towards Crieff, where we intended to sleep, and the next night at Callander. The first part of our road, after having crossed the ferry, was up the glen of the Bran. Looking backwards, we saw Dunkeld very pretty under the hills, and surrounded by rich cultivated ground, but we had not a good distant view of the abbey.

Left our car, and went about a hundred yards from the road to see the Rumbling Brig, which, though well worth our going out of the way even much further, disappointed us, as places in general do which we hear much spoken of as savage, tremendous, etc.,—and no wonder, for they are usually described by people to whom rocks are novelties. The gardener had told us that we should pass through the most populous glen in Scotland, the glen of Amulree. It is not populous in the usual way, with scattered dwellings; but many clusters of houses, hamlets such as we had passed near the Tummel, which had a singular appearance, being like small encampments, were generally without trees, and in high situations—every house the same as its neighbour, whether for men or cattle. There was nothing else remarkable in the glen. We halted at a lonely inn at the foot of a steep barren moor, which we had to cross; then, after descending considerably, came to the narrow glen, which we had approached with no little curiosity, not having been able to procure any distinct description of it.

At Dunkeld, when we were hesitating what road to take, we wished to know whether that glen would be worth visiting, and accordingly put several questions to the waiter, and, among other epithets used in the course of interrogation, we stumbled upon the word 'grand,' to which he replied, 'No, I do not think there are any gentlemen's seats in it.' However, we drew enough from this describer and the gardener to determine us finally to go to Callander, the Narrow Glen being in the way.

Entered the glen at a small hamlet at some distance from the head, and turning aside a few steps, ascended a hillock which commanded a view to the top of it—a very sweet scene, a green valley, not very narrow, with a few scattered trees and huts, almost invisible in a misty gleam of afternoon light. At this hamlet we crossed a bridge, and the road led us down the glen, which had become exceedingly narrow, and so continued to the end: the hills on both sides heathy and rocky, very steep, but continuous; the rocks not single or overhanging, not scooped into caverns or sounding with torrents: there are no trees, no houses, no traces of cultivation, not one outstanding object. It is truly a solitude, the road even making it appear still more so: the bottom of the valley is mostly smooth and level, the brook not noisy: everything is simple and undisturbed, and while we passed through it the whole place was shady, cool, clear, and solemn. At the end of the long valley we ascended a hill to a great height, and reached the top, when the sun, on the point of setting, shed a soft yellow light upon every eminence. The prospect was very extensive; over hollows and plains, no towns, and few houses visible—a prospect, extensive as it was, in harmony with the secluded dell, and fixing its own peculiar character of removedness from the world, and the secure possession of the quiet of nature more deeply in our minds. The following poem was written by William[1] on hearing of a tradition relating to it, which we did not know when we were there:—

> In this still place remote from men
> Sleeps Ossian, in the Narrow Glen,
> In this still place where murmurs on
> But one meek streamlet, only one.
> He sung of battles and the breath
> Of stormy war, and violent death,
> And should, methinks, when all was pass'd,
> Have rightfully been laid at last
> Where rocks were rudely heap'd, and rent
> As by a spirit turbulent;
> Where sights were rough, and sounds were wild,
> And everything unreconciled,
> In some complaining, dim retreat
> Where fear and melancholy meet;
> But this is calm; there cannot be
> A more entire tranquillity.
>
> Does then the bard sleep here indeed?
> Or is it but a groundless creed?
> What matters it? I blame them not
> Whose fancy in this lonely spot
> Was moved, and in this way express'd
> Their notion of its perfect rest.
> A convent, even a hermit's cell
> Would break the silence of this Dell;
> It is not quiet, is not ease,
> But something deeper far than these;
> The separation that is here
> Is of the grave; and of austere
> And happy feelings of the dead:
> And therefore was it rightly said
> That Ossian, last of all his race,
> Lies buried in this lonely place.

1. "Glen Almain, or, the Narrow Glen." Indicated on maps today as Sma' Glen, this glen, is some $6^1/_2$ miles north of Crieff on the A822. A stone marking the resting place William writes about is set between a stream of the River Almond and the road. *Menzies' Tourist's Guide for Scotland* (Edinburgh: 1853) reports the tradition that a servant of General Wade discovered the tomb while constructing a road, and that over the tomb "is laid a stone, Clach-na-Ossian, about 8 feet high and 21 feet in circumference, well known, and often visited by 'the pilgrims of his genius'" (p. 314). Menzies then quotes Wordsworth's "Glen Almain."

Having descended into a broad cultivated vale, we saw nothing remarkable. Observed a gentleman's house,[1] which stood pleasantly among trees. It was dark some time before we reached Crieff, a small town, though larger than Dunkeld.

Saturday, September 10th.—Rose early, and departed without breakfast. We were to pass through one of the most celebrated vales of Scotland, Strath Erne. We found it a wide, long, and irregular vale, with many gentlemen's seats under the hills, woods, copses, frequent cottages, plantations, and much cultivation, yet with an intermixture of barren ground; indeed, except at Killin and Dunkeld, there was always something which seemed to take from the composure and simplicity of the cultivated scenes. There is a struggle to overcome the natural barrenness, and the end not attained, an appearance of something doing or imperfectly done, a passing with labour from one state of society into another. When you look from an eminence on the fields of Grasmere Vale, the heart is satisfied with a simple undisturbed pleasure, and no less, on one of the green or heathy dells of Scotland, where there is no appearance of change to be, or having been, but such as the seasons make. Strath Erne is so extensive a vale that, had it been in England, there must have been much inequality, as in Wensley Dale; but at Wensley there is a unity, a softness, a melting together, which in the large vales of Scotland I never perceived. The difference at Strath Erne may come partly from the irregularity, the undefined outline, of the hills which enclose it; but it is caused still more by the broken surface, I mean broken as to colour and produce, the want of hedgerows, and also the great number of new fir plantations. After some miles it becomes much narrower as we approach nearer the mountains at the foot of the lake of the same name, Loch Erne.

Breakfasted at a small public-house, a wretchedly dirty cottage, but the people were civil, and though we had nothing but barley cakes we made a good breakfast, for there were plenty of eggs. Walked up a high hill to view the seat of Mr. Dundas, now Lord Melville—a spot where, if he have gathered much wisdom from his late disgrace[2] or his long intercourse with the world, he may spend his days as quietly as he need desire. It is a secluded valley, not rich, but with plenty of wood: there are many pretty paths through the woods, and moss huts in different parts. After leaving the cottage where we breakfasted the country was very pleasing, yet still with a want of richness; but this was less perceived, being huddled up in charcoal woods, and the vale narrow. Loch Erne opens out in a

1. "Probably Monzie."
2. Lord Melville had been Treasurer of the Admiralty between 1782 and 1800. He was suspected of mismanagement of the finances of the Admiralty, investigated by a commission of inquiry appointed in 1802, and ultimately impeached (in 1806).

very pleasing manner, seen from a hill along which the road is carried
through a wood of low trees; but it does not improve afterwards, lying
directly from east to west without any perceivable bendings: and the shores
are not much broken or varied, not populous, and the mountains not
sufficiently commanding to make up for the deficiencies. Dined at the head
of the lake.[1] I scarcely know its length, but should think not less than four
or five miles, and it is wide in proportion. The inn is in a small village—a
decent house.

Walked about half a mile along the road to Tyndrum, which is through
a bare glen,[2] and over a mountain pass. It rained when we pursued our
journey again, and continued to rain for several hours. The road which we
were to take was up another glen, down which came a stream that fell into
the lake on the opposite side at the head of it, so, after having crossed the
main vale, a little above the lake, we entered into the smaller glen. The road
delightfully smooth and dry—one gentleman's house very pleasant among
large coppice woods. After going perhaps three miles up this valley, we
turned to the left into another, which seemed to be much more beautiful.
It was a level valley, not—like that which we had passed—a wide sloping
cleft between the hills, but having a quiet, slow-paced stream, which flowed
through level green grounds tufted with trees intermingled with cottages.
The tops of the hills were hidden by mists, and the objects in the valley seen
through misty rain, which made them look exceedingly soft, and indeed
partly concealed them, and we always fill up what we are left to guess at
with something as beautiful as what we see. This valley seemed to have less
of the appearance of barrenness or imperfect cultivation than any of the same
character we had passed through; indeed, we could not discern any traces of
it. It is called Strath Eyer. 'Strath' is generally applied to a broad vale; but
this, though open, is not broad.

We next came to a lake, called Loch Lubnaig, a name which signifies
'winding.' In shape it somewhat resembles Ulswater, but is much narrower
and shorter, being only four miles in length. The character of this lake is
simple and grand. On the side opposite to where we were is a range of steep
craggy mountains, one of which—like Place Fell—encroaching upon the
bed of the lake, forces it to make a considerable bending. I have forgotten
the name of this precipice: it is a very remarkable one, being almost
perpendicular, and very rugged.

We, on the other side, travelled under steep and rocky hills which were
often covered with low woods to a considerable height; there were one or
two farm-houses, and a few cottages. A neat white dwelling on the side of
the hill over against the bold steep of which I have spoken, had been the

1. Lochearnhead.
2. Glen Ogle.

residence of the famous traveller Bruce,[1] who, all his travels ended, had arranged the history of them in that solitude—as deep as any Abyssinian one—among the mountains of his native country, where he passed several years. Whether he died there or not we did not learn; but the manner of his death was remarkable and affecting,—from a fall down-stairs in his own house, after so many dangers through which fortitude and courage had never failed to sustain him. The house stands sweetly, surrounded by coppice-woods and green fields. On the other side, I believe, were no houses till we came near to the outlet, where a few low huts looked very beautiful, with their dark brown roofs near a stream which hurried down the mountain, and after its turbulent course travelled a short way over a level green, and was lost in the lake.

Within a few miles of Callander we come into a grand region; the mountains to a considerable height were covered with wood, enclosing us in a narrow passage; the stream on our right, generally concealed by wood, made a loud roaring; at one place, in particular, it fell down the rocks in a succession of cascades. The scene is much celebrated in Scotland, and is called the Pass of Leny. It was nearly dark when we reached Callander. We were wet and cold, and glad of a good fire. The inn was comfortable; we drank tea; and after tea the waiter presented us with a pamphlet descriptive of the neighbourhood of Callander, which we brought away with us, and I am very sorry I lost it.

1. James Bruce (1730–94) was the Scottish explorer of Africa whose *Travels to Discover the Source of the Nile*, first published in 1790 (Edinburgh: G.G.J. and J. Robinson. 5 vols.) attracted a wide audience.

Though his primary home was at Kinnaird House, in Sterlingshire, Bruce owned property in Ardchullarie More, on the left bank of Loch Lubnaig, between Callander and Strathyre. He lived there part of the time he was preparing his manuscript on his Abyssinian travels for publication.

A "neat white dwelling" like the one Dorothy noticed is still perched on the side of the hill today. One local authority, Elizabeth Beauchamp, in her *Braes O' Balquhidder* p. 3 (Balquhidder: Friends of Balquhidder Church, 1993. 4th ed.) states unequivocally that "It was to this house that the great 18th-century explorer James Bruce of Kinnard retired to write an account of his amazing journeys in Abyssinia." However, with the recent sale of the property came the necessity to examine the deed to it, which reveals that the present house was built in 1910. Most likely, this white house is on the site of the one Dorothy observed.

Bruce was exceptionally tall (6ft. 4in.) and hearty. That he should meet his demise in a household accident—falling down the stairs and breaking his neck—after surviving dangerous travels in Africa struck many as ironic.

FIFTH WEEK

Sunday, September 11th.—Immediately after breakfast, the morning being fine, we set off with cheerful spirits towards the Trossachs, intending to take up our lodging at the house of our old friend the ferryman. A boy accompanied us to convey the horse and car back to Callander from the head of Loch Achray. The country near Callander is very pleasing; but, as almost everywhere else, imperfectly cultivated. We went up a broad vale, through which runs the stream from Loch Ketterine, and came to Loch Vennachar, a larger lake than Loch Achray, the small one which had given us such unexpected delight when we left the Pass of the Trossachs. Loch Vennachar is much larger, but greatly inferior in beauty to the image which we had conceived of its neighbour, and so the reality proved to us when we came up to that little lake, and saw it before us in its true shape in the cheerful sunshine. The Trossachs, overtopped by Benledi and other high mountains, enclose the lake at the head; and those houses which we had seen before, with their corn fields sloping towards the water, stood very prettily under low woods. The fields did not appear so rich as when we had seen them through the veil of mist; but yet, as in framing our expectations we had allowed for a much greater difference, so we were even a second time surprised with pleasure at the same spot.

Went as far as these houses of which I have spoken in the car, and then walked on, intending to pursue the road up the side of Loch Ketterine along which Coleridge had come; but we had resolved to spend some hours in the neighbourhood of the Trossachs, and accordingly coasted the head of Loch Achray, and pursued the brook between the two lakes as far as there was any track. Here we found, to our surprise—for we had expected nothing but heath and rocks like the rest of the neighbourhood of the Trossachs—a secluded farm, a plot of verdant ground with a single cottage and its company of out-houses. We turned back, and went to the very point from which we had first looked upon Loch Achray when we were here with Coleridge. It was no longer a visionary scene: the sun shone into every crevice of the hills, and the mountain-tops were clear. After some time we went into the pass from the Trossachs, and were delighted to behold the forms of objects fully revealed, and even surpassing in loveliness and variety what we had conceived. The mountains, I think, appeared not so high; but on the whole we had not the smallest disappointment; the heather was fading, though still beautiful.

Sate for half-an-hour in Lady Perth's shed[1] and scrambled over the rocks and through the thickets at the head of the lake. I went till I could make my way no further, and left William to go to the top of the hill, whence he had a distinct view, as on a map, of the intricacies of the lake and the course of the river. Returned to the huts, and, after having taken a second dinner of the food we had brought from Callander, set our faces towards the head of Loch Ketterine. I can add nothing to my former description of the Trossachs, except that we departed with our old delightful remembrances endeared, and many new ones. The path or road—for it was neither the one nor the other, but something between both—is the pleasantest I have ever travelled in my life for the same length of way,—now with marks of sledges or wheels, or none at all, bare or green, as it might happen; now a little descent, now a level; sometimes a shady lane, at others an open track through green pastures; then again it would lead us into thick coppice-woods, which often entirely shut out the lake, and again admitted it by glimpses. We have never had a more delightful walk than this evening. Ben Lomond and the three pointed-topped mountains of Loch Lomond, which we had seen from the Garrison, were very majestic under the clear sky, the lake perfectly calm, the air sweet and mild. I felt that it was much more interesting to visit a place where we have been before than it can possibly be the first time, except under peculiar circumstances. The sun had been set for some time, when, being within a quarter of a mile of the ferryman's hut, our path having led us close to the shore of the calm lake, we met two neatly dressed women, without hats, who had probably been taking their Sunday evening's walk. One of them said to us in a friendly, soft tone of voice, 'What! you are stepping westward?' I cannot describe how affecting this simple expression was in that remote place, with the western sky in front, yet glowing with the departed sun. William wrote the following poem[2] long after, in remembrance of his feelings and mine:—

'What! you are stepping westward?' Yea,
'Twould be a wildish destiny
If we, who thus together roam
In a strange land, and far from home,
Were in this place the guests of chance:
Yet who would stop, or fear to advance,
Though home or shelter he had none,
With such a sky to lead him on?

1. According to Stoddart, Lady Perth provided little retreats where travellers could rest and view the area. "The Taste of lady Perth has ... caused wicker huts to be built on the points commanding the most striking views" (*Remarks*, II pp. 307–308).
2. "Stepping Westward."

The dewy ground was dark and cold,
Behind all gloomy to behold,
And stepping westward seem'd to be
A kind of heavenly destiny;
I liked the greeting, 'twas a sound
Of something without place or bound;
And seem'd to give me spiritual right
To travel through that region bright.

The voice was soft; and she who spake
Was walking by her native Lake;
The salutation was to me
The very sound of courtesy;
Its power was felt, and while my eye
Was fix'd upon the glowing sky,
The echo of the voice enwrought
A human sweetness with the thought
Of travelling through the world that lay
Before me in my endless way.

We went up to the door of our boatman's hut as to a home, and scarcely less confident of a cordial welcome than if we had been approaching our own cottage at Grasmere. It had been a very pleasing thought, while we were walking by the side of the beautiful lake, that, few hours as we had been there, there was a home for us in one of its quiet dwellings. Accordingly, so we found it; the good woman, who had been at a preaching by the lake-side, was in her holiday dress at the door, and seemed to be rejoiced at the sight of us. She led us into the hut in haste to supply our wants; we took once more a refreshing meal by her fireside, and, though not so merry as the last time, we were not less happy, bating our regrets that Coleridge was not in his old place. I slept in the same bed as before, and listened to the household stream, which now only made a very low murmuring.

Monday, September 12th.—Rejoiced in the morning to see the sun shining upon the hills when I first looked out through the open window-place at my bed's head. We rose early, and after breakfast, our old companion, who was to be our guide for the day, rowed us over the water to the same point where Coleridge and I had sate down and eaten our dinner, while William had gone to survey the unknown coast. We intended to cross Loch Lomond, follow the lake to Glenfalloch, above the head of it, and then come over the mountains to Glengyle, and so down the glen, and passing Mr. Macfarlane's house, back again to the ferry-house, where we should sleep. So, a third time we went through the mountain hollow, now familiar ground. The inhabitants had not yet got in all their hay, and were at work

in the fields; our guide often stopped to talk with them, and no doubt was called upon to answer many inquiries respecting us two strangers.

At the ferry-house of Inversneyde we had not the happy sight of the Highland girl and her companion, but the good woman received us cordially, gave me milk, and talked of Coleridge, who, the morning after we parted from him, had been at her house to fetch his watch, which he had forgotten two days before. He has since told me that he questioned her respecting the miserable condition of her hut, which, as you may remember,

admitted the rain at the door, and retained it in the hollows of the mud
floor: he told her how easy it would be to remove these inconveniences, and
to contrive something, at least, to prevent the wind from entering at the
window-places, if not a glass window for light and warmth by day.
She replied that this was very true, but if they made any improvements the
laird would conclude that they were growing rich, and would raise their
rent.

The ferryman happened to be just ready at the moment to go over the
lake with a poor man, his wife and child. The little girl, about three years
old, cried all the way, terrified by the water. When we parted from this
family, they going down the lake, and we up it, I could not but think of the
difference in our condition to that poor woman, who, with her husband,
had been driven from her home by want of work, and was now going a
long journey to seek it elsewhere: every step was painful toil, for she had
either her child to bear or a heavy burthen. *I* walked as she did, but pleasure
was my object, and if toil came along with it, even *that* was pleasure,—
pleasure, at least, it would be in the remembrance.

We were, I believe, nine miles from Glenfalloch when we left the boat.
To us, with minds at ease, the walk was delightful; it could not be
otherwise, for we passed by a continual succession of rocks, woods, and
mountains; but the houses were few, and the ground cultivated only in small
portions near the water, consequently there was not that sort of variety
which leaves distinct separate remembrances, but one impression of solitude
and greatness. While the Highlander and I were plodding on together side
by side, interspersing long silences with now and then a question or a
remark, looking down to the lake he espied two small rocky islands, and
pointing to them, said to me, 'It will be gay and dangerous sailing there in
stormy weather when the water is high.' In giving my assent I could not
help smiling, but I afterwards found that a like combination of words is not
uncommon in Scotland, for, at Edinburgh, William being afraid of rain,
asked the ostler what he thought, who, looking up to the sky, pronounced
it to be 'gay and dull,' and therefore rain might be expected. The most
remarkable object we saw was a huge single stone, I believe three or four
times the size of Bowder Stone.[1] The top of it, which on one side was
sloping like the roof of a house, was covered with heather. William climbed
up the rock, which would have been no easy task but to a mountaineer, and
we constructed a rope of pocket-handkerchiefs, garters, plaids, coats, etc.,
and measured its height. It was *so* many times the length of William's
walking-stick, but, unfortunately, having lost the stick, we have lost the
measure. The ferryman told us that a preaching was held there once in three
months by a certain minister—I think of Arrochar—who engages, as a part

1. See note to p. 80.

of his office, to perform the service. The interesting feelings we had connected with the Highland Sabbath and Highland worship returned here with double force. The rock, though on one side a high perpendicular wall, in no place overhung so as to form a shelter, in no place could it be more than a screen from the elements. Why then had it been selected for such a purpose? Was it merely from being a central situation and a conspicuous object? Or did there belong to it some inheritance of superstition from old times? It is impossible to look at the stone without asking, How came it hither? Had then that obscurity and unaccountableness, that mystery of power which is about it, any influence over the first persons who resorted hither for worship? Or have they now on those who continue to frequent it? The lake is in front of the perpendicular wall, and behind, at some distance, and totally detached from it, is the continuation of the ridge of mountains which forms the vale of Loch Lomond—a magnificent temple, of which this spot is a noble Sanctum Sanctorum.

We arrived at Glenfalloch at about one or two o'clock. It is no village; there being only scattered huts in the glen, which may be four miles long, according to my remembrance: the middle of it is very green, and level, and tufted with trees. Higher up, where the glen parts into two very narrow ones, is the house of the laird; I daresay a pretty place. The view from the door of the public-house is exceedingly beautiful; the river flows smoothly into the lake, and the fields were at that time as green as possible. Looking backward, Ben Lomond very majestically shuts in the view. The top of the mountain, as seen here, being of a pyramidal form, it is much grander than with the broken outline, and stage above stage, as seen from the neighbour-hood of Luss. We found nobody at home at the inn,[1] but the ferryman shouted, wishing to have a glass of whisky, and a young woman came from the hay-field, dressed in a white bedgown, without hat or cap. There was no whisky in the house, so he begged a little whey to drink with the fragments of our cold meat brought from Callander. After a short rest in a cool parlour we set forward again, having to cross the river and climb up a steep mountain on the opposite side of the valley. I observed that the people were busy bringing in the hay before it was dry into a sort of 'fauld' or yard, where they intended to leave it, ready to be gathered into the house with the first threatening of rain, and if not completely dry brought out again. Our guide bore me in his arms over the stream, and we soon came to the foot of the mountain. The most easy rising, for a short way at first, was near a naked rivulet which made a fine cascade in one place. Afterwards, the ascent was very laborious, being frequently almost perpendicular.

It is one of those moments which I shall not easily forget, when at that point from which a step or two would have carried us out of sight of the

1. At Inverarnan.

green fields of Glenfalloch, being at a great height on the mountain, we sate down, and heard, as if from the heart of the earth, the sound of torrents ascending out of the long hollow glen. To the eye all was motionless, a perfect stillness. The noise of waters did not appear to come this way or that, from any particular quarter: it was everywhere, almost, one might say, as if 'exhaled' through the whole surface of the green earth. Glenfalloch, Coleridge has since told me, signifies the Hidden Vale; but William says, if we were to name it from our recollections of that time, we should call it the Vale of Awful Sound. We continued to climb higher and higher; but the hill was no longer steep, and afterwards we pursued our way along the top of it with many small ups and downs. The walk was very laborious after the climbing was over, being often exceedingly stony, or through swampy moss, rushes, or rough heather. As we proceeded, continuing our way at the top of the mountain, encircled by higher mountains at a great distance, we were passing, without notice, a heap of scattered stones round which was a belt of green grass—green, and as it seemed rich, where all else was either poor heather and coarse grass, or unprofitable rushes and spongy moss. The Highlander made a pause, saying, 'This place is much changed since I was here twenty years ago.' He told us that the heap of stones had been a hut where a family was then living, who had their winter habitation in the valley, and brought their goats thither in the summer to feed on the mountains, and that they were used to gather them together at night and morning to be milked close to the door, which was the reason why the grass was yet so green near the stones. It was affecting in that solitude to meet with this memorial of manners passed away; we looked about for some other traces of humanity, but nothing else could we find in that place. We ourselves afterwards espied another of those ruins, much more extensive— the remains, as the man told us, of several dwellings. We were astonished at the sagacity with which our Highlander discovered the track, where often no track was visible to us, and scarcely even when he pointed it out. It reminded us of what we read of the Hottentots and other savages. He went on as confidently as if it had been a turnpike road—the more surprising, as when he was there before it must have been a plain track, for he told us that fishermen from Arrochar carried herrings regularly over the mountains by that way to Loch Ketterine when the glens were much more populous than now.

Descended into Glengyle, above Loch Ketterine, and passed through Mr. Macfarlane's grounds, that is, through the whole of the glen, where there was now no house left but his. We stopped at his door to inquire after the family, though with little hope of finding them at home, having seen a large company at work in a hay field, whom we conjectured to be his whole household—as it proved, except a servant-maid, who answered our inquires. We had sent the ferryman forward from the head of the glen to bring the boat round from the place where he left it to the other side of the lake. Passed the same farm-house we had such good reason to remember, and went up to the burying-ground that stood so sweetly near the water-side. The ferryman had told us that Rob Roy's grave was there,[1] so we could not pass on without going up to the spot. There were several tomb-stones, but the inscriptions were either worn-out or unintelligible to us, and the place choked up with nettles and brambles. You will remember the description I have given of the spot. I have nothing here to add, except the following poem which it suggested to William:—

> A famous Man is Robin Hood,
> The English Ballad-singer's joy,
> And Scotland boasts of one as good,
>   She has her own Rob Roy!
>
> Then clear the weeds from off his grave,
> And let us chaunt a passing stave
>   In honour of that Outlaw brave.
>
> Heaven gave Rob Roy a daring heart
> And wondrous length and strength of arm,
> Nor craved he more to quell his foes,
>   Or keep his friends from harm.
>
> Yet Robin was as wise as brave,
> As wise in thought as bold in deed,
> For in the principles of things
>   He sought his moral creed.
>
> Said generous Rob, 'What need of books?
> Burn all the statutes and their shelves:
> They stir us up against our kind,
>   And worse, against ourselves.

1. The grave was not here but at Balquhidder, at the head of Loch Voil, as William would later learn. There was a burial place here, however, and Dorothy incorporated William's poem "Rob Roy's Grave" on the assumption they had correctly identified it as Rob Roy's. In fact, William provided a headnote to that effect for a subsequent publication of the poem: "The history of Rob Roy is sufficiently known; his Grave is near the head of Loch Ketterine, in one of those small Pin-fold-like Burial-grounds, of neglected and desolate appearance, which the Traveller meets with in the Highlands of Scotland." Much later, in 1843, when he was seventy-three years old and casting a retrospective glance on his poetry, he acknowledged: "I have since been told that I was misinformed as to the burial-place of Rob Roy. If so, I may plead in excuse that I wrote on apparently good authority, namely that of a well-educated Lady who lived at the head of the Lake within a mile or less of the point indicated as containing the remains of One so famous in that neighbourhood" (*Fenwick Notes*, pp. 26–7).

'We have a passion; make a law,
Too false to guide us or control:
And for the law itself we fight
  In bitterness of soul.

'And puzzle, blinded thus, we lose
Distinctions that are plain and few:
These find I graven on my heart:
  That tells me what to do.

'The Creatures see of flood and field,
And those that travel on the wind!
With them no strife can last; they live
  In peace, and peace of mind.

'For why? Because the good old rule
Suffices them, the simple plan
That they should take who have the power,
  And they should keep who can.

'A lesson which is quickly learn'd,
A signal this which all can see!
Thus nothing here provokes the strong
  To tyrannous cruelty.

'And freakishness of mind is check'd;
He tamed who foolishly aspires,
While to the measure of their might
  All fashion their desires.

'All kinds and creatures stand and fall
By strength of prowess or of wit,
'Tis God's appointment who must sway,
  And who is to submit.

'Since then,' said Robin, 'right is plain,
And longest life is but a day;
To have my ends, maintain my rights,
  I'll take the shortest way.'

And thus among these rocks he lived
Through summer's heat and winter's snow;
The Eagle, he was lord above,
  And Rob was lord below.

So was it—would at least have been
But through untowardness of fate;
For polity was then too strong:
  He came an age too late.

Or shall we say an age too soon?
For were the bold man living now,
How might he flourish in his pride
    With buds on every bough?

Then Rents and Land-marks, Rights of chase,
Sheriffs and Factors, Lairds and Thanes,
Would all have seem'd but paltry things
    Not worth a moment's pains.

Rob Roy had never linger'd here,
To these few meagre vales confined,
But thought how wide the world, the times
    How fairly to his mind.

And to his Sword he would have said,
'Do thou my sovereign will enact
From land to land through half the earth;
    Judge thou of law and fact.

''Tis fit that we should do our part;
Becoming that mankind should learn
That we are not to be surpass'd
    In fatherly concern.

'Of old things all are over old,
Of good things none are good enough;
I'll shew that I can help to frame
    A world of other stuff.

'I, too, will have my Kings that take
From me the sign of life and death,
Kingdoms shall shift about like clouds
    Obedient to my breath.'

And if the word had been fulfill'd
As might have been, then, thought of joy!
France would have had her present Boast,
    And we our brave Rob Roy.

Oh! say not so, compare them not;
I would not wrong thee, Champion brave!
Would wrong thee nowhere; least of all
    Here, standing by thy Grave.

For thou, although with some wild thoughts,
Wild Chieftain of a savage Clan,
Hadst this to boast of—thou didst love
    The Liberty of Man.

And had it been thy lot to live
With us who now behold the light,
Thou wouldst have nobly stirr'd thyself,
    And battled for the right.

For Robin was the poor man's stay;
The poor man's heart, the poor man's hand,
And all the oppress'd who wanted strength
    Had Robin's to command.

Bear witness many a pensive sigh
Of thoughtful Herdsman when he strays
Alone upon Loch Veol's heights,
    And by Loch Lomond's Braes.

And far and near, through vale and hill,
Are faces that attest the same;
Kindling with instantaneous joy
    At sound of Rob Roy's name.

Soon after we saw our boat coming over the calm water. It was late in the evening, and I was stiff and weary, as well I might, after such a long and toilsome walk, so it was no poor gratification to sit down and be conscious of advancing in our journey without further labour. The stars were beginning to appear, but the brightness of the west was not yet gone;—the lake perfectly still, and when we first went into the boat we rowed almost close to the shore under steep crags hung with birches: it was like a new-discovered country of which we had not dreamed, for in walking down the lake, owing to the road in that part being carried at a considerable height on the hill-side, the rocks and the indentings of the shore had been hidden from us. At this time, those rocks and their images in the calm water composed one mass, the surfaces of both equally distinct, except where the water trembled with the motion of our boat. Having rowed a while under the bold steeps, we launched out further when the shores were no longer abrupt. We hardly spoke to each other as we moved along receding from the west, which diffused a solemn animation over the lake. The sky was cloudless; and everything seemed at rest except our solitary boat, and the mountain-streams,—seldom heard, and but faintly. I think I have rarely experienced a more elevated pleasure than during our short voyage of this night. The good woman had long been looking out for us, and had prepared everything for our refreshment; and as soon as we had finished supper, or rather tea, we went to bed. William, I doubt not, rested well, and, for my part, I slept as soundly on my chaff bed as ever I have done in childhood after the long day's playing of a summer's holiday.

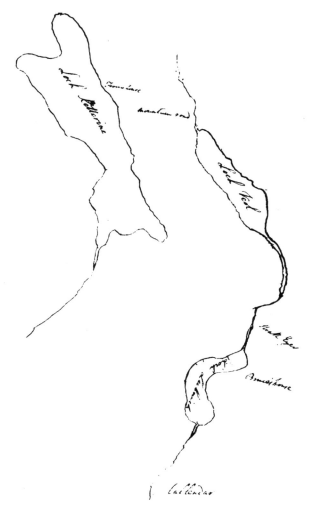

Tuesday, 13th September.—Again a fine morning. I strolled into the green field in which the house stands while the woman was preparing breakfast, and at my return found one of her neighbours sitting by the fire, a feeble paralytic old woman. After having inquired concerning our journey the day before, she said, 'I have travelled far in my time,' and told me she had married an English soldier who had been stationed at the Garrison; they had had many children, who were all dead or in foreign countries; and she had returned to her native place, where now she had lived several years, and was more comfortable than she could ever have expected to be, being very kindly dealt with by all her neighbours. Pointing to the ferryman and his wife, she said they were accustomed to give her a day of their labour in digging peats, in common with others, and in that manner she was provided with fuel, and, by like voluntary contributions, with other necessaries. While this infirm old woman was relating her story in a tremulous voice, I could not but think of the changes of things, and the days of her youth, when the shrill fife, sounding from the walls of the Garrison, made a merry noise through the echoing hills. I asked myself, if she were to be carried again to the deserted spot after her course of life, no doubt a troublesome one, would the silence appear to her the silence of desolation or of peace?

After breakfast we took a final leave of our hostess, and, attended by her husband, again set forward on foot. My limbs were a little stiff, but the morning being uncommonly fine I did not fear to aim at the accomplishment of a plan we had laid of returning to Callander by a considerable circuit. We were to go over the mountains from Loch Ketterine, a little below the ferry-house on the same side of the water, descending to Loch Voil, a lake from which issues the stream that flows through Strath Eyer into Loch Lubnaig. Our road, as is generally the case in passing from one vale into another, was through a settling between the hills, not far from a small stream. We had to climb considerably, the mountain being much higher than it appears to be, owing to its retreating in what looks like a gradual slope from the lake, though we found it steep enough in the climbing. Our guide had been born near Loch Voil, and he told us that at the head of the lake, if we would look about for it, we should see the burying-place of a part of his family, the MacGregors, a clan who had long possessed that district, a circumstance which he related with no unworthy pride of ancestry. We shook hands with him at parting, not without a hope of again entering his hut in company with others whom we loved.

Continued to walk for some time along the top of the hill, having the high mountains of Loch Voil before us, and Ben Lomond and the steeps of Loch Ketterine behind. Came to several deserted mountain huts or shiels, and rested for some time beside one of them, upon a hillock of its green plot of monumental herbage. William here conceived the notion of writing an ode upon the affecting subject of those relics of human society found in that grand and solitary region. The spot of ground where we sate was even beautiful, the grass being uncommonly verdant, and of a remarkably soft and silky texture.

After this we rested no more till we came to the foot of the mountain, where there was a cottage, at the door of which a woman invited me to drink some whey: this I did, while William went to inquire respecting the road at a new stone house a few steps further. He was told to cross the brook, and proceed to the other side of the vale, and that no further directions were necessary, for we should find ourselves at the head of the lake, and on a plain road which would lead us downward. We waded the river and crossed the vale, perhaps half a mile or more. The mountains all round are very high; the vale pastoral and unenclosed, not many dwellings, and but few trees; the mountains in general smooth near the bottom. They are in large unbroken masses, combining with the vale to give an impression of bold simplicity.

Near the head of the lake, at some distance from us, we discovered the burial-place of the MacGregors,[1] and did not view it without some interest, with its ornamental balls on the four corners of the wall, which, I daresay, have been often looked at with elevation of heart by our honest friend of Loch Ketterine. The lake is divided right across by a narrow slip of flat land, making a small lake at the head of the large one. The whole may be about five miles long.

As we descended, the scene became more fertile, our way being pleasantly varied—through coppices or open fields, and passing farm-houses, though always with an intermixture of uncultivated ground. It was harvesttime, and the fields were quietly—might I be allowed to say pensively?—enlivened by small companies of reapers. It is not uncommon in the more lonely parts of the Highlands to see a single person so employed. The following poem was suggested to William by a beautiful sentence in Thomas Wilkinson's 'Tour in Scotland:'[2]—

Behold her single in the field,
You solitary Highland Lass,
Reaping and singing by herself—
Stop here, or gently pass.
Alone she cuts and binds the grain,
And sings a melancholy strain.
Oh! listen, for the Vale profound
Is overflowing with the sound.

No nightingale did ever chaunt
So sweetly to reposing bands
Of travellers in some shady haunt
Among Arabian Sands;
No sweeter voice was ever heard
In spring-time from the cuckoo-bird
Breaking the silence of the seas
Among the farthest Hebrides.

1. Though they apparently did not know the name of the place, they were at Balquhidder, which *is* where Rob Roy is buried.
2. The sentence that suggested this poem, "The Solitary Reaper," was: "Passed a female who was reaping alone; the sweetest human voice I ever heard: her strains were tenderly melancholy, and felt delicious, long after they were heard no more," from an account of a journey in Scotland Wilkinson took in 1787. William Wordsworth saw the manuscript of Wilkinson's journal that would be published in 1824 as *Tours to the British Mountains, with the Descriptive Poems of Lowther, and Emont Vale* (London: Taylor and Hessey).

Will no one tell me what she sings?
Perhaps the plaintive numbers flow
For old unhappy far-off things,
And battles long ago;—
Or is it some more humble lay—
Familiar matter of to-day—
Some natural sorrow, loss, or pain
That has been, and may be again?

Whate'er the theme, the Maiden sung
As if her song could have no ending;
I saw her singing at her work,
And o'er the sickle bending;
I listen'd till I had my fill,
And as I mounted up the hill
The music in my heart I bore
Long after it was heard no more.

Towards the foot of the lake, on the opposite side, which was more
barren than that on which we travelled, was a bare road up a steep hill,
which leads to Glen Finlas, formerly a royal forest. It is a wild and rocky
glen, as we had been told by a person who directed our notice to its outlet
at Loch Achray. The stream which passes through it falls into that lake near
the head. At the end of Loch Voil the vale is wide and populous—large
pastures with many cattle, large tracts of corn. We walked downwards a little
way, and then crossed over to the same road along which we had travelled
from Loch Erne to Callander, being once again at the entrance of Strath
Eyer. It might be about four or five o'clock in the afternoon; we were ten
miles from Callander, exceedingly tired, and wished heartily for the poor
horse and car. Walked up Strath Eyer, and saw in clear air and sunshine
what had been concealed from us when we travelled before in the mist and
rain. We found it less woody and rich than it had appeared to be, but, with
all deductions, a very sweet valley.

Not far from Loch Lubnaig, though not in view of it, is a long village,
with two or three public-houses, and being in despair of reaching Callander
that night without over-fatigue we resolved to stop at the most respectable-
looking house, and, should it not prove wretched indeed, to lodge there if
there were beds for us: at any rate it was necessary to take some refreshment.
The woman of the house spoke with gentleness and civility, and had a good
countenance, which reconciled me to stay, though I had been averse to the
scheme, dreading the dirt usual in Scotch public-houses by the way-side.
She said she had beds for us, and clean sheets, and we desired her to prepare
them immediately. It was a two-storied house, light built, though in other
respects no better than the huts, and—as all the slated cottages are—much

more uncomfortable in appearance, except that there was a chimney in the kitchen. At such places it is fit that travellers should make up their minds to wait at least an hour longer than the time necessary to prepare whatever meal they may have ordered, which we, I may truly say, did with most temperate philosophy. I went to talk with the mistress, who was making barley cakes, which she wrought out with her hands as thin as the oaten bread we make in Cumberland. I asked her why she did not use a rolling-pin, and if it would not be much more convenient, to which she returned me no distinct answer, and seemed to give little attention to the question: she did not know, or that was what they were used to, or something of the sort. It was a tedious process, and I thought could scarcely have been managed if the cakes had been as large as ours; but they are considerably smaller, which is a great loss of time in the baking.

This woman, whose common language was the Gaelic, talked with me a very good English, asking many questions, yet without the least appearance of an obtrusive or impertinent curiosity; and indeed I must say that I never, in those women with whom I conversed, observed anything on which I could put such a construction. They seemed to have a faith ready for all; and as a child when you are telling him stories, asks for 'more, more,' so they appeared to delight in being amused without effort of their own minds. Among other questions she asked me the old one over again, if I was married; and when I told her that I was not, she appeared surprised, and, as if recollecting herself, said to me, with a pious seriousness and perfect simplicity, 'To be sure, there is a great promise for virgins in Heaven;' and then she began to tell how long she had been married, that she had had a large family and much sickness and sorrow, having lost several of her children. We had clean sheets and decent beds.

Wednesday, September 14th.—Rose early, and departed before breakfast. The morning was dry, but cold. Travelled as before, along the shores of Loch Lubnaig, and along the pass of the roaring stream of Leny, and reached Callander at a little past eight o'clock. After breakfast set off towards Stirling, intending to sleep there; the distance eighteen miles. We were now entering upon a populous and more cultivated country, having left the mountains behind, therefore I shall have little to tell; for what is most interesting in such a country is not to be seen in passing through it as we did. Half way between Callander and Stirling is the village of Doune, and a little further on we crossed a bridge over a pleasant river, the Teith. Above the river stands a ruined castle of considerable size, upon a woody bank. We wished to have had time to go up to the ruin. Long before we reached the town of Stirling, saw the Castle, single, on its stately and commanding eminence. The rock or hill rises from a level plain; the print in Stoddart's book does indeed give a good notion of its form. The surrounding plain appears to be of a rich soil, well cultivated. The crops of ripe corn were abundant. We found the town quite full; not a vacant room in the inn, it being the time of the assizes: there was no lodging for us, and hardly even the possibility of getting anything to eat in a bye-nook of the house. Walked up to the Castle. The prospect from it is very extensive, and must be exceedingly grand on a fine evening or morning, with the light of the setting or rising sun on the distant mountains, but we saw it at an unfavourable time of day, the mid-afternoon, and were not favoured by light and shade. The Forth makes most intricate and curious turnings, so that it is difficult to trace them, even when you are overlooking the whole. It flows through a perfect level, and in one place cuts its way in the form of a large figure of eight. Stirling is the largest town we had seen in Scotland, except Glasgow. It is an old irregular place; the streets towards the Castle on one side very steep. On the other, the hill or rock rises from the fields. The architecture of a part of the Castle is very fine, and the whole building in good repair: some parts indeed, are modern. At Stirling we bought Burns's Poems in one volume, for two shillings. Went on to Falkirk, ten or eleven miles. I do not recollect anything remarkable after we were out of sight of Stirling Castle, except the Carron Ironworks, seen at a distance;—the sky above them was red with a fiery light. In passing through a turnpike gate we were greeted by a Highland drover, who, with many others, was coming from a fair at Falkirk, the road being covered all along with horsemen and cattle. He spoke as if we had been well known to him, asking us how we had fared on our journey. We were at a loss to conceive why he should interest himself about us, till he said he had passed us on the Black Mountain, near King's House. It was pleasant to observe the effect of solitary places in making men friends, and to see so much kindness, which had been produced in such a chance encounter, retained in a crowd. No beds in the inns at Falkirk—every room taken up by the people come to the fair. Lodged in a private house, a neat clean place—kind treatment from the old man and his daughter.

Thursday, September 15th.—Breakfasted at Linlithgow, a small town. The house is yet shown from which the Regent Murray was shot.[1] The remains of a royal palace, where Queen Mary was born,[2] are of considerable extent; the banks of gardens and fish-ponds may yet be distinctly traced, though the whole surface is transformed into smooth pasturage where cattle graze. The

1. James Stuart (c.1531–70), Earl of Murray, regent of Scotland, the illegitimate son of James V of Scotland, was murdered—shot by Hamilton of Bothwellhaugh from a window as he rode through Linlithgow on 21 January 1570, headed to a trial in Edinburgh.
2. Mary, Queen of Scots, who was the half-sister of Regent Murray, was born in Linlithgow Palace on 8 December 1542. The palace, some seventeen miles west of Edinburgh, was extensively ruined in 1746 by a fire accidentally caused by one of the soldiers garrisoned there after the 1745 Jacobite uprising.

castle stands upon a gentle eminence, the prospect not particularly pleasing, though not otherwise; it is bare and wide. The shell of a small ancient church is standing, into which are crammed modern pews, galleries, and pulpit—very ugly, and discordant with the exterior. Nothing very interesting till we came to Edinburgh. Dined by the way at a small town or village upon a hill, the back part of the houses on one side overlooking an extensive prospect over flat corn fields. I mention this for the sake of a pleasant hour we passed sitting on the bank, where we read some of Burns's poems in the volume which we had bought at Stirling.

Arrived at Edinburgh a little before sunset. As we approached, the Castle rock resembled that of Stirling—in the same manner appearing to rise from a plan of cultivated ground, the Firth of Forth being on the other side, and not visible. Drove to the White Hart in the Grassmarket, an inn which had been mentioned to us, and which we conjectured would better suit us than one in a more fashionable part of the town. It was not noisy, and tolerably cheap. Drank tea, and walked up to the Castle, which luckily was very near. Much of the daylight was gone, so that except it had been a clear evening, which it was not, we could not have seen the distant prospect.

Friday, September 16th.—The sky the evening before, as you may remember the ostler told us, had been 'gay and dull,' and this morning it was downright dismal: very dark, and promising nothing but a wet day, and before breakfast was over the rain began, though not heavily. We set out upon our walk, and went through many streets to Holyrood House, and thence to the hill called Arthur's Seat, a high hill, very rocky at the top, and below covered with smooth turf, on which sheep were feeding. We climbed up till we came to St. Anthony's Well and Chapel, as it is called, but it is more like a hermitage than a chapel,—a small ruin, which from its situation is exceedingly interesting, though in itself not remarkable. We sate down on a stone not far from the chapel, overlooking a pastoral hollow as wild and solitary as any in the heart of the Highland mountains: there, instead of the roaring of torrents, we listened to the noises of the city, which were blended in one loud indistinct buzz,—a regular sound in the air, which in certain moods of feeling, and at certain times, might have a more tranquillizing effect upon the mind than those which we are accustomed to hear in such places. The Castle rock looked exceedingly large through the misty air: a cloud of black smoke overhung the city, which combined with the rain and mist to conceal the shapes of the houses,—an obscurity which added much to the grandeur of the sound that proceeded from it. It was impossible to think of anything that was little or mean, the goings-on of trade, the strife of men, or every-day city business:—the impression was one, and it was visionary; like the conceptions of our childhood of Bagdad or Balsora when we have been reading the Arabian Nights' Entertainments. Though the rain was very heavy we remained upon the hill for some time, then returned by the same road by which we had come, through green flat fields, formerly the pleasure-grounds of Holyrood House, on the edge of which stands the old roofless chapel, of venerable architecture. It is a pity that it should be suffered to fall down, for the walls appear to be yet entire. Very near to the chapel is Holyrood House, which we could not but lament has nothing ancient in its appearance, being sash-windowed and not an irregular pile. It is very like a building for some national establishment,—a hospital for soldiers or sailors. You have a description of it in Stoddart's Tour,[1] therefore I need not tell you what we saw there.

When we found ourselves once again in the streets of the city, we lamented over the heavy rain, and indeed before leaving the hill, much as we were indebted to the accident of the rain for the peculiar grandeur and affecting wildness of those objects we saw, we could not but regret that the Firth of Forth was entirely hidden from us, and all distant objects, and we strained our eyes till they ached, vainly trying to pierce through the thick mist. We walked industriously through the streets, street after street, and, in spite of wet and dirt, were exceedingly delighted. The old town, with its irregular houses, stage above stage, seen as we saw it, in the obscurity of a rainy day, hardly resembles the work of men, it is more like a piling up of rocks, and I cannot attempt to describe what we saw so imperfectly, but must say that, high as my expectations had been raised, the city of Edinburgh far surpassed all expectation. Gladly would we have stayed another day, but could not afford more time, and our notions of the weather of Scotland were so dismal, notwithstanding we ourselves had been so much favoured, that we had no hope of its mending. So at about six o'clock in the evening we departed, intending to sleep at an inn in the village of Roslin,

1. Stoddart wrote: "Holy Rood House is named, from the abbey above mentioned ['Sanctae Crucis, the Holy *Rood* or Cross'] which was erected by David I. A.D. 1128, and converted into a royal palace by James V. in 1528, but not completed until 1664, in the reign of Charles II. by the celebrated Scotch architect Sir William Bruce. When I first saw it, the gloomy majesty, which it still retains, was somewhat enlivened, by the presence of Monsieur and his suite. The inhabitants of Edinburgh showed every respect to their noble visitor, who, on his part, repaid their attentions by every means in his power; but his unfortunate situation allowed only a diminished splendour; and at his departure, the Abbey (for so it is still called) relapsed into its former dreariness and desertion.

The private apartments, appropriated to some of the nobility, contain some good paintings; but very little of what is shown is either grand, or beautiful. The small chamber from which Rizzio was dragged, in the presence of Queen Mary, to assassination, is, like all that part of the palace, exceedingly wretched and desolate. The two portraits of that interesting woman are execrable daubs, without beauty or expression, and totally unlike each other. The gallery of one hundred and eleven monarchs, is a spurious collection of pictures without merit; and, in short, the only thing here deserving attention is the ruinous chapel. This latter was a part of the ancient abbey, and was built in the light and elegant Gothic architecture of the fifteenth century; it is now roofless, but loses much of its picturesque effect, by being closely attached to so regular and formal an edifice as the palace" (*Remarks*, I pp. 76–7).

Fifth Week
11–17 September

156. Loch Venachar. ("Loch Vennachar.")
"We went up a broad vale . . . and came to Loch Vennachar . . ." (p. 180)

157. Loch Achray. Near Callander Kirk, Trossachs.
"...coasted the head of Loch Achray..." (p. 180)

158. Glen Falloch. ("Glenfalloch.") Inverarnan Inn. Rear entrance.
"The view from the door of the public-house is exceedingly beautiful..." (p. 185)

159. Glen Falloch. ("Glenfalloch.") Flowing river.
". . . the river flows smoothly into the lake . . ." (p. 185)

160. Glen Falloch. ("Glenfalloch.") Beienglas Farm and "steep mountain" across from inn.
"After a short rest in cool parlour we set forward again, having to cross the river and climb
up a steep mountain on the opposite side of the valley." (p. 185)

161. Portnellan, on Loch Katrine. MacGregor burial place mistaken by William for Rob Roy's grave site.

"... the burying-ground that stood so sweetly near the water-side." (p. 187)

162. Balquidder. Burial place of the MacGregors.

"Near the head of the lake [Voil], at some distance from us, we discovered the burial-place of the MacGregors ..." (p. 193)

163. Balquidder. Grave site of MacGregors.

"... and did not view it without some interest, with its ornamental balls on the four corners of the wall ..." (p. 193)

164. Loch Voil. Near Balquidder.
"The whole may be about five miles long." (p. 193)
"As we descended, the scene became more fertile, our way being pleasantly varied . . . It
was harvest-time, and the fields were quietly—might I be allowed to say pensively?—
enlivened by small companies of reapers. It is not uncommon . . . to see a single person so
employed." (p. 193)

165. Balquhidder Glen. The solitary reaper.

Behold her single in the field,
Yon solitary Highland Lass,
Reaping and singing by herself—
(William Wordsworth, p. 193)

166. Callander.
"Rose early, and departed before breakfast. The morning was dry, but cold. Travelled as before, along the shores of Loch Lubnaig, and along the pass of the roaring stream of Leny, and reached Callander at a little past eight o'clock." (p. 195)

167. Doune Castle.
"Above the river stands a ruined castle of considerable size, upon a woody bank: We wished to have had time to go up to the ruin." (p. 195)

168. Stirling. Stirling Castle.
". . . saw the Castle, single, on its stately and commanding eminence. The rock or hill rises from a level plain . . . The surrounding plain appears to be of a rich soil . . ." (p. 195)

169. Stirling. Town, seen from the Castle.
"Stirling is the largest town we had seen in Scotland, except Glasgow." (p. 196)

170. Stirling. Winding street.
   "It is an old irregular place; the streets towards the Castle on one side very steep." (p. 196)

171. Stirling. Bookstore near Castle.
   "At Stirling we bought Burns's Poems in one volume, for two shillings." (p. 196)

172. Linlithgow. Palace. ("Castle.")
"The castle stands upon a gentle eminence . . ." (pp. 196–97)

173. Edinburgh. Grassmarket. The White Hart Inn.
"Arrived at Edinburgh a little before sunset . . . Drove to the White Hart in the
Grassmarket, an inn which had been mentioned to us, and which we conjectured would
better suit us than one in a more fashionable part of the town." (p. 197)

174. Edinburgh. Edinburgh Castle.
"Drank tea, and walked up to the Castle, which luckily was very near." (p. 197)

175. Edinburgh. Holyrood House.
". . . this morning it was downright dismal: very dark, and promising nothing but a wet day, and before breakfast was over the rain began, though not heavily. We set out upon our walk, and went through many streets to Holyrood House . . ." (p. 197)

176. Edinburgh. Arthur's Seat.
"... and thence to the hill called Arthur's Seat, a high hill, very rocky at the top ..."
(p. 197)

177. Edinburgh. St. Anthony's Well and Chapel, on Arthur's Seat.
"We climbed up till we came to St. Anthony's Well and Chapel, as it is called, but it is more like a hermitage than a chapel—a small ruin ..."
(p. 197)

178. Edinburgh. View from ruin on Arthur's Seat.
"We sate down on a stone not far from the chapel, overlooking a pastoral hollow as wild and solitary as any in the heart of the Highland mountains ..." (p. 197)

179. Edinburgh. Roofless chapel at Holyrood House.
   "[We] returned by the same road by which we had come, through green flat fields, formerly the pleasure-grounds of Holyrood House, on the edge of which stands the old roofless chapel, of venerable architecture." (p. 198)

180. Edinburgh. Street Scene.
   "The old town, with its irregular houses, stage above stage, seen as we saw it, in the obscurity of a rainy day, hardly resembles the work of men . . . and I cannot attempt to describe what we saw so imperfectly, but must say that, high as my expectations had been raised, the city of Edinburgh far surpassed all expectation." (p. 198)

181. Roslin. Rosslyn Castle. ("Roslin Castle.")
"Roslin Castle stands upon a woody bank . . . We looked down upon the ruin from higher
ground." (p. 199)

182. Roslin. Rosslyn Chapel.
"Near it stands the Chapel, a most elegant building, a ruin, though the walls and roof are
entire." (p. 199)

183. Rosslyn Glen.
"I never passed through a more delicious dell than the glen of Roslin . . ." (p. 199)

184. Rosslyn Glen. Hawthornden, Drummond's house.
"About a mile from the Castle, on the contrary side of the water, upon the edge of a very steep bank, stands Hawthornden, the house of Drummond the poet, whither Ben Jonson came on foot from London to visit his friend." (p. 199)

185. Lasswade. Scott's cottage.
". . . and waited some time in a large sitting-room. Breakfasted with them . . ." (p. 199)

186. Roslin. The Old Rosslyn Inn.
  "We ordered dinner on our return to the inn . . ."
  (p. 200)
    The building adjoins the grounds of Rosslyn Chapel. In addition to the Wordsworths, Boswell, Johnson, Burns and Scott also "tarried awhile" (as the commemorative plaque puts it) at this inn. The date over the lintel is 1660.

187. Roslin. Detail on Rosslyn Chapel.
  "The stone both of the roof and walls is sculptured with leaves and flowers . . ." (p. 200)

about five miles from Edinburgh. The rain continued till we were almost at Roslin; but then it was quite dark, so we did not see the Castle that night.

Saturday, September 17th.—The morning very fine. We rose early and walked through the glen of Roslin, past Hawthornden, and considerably further, to the house of Mr. Walter Scott at Lasswade. Roslin Castle stands upon a woody bank above a stream, the North Esk, too large, I think, to be called a brook, yet an inconsiderable river. We looked down upon the ruin from higher ground. Near it stands the Chapel, a most elegant building, a ruin, though the walls and roof are entire. I never passed through a more delicious dell than the glen of Roslin, though the water of the stream is dingy and muddy. The banks are rocky on each side, and hung with pine wood. About a mile from the Castle, on the contrary side of the water, upon the edge of a very steep bank, stands Hawthornden, the house of Drummond the poet, whither Ben Jonson came on foot from London to visit his friend.[1] We did hear to whom the house at present belongs, and some other particulars, but I have a very indistinct recollection of what was told us, except that many old trees had been lately cut down. After Hawthornden the glen widens, ceases to be rocky, and spreads out into a rich vale, scattered over with gentlemen's seats.

Arrived at Lasswade before Mr. and Mrs. Scott had risen, and waited some time in a large sitting-room. Breakfasted with them,[2] and stayed till two o'clock, and Mr. Scott accompanied us back almost to Roslin, having given us directions respecting our future journey, and promised to meet us at Melrose two days after.

1. The Scottish poet William Drummond (1585–1649) was born at Hawthornden and upon his father's death became laird of Hawthornden. Well educated and well read Drummond claimed among his literary friends the poet Michael Drayton and the dramatist Ben Jonson.' In August 1618 the middle-aged Jonson walked from London to Edinburgh for the express purpose, according to early biographers, of meeting Drummond. They did indeed meet in Edinburgh, and Jonson visited Drummond at Hawthornden at Christmas for two weeks or more. Dorothy Wordsworth writes in her journal for 11 February 1802 that she read Thomas Fuller's *Life of Ben Jonson* (1662), to William.

2. John Gibson Lockhart, Scott's son-in-law and biographer, gave this account of the meeting between the Wordsworths and the Scotts: "On the morning of the 17th of September, having left their carriage at Roslin, they walked down the valley to Lasswade, and arrived there before Mr. and Mrs. Scott had risen. 'We were received,' Mr. Wordsworth has told me, 'with that frank cordiality which; under whatever circumstances I afterwards met him, always marked his manners; and, indeed, I found him then in every respect—except, perhaps, that his animal spirits were somewhat higher—precisely the same man that you knew him in later life; the same lively, entertaining conversation, full of anecdote, and averse from disquisition; the same unaffected modesty about himself; the same cheerful and benevolent and hopeful views of man and the world. He partly read and partly recited, sometimes in an enthusiastic style of chant, the first four cantos of the Lay of the Last Minstrel; and the novelty of the manners, the clear picturesque descriptions, and the easy glowing energy of much of the verse, greatly delighted me" (*Narrative of the Life of Sir Walter Scott, Bart, Begun by Himself and Continued by J.G. Lockhart*. London: J.M. Dent & Sons Ltd, 1931, pp. 116–17).

We ordered dinner on our return to the inn, and went to view the inside of the Chapel of Roslin, which is kept locked up, and so preserved from the injuries it might otherwise receive from idle boys; but as nothing is done to keep it together, it must in the end fall. The architecture within is exquisitely beautiful. The stone both of the roof and walls is sculptured with leaves and flowers, so delicately wrought that I could have admired them for hours, and the whole of their groundwork is stained by time with the softest colours. Some of those leaves and flowers were tinged perfectly green, and at one part the effect was most exquisite: three or four leaves of a small fern, resembling that which we call adder's tongue, grew round a cluster of them at the top of a pillar, and the natural product and the artificial were so intermingled that at first it was not easy to distinguish the living plant from the other, they being of an equally determined green, though the fern was of a deeper shade.

We set forward again after dinner. The afternoon was pleasant. Travelled through large tracts of ripe corn, interspersed with larger tracts of moorland—the houses at a considerable distance from each other, no longer thatched huts, but farm-houses resembling those of the farming counties in England, having many corn-stacks close to them. Dark when we reached Peebles; found a comfortable old-fashioned public-house, had a neat parlour, and drank tea.

SIXTH WEEK

Sunday, September 18th.—The town of Peebles is on the banks of the Tweed. After breakfast walked up the river to Neidpath Castle, about a mile and a half from the town. The castle stands upon a green hill, overlooking the Tweed, a strong square-towered edifice, neglected and desolate, though not in ruin, the garden overgrown with grass, and the high walls that fenced it broken down. The Tweed winds between green steeps, upon which, and close to the river side, large flocks of sheep pasturing; higher still are the grey mountains; but I need not describe the scene, for William has done it better than I could do in a sonnet which he wrote the same day;[1] the five last lines, at least, of his poem will impart to you more of the feeling of the place than it would be possible for me to do:—

> Degenerate Douglass! thou unworthy Lord
> Whom mere despite of heart could so far please,
> And love of havoc (for with such disease
> Fame taxes him) that he could send forth word
> To level with the dust a noble horde,
> A brotherhood of venerable trees,
> Leaving an ancient Dome and Towers like these
> Beggar'd and outraged! Many hearts deplored
> The fate of those old trees; and oft with pain
> The Traveller at this day will stop and gaze
> On wrongs which Nature scarcely seems to heed;
> For shelter'd places, bosoms, nooks, and bays,
> And the pure mountains, and the gentle Tweed,
> And the green silent pastures yet remain.

I was spared any regret for the fallen woods when we were there, not then knowing the history of them. The soft low mountains, the castle, and the decayed pleasure-grounds, the scattered trees which have been left in different parts, and the road carried in a very beautiful line along the side of the hill, with the Tweed murmuring through the unfenced green pastures spotted with sheep, together composed an harmonious scene, and I wished for nothing that was not there. When we were with Mr. Scott he spoke of

---

1. "Sonnet, Composed at——Castle" (Neidpath Castle) targets William Douglas, 4th Duke of Queensberry (1725–1810). Old "Q," as he was known, was notorious for his gambling debts (hence "degenerate"). Wordsworth deplored his wanton act in cutting down the ancient trees around the castle.

cheerful days he had spent in that castle not many years ago, when it was inhabited by Professor Ferguson and his family, whom the Duke of Queensberry, its churlish owner, forced to quit it. We discovered a very fine echo within a few yards of the building.

The town of Peebles looks very pretty from the road in returning: it is an old town, built of grey stone, the same as the castle. Well-dressed people were going to church. Sent the car before, and walked ourselves, and while going along the main street William was called aside in a mysterious manner by a person who gravely examined him—whether he was an Irishman or a foreigner, or what he was; I suppose our car was the occasion of suspicion at a time when every one was talking of the threatened invasion.[1] We had a day's journey before us along the banks of the Tweed, a name which has been sweet to my ears almost as far back as I can remember anything. After the first mile or two our road was seldom far from the river, which flowed in gentleness, though perhaps never silent; the hills on either side high and sometimes stony, but excellent pasturage for sheep. In some parts the vale was wholly of this pastoral character, in others we saw extensive tracts of corn ground, even spreading along whole hill-sides, and without visible fences, which is dreary in a flat country; but there is no dreariness on the banks of the Tweed,—the hills, whether smooth or stony, uncultivated or covered with ripe corn, had the same pensive softness. Near the corn tracts were large farm-houses, with many corn-stacks; the stacks and house and out-houses together, I recollect, in one or two places upon the hills, at a little distance, seemed almost as large as a small village or hamlet. It was a clear autumnal day, without wind, and, being Sunday, the business of the harvest was suspended, and all that we saw, and felt, and heard, combined to excite one sensation of pensive and still pleasure.

Passed by several old halls yet inhabited, and others in ruin; but I have hardly a sufficiently distinct recollection of any of them to be able to describe them, and I now at this distance of time regret that I did not take notes. In one very sweet part of the vale a gate crossed the road, which was opened by an old woman who lived in a cottage close to it; I said to her, 'You live in a very pretty place!' 'Yes,' she replied, 'the water of Tweed is a bonny water.' The lines of the hills are flowing and beautiful, the reaches of the vale long; in some places appear the remains of a forest, in others you will see as lovely a combination of forms as any traveller who goes in search of the picturesque[2] need desire, and yet perhaps without a single tree; or at

1. The reference here is to an Irish-supported French invasion of Britain. (See p. 10.)
2. For an excellent discussion of the picturesque and Dorothy Wordsworth's awareness of it see: John R. Nabholtz's "Dorothy Wordsworth and the Picturesque" in *Studies in Romanticism*, III 2, Winter 1964. Nabholtz notes similarities between Dorothy's responses to Scottish landscapes and those of William Gilpin and suggests that her sensitivity to the absence of trees in some settings corresponds to aesthetic values articulated by Uvedale Price in his *Essay on the Picturesque*, 1794.

least if trees there are, they shall be very few, and he shall not care whether they are there or not.

The road took us through one long village, but I do not recollect any other; yet I think we never had a mile's length before us without a house, though seldom several cottages together. The loneliness of the scattered dwellings, the more stately edifices decaying or in ruin, or, if inhabited, not in their pride and freshness, aided the general effect of the gently varying scenes, which was that of tender pensiveness; no bursting torrents when we were there, but the murmuring of the river was heard distinctly, often blended with the bleating of sheep. In one place we saw a shepherd lying in the midst of a flock upon a sunny knoll, with his face towards the sky,— happy picture of shepherd life.

The transitions of this vale were all gentle except one, a scene of which a gentleman's house was the centre, standing low in the vale, the hills above it covered with gloomy fir plantations, and the appearance of the house itself, though it could scarcely be seen, was gloomy. There was an allegorical air—a person fond of Spenser will understand me[1]—in this uncheerful spot, single in such a country,

> The house is hears'd about with a black wood.

We have since heard that it was the residence of Lord Traquair, a Roman Catholic nobleman, of a decayed family.

We left the Tweed when we were within about a mile and a half or two miles of Clovenford, where we were to lodge. Turned up the side of a hill, and went along sheep-grounds till we reached the spot—a single stone house, without a tree near it or to be seen from it. On our mentioning Mr. Scott's name the woman of the house showed us all possible civility, but her slowness was really amusing. I should suppose it is a house little frequented, for there is no appearance of an inn. Mr. Scott, who she told me was a very clever gentlemen, 'goes there in the fishing season;' but indeed Mr. Scott is

---

1. The line she quotes to illustrate her sense of "an allegorical air" is not from Spenser but Richard Crashaw (?1612–49), "Sospetto d' Herode," (Herod's Suspicion) in *Steps to the Temple, with Other Delights of the Muses,* 1646. The setting of the stanza from which the line comes is far more grisly than the "uncheerful spot" Dorothy is responding to:

> The house is hears'd about with a black wood,
> Which nods with many a heavy headed tree.
> Each flowers a pregnant poyson, try'd and good,
> Each herbe a Plague. The winds sighes timed-bee
> By a black Fount, which weeps into a flood.
> Through the thick shades obscurely might you see
> Minotaures, Cyclopses, with a darke drove
> Of Dragons, Hydraes, Sphinxes, fill the Grove.

The poem is from Crashaw's translation of an Italian work, *Slaughter of the Innocents,* by Giambattista Marino (1569–1625).

respected everywhere: I believe that by favour of his name one might be hospitably entertained throughout all the borders of Scotland. We dined and drank tea—did not walk out, for there was no temptation; a confined barren prospect from the window.

At Clovenford, being so near to the Yarrow, we could not but think of the possibility of going thither, but came to the conclusion of reserving the pleasure for some future time, in consequence of which, after our return, William wrote the poem which I shall here transcribe:[1]—

> From Stirling Castle we had seen
> The mazy Forth unravell'd,
> Had trod the banks of Clyde and Tay,
> And with the Tweed had travell'd.
> And when we came to Clovenford,
> Then said my winsome Marrow,
> 'Whate'er betide we'll turn aside
> And see the Braes of Yarrow.'
>
> 'Let Yarrow Folk frae Selkirk Town,
> Who have been buying, selling,
> Go back to Yarrow:—'tis their own,
> Each Maiden to her dwelling.
> On Yarrow's banks let herons feed,
> Hares couch, and rabbits burrow,
> But we will downwards with the Tweed,
> Nor turn aside to Yarrow.
>
> 'There's Gala Water, Leader Haughs,
> Both lying right before us;
> And Dryburgh, where with chiming Tweed
> The lintwhites sing in chorus.
> There's pleasant Teviot Dale, a land
> Made blithe with plough and harrow.
> Why throw away a needful day,
> To go in search of Yarrow?
>
> 'What's Yarrow but a river bare,
> That glides the dark hills under?
> There are a thousand such elsewhere,
> As worthy of your wonder.'
> Strange words they seem'd of slight and scorn,
> My true-love sigh'd for sorrow,

1. The poem is "Yarrow Unvisited." On two subsequent journeys to Scotland William visited Yarrow and wrote "Yarrow Visited, September, 1814" and "Yarrow Revisited," in September or October 1831. James Hogg, the Ettrick Poet, accompanied Wordsworth on the first visit, Scott on the second.

And look'd me in the face to think
I thus could speak of Yarrow.

'Oh! green,' said I, 'are Yarrow's Holms,
And sweet is Yarrow flowing,
Fair hangs the apple frae the rock,
But we will leave it growing.
O'er hilly path and open Strath
We'll wander Scotland thorough,
But though so near we will not turn
Into the Dale of Yarrow.

'Let beeves and home-bred kine partake
The sweets of Burnmill Meadow,
The swan on still St. Mary's Lake
Float double, swan and shadow.
We will not see them, will not go,
To-day nor yet to-morrow;
Enough if in our hearts we know
There's such a place as Yarrow.

'Be Yarrow stream unseen, unknown,
It must, or we shall rue it,
We have a vision of our own,
Ah! why should we undo it?
The treasured dreams of times long past,
We'll keep them, "winsome Marrow,"
For when we're there, although 'tis fair,
'Twill be another Yarrow.

'If care with freezing years should come,
And wandering seem but folly,
Should we be loth to stir from home,
And yet be melancholy,
Should life be dull and spirits low,
'Twill soothe us in our sorrow
That earth has something yet to show—
The bonny Holms of Yarrow.'

The next day we were to meet Mr. Scott, and again join the Tweed. I
wish I could have given you a better idea of what we saw between Peebles
and this place. I have most distinct recollections of the effect of the whole
day's journey; but the objects are mostly melted together in my memory,
and though I should recognise them if we revisit the place, I cannot call
them out so as to represent them to you with distinctness. William, in
attempting in verse to describe this part of the Tweed, says of it,

> More pensive in sunshine
> Than others in moonshine.

which perhaps may give you more power to conceive what it is than all I
have said.

Monday, September 19th.—We rose early, and went to Melrose, six miles,
before breakfast. After ascending a hill, descended, and overlooked a dell, on
the opposite side of which was an old mansion, surrounded with trees and
steep gardens, a curious and pleasing, yet melancholy spot; for the house and
gardens were evidently going to decay, and the whole of the small dell,
except near the house, was unenclosed and uncultivated, being a sheep-walk
to the top of the hills. Descended to Gala Water, a pretty stream, but much
smaller than the Tweed, into which the brook flows from the glen I have
spoken of. Near the Gala is a large modern house, the situation very
pleasant, but the old building which we had passed put to shame the fresh
colouring and meagre outline of the new one. Went through a part of the
village of Galashiels, pleasantly situated on the bank of the stream; a pretty
place it once has been, but a manufactory is established there; and a townish
bustle and ugly stone houses are fast taking place of the brown-roofed
thatched cottages, of which a great number yet remain, partly overshadowed
by trees. Left the Gala, and, after crossing the open country, came again to
the Tweed, and pursued our way as before near the river, perhaps for a mile
or two, till we arrived at Melrose. The valley for this short space was not so
pleasing as before, the hills more broken, and though the cultivation was
general, yet the scene was not rich, while it had lost its pastoral simplicity.
At Melrose the vale opens out wide; but the hills are high all round—single
distinct risings. After breakfast we went out, intending to go to the Abbey,
and in the street met Mr. Scott, who gave us a cordial greeting, and
conducted us thither himself. He was here on his own ground, for he is
familiar with all that is known of the authentic history of Melrose and the
popular tales connected with it. He pointed out many pieces of beautiful
sculpture in obscure corners which would have escaped our notice. The
Abbey has been built of a pale red stone; that part which was first erected
of a very durable kind, the sculptured flowers and leaves and other minute
ornaments being as perfect in many places as when first wrought. The ruin
is of considerable extent, but unfortunately it is almost surrounded by
insignificant houses, so that when you are close to it you see it entirely
separated from many rural objects, and even when viewed from a distance
the situation does not seem to be particularly happy, for the vale is broken
and disturbed, and the Abbey at a distance from the river, so that you do not
look upon them as companions of each other. And surely this is a national
barbarism: within these beautiful walls is the ugliest church that was ever

beheld—if it had been hewn out of the side of a hill it could not have been more dismal; there was no neatness, nor even decency, and it appeared to be so damp, and so completely excluded from fresh air, that it must be dangerous to sit in it; the floor is unpaved, and very rough. What a contrast to the beautiful and graceful order apparent in every part of the ancient design and workmanship! Mr. Scott went with us into the gardens and orchards of a Mr. Riddel, from which we had a very sweet view of the Abbey through trees, the town being entirely excluded. Dined with Mr. Scott at the inn; he was now travelling to the assizes at Jedburgh in his character of Sheriff of Selkirk, and on that account, as well as for his own sake, he was treated with great respect, a small part of which was vouchsafed to us as his friends, though I could not persuade the woman to show me the beds, or to make any sort of promise till she was assured from the Sheriff himself that he had no objection to sleep in the same room with William.

Tuesday, September 20th.—Mr. Scott departed very early for Jedburgh, and we soon followed, intending to go by Dryburgh to Kelso. It was a fine morning. We went without breakfast, being told that there was a public-house at Dryburgh. The road was very pleasant, seldom out of sight of the Tweed for any length of time, though not often close to it. The valley is not so pleasantly defined as between Peebles and Clovenford, yet so soft and beautiful, and in many parts pastoral, but that peculiar and pensive simplicity which I have spoken of before was wanting, yet there was a fertility chequered with wildness which to many travellers would be more than a compensation. The reaches of the vale were shorter, the turnings more rapid, the banks often clothed with wood. In one place was a lofty scar, at another a green promontory, a small hill skirted by the river, the hill above irregular and green, and scattered over with trees. We wished we could have brought the ruins of Melrose to that spot, and mentioned this to Mr. Scott, who told us that the monks had first fixed their abode there, and raised a temporary building of wood. The monastery of Melrose was founded by a colony from Rievaux Abbey in Yorkshire, which building it happens to resemble in the colour of the stone, and I think partly in the style of architecture, but is much smaller, that is, has been much smaller, for there is not at Rievaux any one single part of the ruin so large as the remains of the church at Melrose, though at Rievaux a far more extensive ruin remains. It is also much grander, and the situation at present much more beautiful, that ruin not having suffered like Melrose Abbey from the encroachments of a town. The architecture at Melrose is, I believe, superior in the exactness and taste of some of the minute ornamental parts; indeed, it is impossible to conceive anything more delicate than the workmanship, especially in the imitations of flowers.

We descended to Dryburgh after having gone a considerable way upon high ground. A heavy rain when we reached the village, and there was no public-house. A well-dressed, well-spoken woman courteously—shall I say charitably?—invited us into her cottage, and permitted us to make breakfast; she showed us into a neat parlour, furnished with prints, a mahogany table, and other things which I was surprised to see, for her husband was only a day-labourer, but she had been Lady Buchan's waiting-maid, which accounted for these luxuries and for a noticeable urbanity in her manners. All the cottages in this neighbourhood, if I am not mistaken, were covered with red tiles, and had chimneys. After breakfast we set out in the rain to the ruins of Dryburgh Abbey, which are near Lord Buchan's house, and, like Bothwell Castle, appropriated to the pleasure of the owner. We rang a bell at the gate, and, instead of a porter, an old woman came to open it through a narrow side-alley cut in a thick plantation of evergreens. On entering, saw the thatch of her hut just above the trees, and it looked very pretty, but the poor creature herself was a figure to frighten a child,—bowed almost double, having a hooked nose and overhanging eyebrows, a complexion stained brown with smoke, and a cap that might have been worn for months and never washed. No doubt she had been cowering over her peat fire, for if she had emitted smoke by her breath and through every pore, the odour could not have been stronger. This ancient woman, by right of office, attended us to show off the curiosities, and she had her tale as perfect, though it was not quite so long a one, as the gentleman Swiss, whom I remember to have seen at Blenheim with his slender wand and dainty white clothes. The house of Lord Buchan and the Abbey stand upon a large flat peninsula, a green holm almost covered with fruit-trees. The ruins of Dryburgh are much less extensive than those of Melrose, and greatly inferior both in the architecture and stone, which is much mouldered away. Lord Buchan has trained pear-trees along the walls, which are bordered with flowers and gravel walks, and he has made a pigeon-house, and a fine room in the ruin, ornamented with a curiously-assorted collection of busts of eminent men, in which lately a ball was given; yet, deducting for all these improvements, which are certainly much less offensive than you could imagine, it is a very sweet ruin, standing so enclosed in wood, which the towers overtop, that you cannot know that it is not in a state of natural desolation till you are close to it. The opposite bank of the Tweed is steep and woody, but unfortunately many of the trees are firs. The old woman followed us after the fashion of other guides, but being slower of foot than a younger person, it was not difficult to slip away from the scent of her poor smoke-dried body. She was sedulous in pointing out the curiosities, which, I doubt not, she had a firm belief were not to be surpassed in England or Scotland.

Having promised us a sight of the largest and oldest yew-tree ever seen, she conducted us to it; it was a goodly tree, but a mere dwarf compared with several of our own country—not to speak of the giant of Lorton.[1] We returned to the cottage, and waited some time in hopes that the rain would abate, but it grew worse and worse, and we were obliged to give up our journey to Kelso, taking the direct road to Jedburgh.

We had to ford the Tweed, a wide river at the crossing-place. It would have been impossible to drive the horse through, for he had not forgotten the fright at Connel Ferry, so we hired a man to lead us. After crossing the water, the road goes up the bank, and we had a beautiful view of the ruins of the Abbey, peering above the trees of the woody peninsula, which, in shape, resembles that formed by the Tees at Lickburn, but is considerably smaller. Lord Buchan's house is a very neat, modest building, and almost hidden by trees. It soon began to rain heavily. Crossing the Teviot by a stone bridge—the vale in that part very wide—there was a great deal of ripe corn, but a want of trees, and no appearance of richness. Arrived at Jedburgh half an hour before the Judges were expected out of Court to dinner.

We gave in our passport—the name of Mr. Scott, the Sheriff—and were very civilly treated, but there was no vacant room in the house except the Judge's sitting-room, and we wanted to have a fire, being exceedingly wet and cold. I was conducted into that room, on condition that I would give it up the moment the Judge came from Court. After I had put off my wet clothes I went up into a bed-room, and sate shivering there, till the people of the inn had procured lodgings for us in a private house.

We were received with hearty welcome by a good woman, who, though above seventy years old,[2] moved about as briskly as if she was only seventeen. Those parts of the house which we were to occupy were neat and clean; she showed me every corner, and, before I had been ten minutes in the house, opened her very drawers that I might see what a stock of linen she had; then asked me how long we should stay, and said she wished we were come for three months. She was a most remarkable person; the alacrity with which she ran up-stairs when we rung the bell, and guessed at, and strove to prevent, our wants was surprising; she had a quick eye, and keen strong features, and a joyousness in her motions, like what used to be in old Molly[3] when she was particularly elated. I found afterwards that she had been subject to fits of dejection and ill-health: we then conjectured that her

1. Dorothy and William took a short excursion in the Irish jaunting car in the fall of 1804 (see Mark Reed, *Wordsworth: The Chronology of the Middle Years, 1800–1815*. Cambridge, Mass.: Harvard University Press, 1975, p. 271) which included a drive to Lorton Vale, near Cockermouth, where William was born. Here they saw a large solitary yew tree, described by William in his poem "Yew-Trees" as the "pride of Lorton Vale" and "Of vast circumference and gloom profound."
2. The "good woman" was called Nellie Mitchell.
3. Mary (Molly) Fisher, a servant in the Wordsworth household, lived in a house across the road from Dove Cottage with her brother and his wife.

overflowing gaiety and strength might in part be attributed to the same cause
as her former dejection. Her husband was deaf and infirm, and state in a
chair with scarcely the power to move a limb—and affecting contrast! The
old woman said they had been a very hard-working pair; they had wrought
like slaves at their trade—her husband had been a currier; and she told me
how they had portioned off their daughters with money, and each a feather-
bed, and that in their old age they had laid out the little they could spare in
building and furnishing that house, and she added with pride that she had
lived in her youth in the family of Lady Egerton, who was no high lady, and
now was in the habit of coming to her house whenever she was at Jedburgh,
and a hundred other things; for when she once began with Lady Egerton,
she did not know how to stop, nor did I wish it, for she was very
entertaining. Mr. Scott sate with us an hour or two, and repeated a part of
the Lay of the Last Minstrel. When he was gone our hostess came to see if
we wanted anything, and to wish us good-night. On all occasions her
manners were governed by the same spirit: there was no withdrawing one's
attention from her. We were so much interested that William, long afterwards, thought it worth while to express in verse[1] the sensations which she
had excited, and which then remained as vividly in his mind as at the
moment when we lost sight of Jedburgh:—

> Age! twine thy brows with fresh spring flowers,
> And call a train of laughing Hours;
> And bid them dance, and bid them sing,
> And Thou, too, mingle in the Ring!
> Take to thy heart a new delight!
> If not, make merry in despite
> That one should breathe who scorns thy power.
> —But dance! for under Jedborough Tower
> A Matron dwells who, tho' she bears
> Our mortal complement of years,
> Lives in the light of youthful glee,
> And she will dance and sing with thee.
>
> Nay! start not at that Figure—there!
> Him who is rooted to his Chair!
> Look at him, look again; for He
> Hath long been of thy Family.
> With legs that move not, if they can,
> And useless arms, a Trunk of Man,
> He sits, and with a vacant eye;
> A Sight to make a Stranger sigh!

1. "The Matron of Jedborough and Her Husband."

Deaf, drooping, such is now his doom;
His world is in that single room—
Is this a place for mirthful cheer?
Can merry-making enter here?

The joyous Woman is the Mate
Of him in that forlorn estate;
He breathes a subterraneous damp;
But bright as Vesper shines her lamp,
He is as mute as Jedborough Tower,
She jocund as it was of yore
With all its bravery on, in times
When all alive with merry chimes
Upon a sun-bright morn of May
It roused the Vale to holiday.

I praise thee, Matron! and thy due
Is praise, heroic praise and true.
With admiration I behold
Thy gladness unsubdued and bold:
Thy looks, thy gestures, all present
The picture of a life well spent;
This do I see, and something more,
A strength unthought of heretofore.
Delighted am I for thy sake,
And yet a higher joy partake:
Our human nature throws away
Its second twilight, and looks gay,
A Land of promise and of pride
Unfolding, wide as life is wide.

Ah! see her helpless Charge! enclosed
Within himself as seems, composed;
To fear of loss and hope of gain,
The strife of happiness and pain—
Utterly dead! yet in the guise
Of little Infants when their eyes
Begin to follow to and fro
The persons that before them go,
He tracks her motions, quick or slow.
Her buoyant spirits can prevail
Where common cheerfulness would fail.
She strikes upon him with the heat
Of July suns; he feels it sweet;

An animal delight, though dim!
'Tis all that now remains for him!

I look'd, I scann'd her o'er and o'er,
And, looking, wondered more and more:
When suddenly I seem'd to espy
A trouble in her strong black eye,
A remnant of uneasy light,
A flash of something over-bright!
Not long this mystery did detain
My thoughts. She told in pensive strain
That she had borne a heavy yoke,
Been stricken by a twofold stroke;
Ill health of body, and had pined
Beneath worse ailments of the mind.

So be it!—but let praise ascend
To Him who is our Lord and Friend!
Who from disease and suffering
As bad almost as Life can bring,
Hath call'd for thee a second Spring;
Repaid thee for that sore distress
By no untimely joyousness;
Which makes of thine a blissful state;
And cheers thy melancholy Mate!

Wednesday, September 21st.—The house where we lodged was airy, and even cheerful, though one of a line of houses bordering on the churchyard, which is the highest part of the town, overlooking a great portion of it to the opposite hills. The kirk is, as at Melrose, within the walls of a conventual church; but the ruin is much less beautiful, and the church a very neat one. The churchyard was full of graves, and exceedingly slovenly and dirty; one most indecent practice I observed: several women brought their linen to the flat table-tombstones, and, having spread it upon them, began to batter as hard as they could with a wooden roller, a substitute for a mangle.

After Mr. Scott's business in the Courts was over, he walked with us up the Jed—'sylvan Jed' it has been properly called by Thomson—for the banks are yet very woody, though wood in large quantities has been felled within a few years. There are some fine red scars near the river, in one or two of which we saw the entrances to caves, said to have been used as places of refuge in times of insecurity.

Walked up to Ferniehurst, an old hall, in a secluded situation, now inhabited by farmers; the neighbouring ground had the wildness of a forest, being irregularly scattered over with fine old trees. The wind was tossing their branches, and sunshine dancing among the leaves, and I happened to exclaim, 'What a life there is in trees!' on which Mr. Scott observed that the words reminded him of a young lady who had been born and educated on an island of the Orcades, and came to spend a summer at Kelso and in the neighbourhood of Edinburgh. She used to say that in the new world into which she was come nothing had disappointed her so much as trees and woods; she complained that they were lifeless, silent, and, compared with the grandeur of the ever-changing ocean, even insipid. At first I was surprised, but the next moment I felt that the impression was natural. Mr. Scott said that she was a very sensible young woman, and had read much. She talked with endless rapture and feeling of the power and greatness of the ocean; and with the same passionate attachment returned to her native island without any probability of quitting it again.

The valley of the Jed is very solitary immediately under Ferniehurst; we walked down the river, wading almost up to the knees in fern, which in many parts overspread the forest-ground. It made me think of our walks at Allfoxden, and of *our own* park—though at Ferniehurst is no park at present—and the slim fawns that we used to startle from their couching-places among the fern at the top of the hill. We were accompanied on our walk by a young man from the Braes of Yarrow, an acquaintance of Mr. Scott's, who, having been much delighted with some of William's poems which he had chanced to see in a newspaper, had wished to be introduced to him; he lived in the most retired part of the dale of Yarrow, where he had a farm: he was fond of reading, and well informed, but at first meeting as shy as any of our Grasmere lads, and not less rustic in his appearance. He had been in the Highlands, and gave me such an account of Loch Rannoch as made us regret that we had not persevered in our journey thither, especially as he told us that the bad road ended at a very little distance from the place where we had turned back, and that we should have come into another good road, continued all along the shore of the lake. He also mentioned that there was a very fine view from the steeple at Dunkeld.

The town of Jedburgh, in returning along the road, as it is seen through the gently winding narrow valley, looks exceedingly beautiful on its low eminence, surmounted by the conventual tower, which is arched over, at the summit, by light stone-work resembling a coronet; the effect at a distance is very graceful. The hills all round are high, and rise rapidly from the town, which though it stands considerably above the river, yet, from every side except that on which we walked, appears to stand in a bottom.

We had our dinner sent from the inn, and a bottle of wine, that we might not disgrace the Sheriff, who supped with us in the evening,—stayed late, and repeated some of his poem.

Thursday, September 22d.—After breakfast, the minister, Dr. Somerville, called upon us with Mr. Scott, and we went to the manse, a very pretty house, with pretty gardens, and in a beautiful situation, though close to the town. Dr. Somerville and his family complained bitterly of the devastation that had been made among the woods within view from their windows, which looked up the Jed. He conducted us to the church, which under his directions has been lately repaired, and is a very neat place within. Dr. Somerville spoke of the dirt and other indecencies in the churchyard, and said that he had taken great pains to put a stop to them, but wholly in vain. The business of the assizes closed this day, and we went into Court to hear the Judge pronounce his charge, which was the most curious specimen of old woman's oratory and newspaper-paragraph loyalty that was ever heard. When all was over they returned to the inn in procession, as they had come, to the sound of a trumpet, the Judge first, in his robes of red, the Sheriffs next, in large cocked hats, and inferior officers following, a show not much calculated to awe the beholders. After this we went to the inn. The landlady and her sister inquired if we had been comfortable, and lamented that they had not had it in their power to pay us more attention. I began to talk with them, and found out that they were from Cumberland: they knew Captain and Mrs. Wordsworth, who had frequently been at Jedburgh, Mrs. Wordsworth's sister having married a gentleman of that neighbourhood. They spoke of them with great pleasure. I returned to our lodgings to take leave of the old woman, who told me that I had behaved 'very discreetly,' and seemed exceedingly sorry that we were leaving her so soon. She had been out to buy me some pears, saying that I must take away some 'Jedderd' pears. We learned afterwards that Jedburgh is famous in Scotland for pears, which were first cultivated there in the gardens of the monks.

Mr. Scott was very glad to part from the Judge and his retinue, to travel with us in our car to Hawick; his servant drove his own gig. The landlady, very kindly, had put up some sandwiches and cheese-cakes for me, and all the family came out to see us depart. Passed the monastery gardens, which are yet gardens, where there are many remarkably large old pear-trees. We soon came into the vale of Teviot, which is open and cultivated, and scattered over with hamlets, villages, and many gentlemen's seats, yet, though there is no inconsiderable quantity of wood, you can never, in the wide and cultivated parts of the Teviot, get rid of the impression of barrenness, and the fir plantations, which in this part are numerous, are for ever at war with simplicity. One beautiful spot I recollect of a different character, which Mr. Scott took us to see a few yards from the road. A stone bridge crossed the water at a deep and still place, called Horne's Pool, from a contemplative schoolmaster, who had lived not far from it, and was accustomed to walk thither, and spend much of his leisure near the river. The valley was here narrow and woody. Mr. Scott pointed out to us

Sixth Week
18–24 September

188. Peebles. Neidpath Castle.
"The castle stands upon a green hill, overlooking the Tweed, a strong square-towered edifice,
neglected and desolate, though not in ruin . . ." (p. 201)

Leaving an ancient Dome and Towers like these
Beggar'd and outraged!
(William Wordsworth, p. 201)

189. Banks of the River Tweed. Near Peebles.
"We had a day's journey before us along the banks of the Tweed, a name which has been sweet to my ears almost as far back as I can remember anything." (p. 202)

190. Clovenfords. ("Clovenford.") Clovenfords Hotel.
"I should suppose it is a house little frequented, for there is no appearance of an inn . . . Mr. Scott is respected everywhere: I believe that by favour of his name one might be hospitably entertained throughout all the borders of Scotland." (pp. 203–204)

191. Yarrow. Ruin. Unvisited.
"At Clovenford, being so near to the Yarrow, we could not but think of the possibility of going thither, but . . ."
(p. 204)

192. Melrose. Detail on Abbey.
"He [Scott] pointed out many pieces of beautiful sculpture in obscure corners which would have escaped our notice." (p. 208)

193. Melrose. Melrose Abbey.
"The ruin is of considerable extent, but unfortunately it is almost surrounded by insignificant houses . . . and even when viewed from a distance the situation does not seem to be particularly happy, for the vale is broken and disturbed . . ." (p. 206)

194. Dryburgh. Dryburgh Abbey.
"The ruins of Dryburgh are much less extensive than those of Melrose, and greatly inferior both in the architecture and stone, which is much mouldered away." (p. 208)

195. Jedburgh. Square, with Sheriff Court.
"Arrived at Jedburgh half an hour before the Judges were expected out of Court to dinner." (p. 209)

196. Jedburgh. Nellie Mitchell's house, in which the Wordsworths stayed.
"We were received with hearty welcome by a good woman, who, though above seventy years old, moved about as briskly as if she was only seventeen. Those parts of the house which we were to occupy were neat and clean . . ." (p. 209)

197. Jedburgh. Jedburgh Tower.

—But dance! For under Jedborough Tower
A Matron dwells who, tho' she bears
Our mortal complement of years,
Lives in the light of youthful glee,
And she will dance and sing with thee.
(William Wordsworth, p. 210)

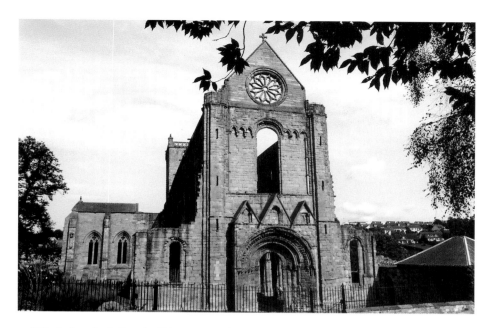

198. Jedburgh. Jedburgh Abbey. From the west, where Dorothy's "private house" was.
"The kirk is, as at Melrose, within the walls of a conventual church; but the ruin is much less beautiful, and the church a very neat one." (p. 212)

199. Jedburgh. Graves in churchyard.
"The churchyard was full of graves, and exceedingly slovenly and dirty; one most indecent practice I observed: several women brought their linen to the flat table-tombstones, and, having spread it upon them, began to batter as hard as they could with a wooden roller, a substitute for a mangle." (p. 212)

200. Ferniehurst Castle.
"Walked up to Ferniehurst, an old hall, in a secluded situation . . ." (p. 212)

201. Jedburgh. Abbey, from the south.
"The town of Jedburgh, in returning along the road, as it is seen through the gently winding narrow valley, looks exceedingly beautiful on its low eminence, surmounted by the conventual tower, which is arched over, at the summit, by light stone-work resembling a coronet . . ." (p. 213)

202. Vale of Teviot. View of Minto.
"Mr. Scott pointed out to us Ruberslaw, Minto Crags, and every other remarkable object in or near the vale of Teviot . . ." (pp. 214–15)

203. Hawick. Tower Hotel. (Tower Inn.)
"Arrived at Hawick to dinner; the inn is a large old house with walls above a yard thick,
formerly a gentleman's house." (p. 215)

204. Hawick. View from the top of a hill.
"Before breakfast, walked with Mr. Scott along a high road for about two miles, up a bare
hill . . . From the top of the hill we had an extensive view over the moors of Liddisdale,
and saw the Cheviot Hills." (p. 215)

205. Branxholm Castle. ("Branxholm Hall.")
"Passed Branxholm Hall, one of the mansions belonging to the Duke of Buccleuch, which we looked at with particular interest for the sake of the Lay of the Last Minstrel." (p. 216)

206. Mosspaul. ("Moss Paul.") Mosspaul Hotel.
"We saw a single stone house a long way before us, which we conjectured to be, as it proved, Moss Paul, the inn where we were to bait. The scene, with this single dwelling, was melancholy and wild . . ." (p. 216)

207. Langholm. Town, River Esk.
"The town, as we approached, from a hill, looked very pretty, the houses being roofed with blue slates, and standing close to the river Esk, here a large river, that scattered its waters wide over a stony channel." (p. 217)

208. Threlkeld. Salutation Inn, Saddleback in background.
"—A beautiful autumnal day. Breakfasted at a public-house by the road-side; dined at Threlkeld . . ." (p. 217)

209. Grasmere. Dove Cottage.
". . . arrived at home between eight and nine o'clock . . ." (p. 217)

210. Grasmere. Interior, with open window.

Ruberslaw, Minto Crags, and every other remarkable object in or near the vale of Teviot, and we scarcely passed a house for which he had not some story. Seeing us look at one, which stood high on the hill on the opposite side of the river, he told us that a gentleman lived there who, while he was in India, had been struck with the fancy of making his fortune by a new speculation, and so set about collecting the gods of the country, with infinite pains and no little expense, expecting that he might sell them for an enormous price. Accordingly, on his return they were offered for sale, but no purchasers came. On the failure of this scheme, a room was hired in London in which to exhibit them as a show; but alas! nobody would come to see; and this curious assemblage of monsters is now, probably, quietly lodged in the vale of Teviot. The latter part of this gentleman's history is more affecting:—he had an only daughter, whom he had accompanied into Spain two or three years ago for the recovery of her health, and so for a time saved her from a consumption, which now again threatened her, and he was about to leave his pleasant residence, and attend her once more on the same errand, afraid of the coming winter.

We passed through a village, whither Leyden, Scott's intimate friend, the author of Scenes of Infancy, was used to walk over several miles of moorland country every day to school, a poor barefooted boy. He is now in India, applying himself to the study of Oriental literature, and, I doubt not, it is his dearest thought that he may come and end his days upon the banks of Teviot, or some other of the Lowland streams—for he is, like Mr. Scott, passionately attached to the district of the Borders.

Arrived at Hawick to dinner; the inn is a large old house[1] with walls above a yard thick, formerly a gentleman's house. Did not go out this evening.

Friday, September 23d.—Before breakfast, walked with Mr. Scott along a high road for about two miles, up a bare hill. Hawick is a small town. From the top of the hill we had an extensive view over the moors of Liddisdale, and saw the Cheviot Hills. We wished we could have gone with Mr. Scott into some of the remote dales of this country, where in almost every house he can find a home and a hearty welcome. But after breakfast we were obliged to part with him, which we did with great regret: he would gladly

1. Called today the Tower Hotel. A plaque on the building, which is being renovated, reads:

TO THIS INN,
THE ANCIENT DWELLING OF THE DRUMLANRIG FAMILY
SIR WALTER SCOTT
CONDUCTED WILLIAM WORDSWORTH AND HIS SISTER DOROTHY
ON 22ND SEPTEMBER 1803
WHERE SIR WALTER AND THEY
RESIDED OVER NIGHT.

have gone with us to Langholm, eighteen miles further. Our way was through the vale of Teviot, near the banks of the river.

Passed Branxholm Hall, one of the mansions belonging to the Duke of Buccleuch, which we looked at with particular interest for the sake of the Lay of the Last Minstrel. Only a very small part of the original building remains: it is a large strong house, old, but not ancient in its appearance—stands very near the river-side; the banks covered with plantations.

A little further on, met the Edinburgh coach with several passengers, the only stage-coach that had passed us in Scotland. Coleridge had come home by that conveyance only a few days before. The quantity of arable land gradually diminishes, and the plantations become fewer, till at last the river flows open to the sun, mostly through unfenced and untilled grounds, a soft pastoral district, both the hills and the valley being scattered over with sheep: here and there was a single farm-house, or cluster of houses, and near them a portion of land covered with ripe corn.

Near the head of the vale of Teviot, where that stream is but a small rivulet, we descended towards another valley, by another small rivulet. Hereabouts Mr. Scott had directed us to look about for some old stumps of trees, said to be the place where Johnny Armstrong was hanged; but we could not find them out. The valley into which we were descending, though, for aught I know, it is unnamed in song, was to us more interesting than the Teviot itself. Not a spot of tilled ground was there to break in upon its pastoral simplicity; the same soft yellow green spread from the bed of the streamlet to the hill-tops on each side, and sheep were feeding everywhere. It was more close and simple than the upper end of the vale of Teviot, the valley being much narrower, and the hills equally high and not broken into parts, but on each side a long range. The grass, as we had first seen near Crawfordjohn, had been mown in the different places of the open ground, where it might chance to be best; but there was no part of the surface that looked perfectly barren, as in those tracts.

We saw a single stone house a long way before us, which we conjectured to be, as it proved, Moss Paul, the inn where we were to bait. The scene, with this single dwelling, was melancholy and wild, but not dreary, though there was no tree nor shrub; the small streamlet glittered, the hills were populous with sheep; but the gentle bending of the valley, and the correspondent softness in the forms of the hills, were of themselves enough to delight the eye. At Moss Paul we fed our horse;—several travellers were drinking whisky. We neither ate nor drank, for we had, with our usual foresight and frugality in travelling, saved the cheese-cakes and sandwiches which had been given us by our countrywoman at Jedburgh the day before. After Moss Paul, we ascended considerably, then went down other reaches of the valley, much less interesting, stony and barren. The country afterwards not peculiar, I should think, for I scarcely remember it.

Arrived at Langholm at about five o'clock. The town, as we approached, from a hill, looked very pretty, the houses being roofed with blue slates, and standing close to the river Esk, here a large river, that scattered its waters wide over a stony channel. The inn neat and comfortable—exceedingly clean: I could hardly believe we were still in Scotland.

After tea walked out; crossed a bridge, and saw, at a little distance up the valley. Langholm House, a villa of the Duke of Buccleuch: it stands upon a level between the river and a steep hill, which is planted with wood. Walked a considerable way up the river, but could not go close to it on account of the Duke's plantations, which are locked up. When they ended, the vale became less cultivated; the view through the vale towards the hills very pleasing, though bare and cold.

Saturday, September 24th.—Rose very early and travelled about nine miles to Longtown, before breakfast, along the banks of the Esk. About half a mile from Langholm crossed a bridge. At this part of the vale, which is narrow, the steeps are covered with old oaks and every variety of trees. Our road for some time through the wood, then came to a more open country, exceedingly rich and populous; the banks of the river frequently rocky, and hung with wood; many gentlemen's houses. There was the same rich variety while the river continued to flow through Scottish grounds; but not long after we had passed through the last turnpike gate in Scotland and the first in England—but a few yards asunder—the vale widens, and its aspect was cold, and even dreary, though Sir James Graham's plantations are very extensive. His house, a large building, stands in this open part of the vale. Longtown was before us, and ere long we saw the well-remembered guide-post, where the circuit of our six weeks' travels had begun, and now was ended.

We did not look along the white line of the road to Solway Moss without some melancholy emotion, though we had the fair prospect of the Cumberland mountains full in view, with the certainty, barring accidents, of reaching our own dear home the next day. Breakfasted at the Graham's Arms. The weather had been very fine from the time of our arrival at Jedburgh, and this was a very pleasant day. The sun 'shone fair on Carlisle walls' when we first saw them from the top of the opposite hill. Stopped to look at the place on the sand near the bridge where Hatfield had been executed. Put up at the same inn as before, and were recognised by the woman who had waited on us. Everybody spoke of Hatfield as an injured man. After dinner went to a village six miles further,' where we slept.

Sunday, September 25th, 1803.—A beautiful autumnal day. Breakfasted at a public-house by the road-side; dined at Threlkeld; arrived at home be-

1. Probably Dalston.

tween eight and nine o'clock, where we found Mary in perfect health, Joanna Hutchinson with her, and little John asleep in the clothes-basket by the fire.

SONNET COMPOSED BETWEEN DALSTON AND GRASMERE, SEPTEMBER *25, 1803.*

FLY, some kind spirit, fly to Grasmere Vale!
Say that we come, and come by this day's light
Glad tidings!—spread them over field and height,
But, chiefly, let one Cottage hear the tale!
There let a mystery of joy prevail,
The kitten frolic with unruly might,
And Rover whine as at a second sight
Of near-approaching good, that will not fail:
And from that Infant's face let joy appear;
Yea, let our Mary's one companion child,
That hath her six weeks' solitude beguiled
With intimations manifold and dear,
While we have wander'd over wood and wild—
Smile on its Mother now with bolder cheer!

APPENDIX 1

John Hatfield, or Hadfield, as Molly Lefebure contends his name is correctly spelled (in *The Bondage of Opium*, Appendix), was an intriguing fraud—an imposter, a bigamist, an incorrigible womanizer, a swindler, an ex-convict, and, most significantly for a court and jury seeking to nail him for something that would make him pay for cumulative offences, a forger. In a sensational trial in Carlisle at the town hall during the 1803 August assizes, he was indicted on two counts of forgery and one count of defrauding the Post Office by franking letters under the name of a Member of Parliament. He was convicted and sentenced to death, forgery being a capital offence. The Wordsworth–Coleridge party arrived in Carlisle the day after his trial, and on the same day, 16 August, that he was sentenced; by the time Dorothy and William Wordsworth passed through Carlisle again at the end of the Scottish journey, Hatfield had been hanged.

The conduct that most outraged the Lake District was Hatfield's betrayal of Mary Robinson, the daughter of the landlord of the Fish Inn in Buttermere, whose reputation for natural country beauty inspired local affection and pride and, brought tourists simply to gape at her as she went about her work helping her parents serve guests at the inn. Indeed, some ten years before the Hatfield incident, when she was still a young woman of fourteen, Mary had been cited as one of the attractions of the Lakes in the guide book *A Fortnight's Ramble into the Lakes in Westmorland, Lancashire, and Cumberland*, by A. Rambler [Joseph Budworth/Palmer], (London: 1792. Repr. Upper Basildon, Berkshire: Preston Publishing, 1990). On 2 October 1802 John Hatfield married the Beauty of Buttermere, as she had been known, and swept her off to the Scottish border country. The man Mary believed she was marrying was someone considerably above her station—the Honourable Augustus Hope, MP for Linlithgowshire, brother of the 3rd Earl of Hopetoun. Colonel Hope, as he had been known in Keswick, where he had been living at the Queen's Head, charmed (and deceived) both men and women in Keswick society. While courting Mary, riding nine miles from Keswick to Buttermere ostensibly to indulge his interest in fishing (for char, which was plentiful in Buttermere), "Colonel Hope" had been busy establishing an exploitative relationship with Colonel Nathaniel Montgomery Moore, MP, a tourist, in Keswick with his wife and wealthy young ward, to whom Hatfield also became engaged. The day before he married the Beauty of Buttermere, "Colonel Hope" sent a letter to Colonel Moore asking him to cash a draft for £30. The draft, drawn upon Mr. John Gregory Crump, had been forged.

News of the marriage between the renowned local maid Mary and the colorful visitor at the Queen's Head, "Colonel Hope," swept Keswick. When word reached the honeymooning Hatfield that his honesty was being questioned, he returned to Buttermere with his new wife and proceeded to Keswick, where with stunning audacity he would attempt to salvage his reputation. However, the Queen's Head was currently host to a new visitor, a barrister who knew the real Alexander Augustus Hope, MP and was able to confirm that the "Colonel Hope" on hand was an imposter. Hatfield malingered stylishly, then fled. The abandoned Maid of Buttermere found in the false bottom of a dressing-box Hatfield had left behind a cache of incriminating letters from his previous wife and children and was thus harshly divested of any remaining illusions.

Coleridge had played a significant hand in exposing Hatfield through five articles he wrote for the London *Morning Post* which were run almost immediately in other papers. The first of two pieces entitled "Romantic Marriage" came out on 11 October 1802, a Monday, a slow day for news, and commanded national attention sufficient to create a ready audience for the second, which appeared on 22 October. On 5 November a one-paragraph piece entitled "The Fraudulent Marriage" appeared, giving an account of the contents of the dressing-box Hatfield left behind and proof of bigamy. Two pieces entitled "The Keswick Imposter," appearing on 20 November and 31 December, completed Coleridge's damning portrait of Hatfield.

On the last day of Hatfield's trial in Carlisle Coleridge made his presence known in an odd way: "I alarmed the whole Court, Judges, Counsellors, Tipstaves, Jurymen, Witnesses, & Spectators by hallooing to Wordsworth who was in a window on the side of the Hall—*Dinner!*" (*Notebooks*, ɪ p. 1432). The visit with Hatfield afterwards at the jail, was "impelled by Miss Wordsworth," according to Coleridge, who found his imposter "*vain*, a hypocrite" adding, "It is not by mere Thought, I can understand this man" (p. 1432).

In his journalism Coleridge had identified a case that was to fascinate writers from the Lake poets to the present. Stage productions and novels grew out of the travails of Mary and the dashing fraud she married. Coleridge himself appears to have considered writing a comic epic and a novel. Wordsworth reacted in a different spirit. He was disturbed when in July 1803 Sadler's Wells turned the story of Mary of Buttermere into a play, *The Beauty of Buttermere*, for he perceived the dramatization of the local woman's life and circumstances as

> too holy [a] theme for such a place,
> And doubtless treated with irreverance,
> Albeit with their very best of skill—
> I mean . . . a story drawn
> From our own ground, the Maid of Buttermere.
> *The Prelude*, Book Seventh ll. 318–22

One three-volume novel published in 1841 entitled *James Hatfield and the Beauty of Buttermere: A Story of Modern Times* gives no author but boasts illustrations by Cruikshank. The most recent study is a marvelously effective interweaving of documentation and narrative by Cumbrian-born Melvyn Bragg: *The Maid of Buttermere*. London: Hodder and Stoughton Ltd, 1987; Sceptre Paperback, 1988.

APPENDIX 2

Stoddart mentions only one cave: "Half way up one of these terrific cliffs, a cave is pointed out (for few I believe attempt to scale it), still called Wallace's Cave, and said to have been the retreat of that hero, when pursued by the English" (*Remarks*, I 163). A guide book for walkers in Lanark today also indicates only one cave and advises against attempting to visit it. The cave is directly below the tall Cartland Bridge (designed by Thomas Telford in 1822) which takes traffic over the 130-foot gorge of the Mouse Water. William Wallace (*c.*1270–1305) was the second son of a knight in a family that opposed the increasing presence of English force in Scotland. His historical image has in recent years been "revisioned," and he has drawn international attention through the film *Braveheart* (dir. Mel Gibson) which depicts him as passionately courageous, cunning, and brilliant in his leadership in the Scottish cause for separatism. Ceremonies continue to commemorate him in Lanark.

The William Wallace Society represents a Scottish point of view that is still alive in the following summary of the events of Wallace's life relevant to Lanark:

> William embarked on a campaign of guerilla warfare making trouble for the English garrisons throughout the land. The English Sheriff at Lanark had William's wife murdered for assisting him to escape capture in the town and in revenge Wallace killed the Sheriff. The local people joined forces to slaughter the entire English garrison in the town and when news of these events spread Wallace's army grew. They learned of a large English force camped near Biggar and, taking them by surprise, won a great victory. Wallace was declared Guardian of Scotland at the Forest Kirk (near Carluke) and as the ranks of his army of ordinary people and lesser knights grew, he chose a strategic position to the north of Stirling Brig for his next encounter with an English Army. Wallace's famous victory there was so complete that all English forces were driven from the land. It was not long before another English army was sent north and this time they caught up with him at Falkirk. The site of the battle suited the English cavalry and as the Scots nobles had refused to assist Wallace his army was no match for them. The Scots were defeated but Wallace escaped and, though resigning as guardian, continued his guerilla operations against the occupying force. The English King offered inducements to the Scots nobles to capture Wallace and on the 5th of August 1305 he was betrayed by Sir John Stewart of Menteith and handed to the English. Wallace was rushed to London where he was sentenced to die as a traitor. In Lanark the site of Wallace's wife's house in the Castlegate is marked by a plaque and his statue looks out from the steeple of St. Nicholas Church:

(*Souvenir Programme of March and Wreath Laying Ceremony Commemorating Wallace in Lanark, 20 August 1994*, William Wallace Society, Lanark.)

APPENDIX 3

The inscription reads:

SISTE, VIATOR!
SI LIPORIS, INGENIIQUE VENAM BENIGNAM,
SI MORUM CALLIDISSIMUM PICTOREM,
UNQUAM ES MIRATUS
IMMORARE PALULUM MEMORIAE
TOBIAE SMOLLETT, M.D.
VIRI VIRTUTIBUS HISCE
QUAS IN HOMINE ET CIVE
ET LAUDES ET IMITERIS,
HAUD MEDIOCRITER ORNATI:
QUI IN LITERIS VAR IS VERSATUS
POSTQUAM FELICITATE SIBI PROPRIA,
SESE POSTERIS COMMENDAVERAT,
MORTE ACERBA RAPTUS,
ANNO AETATIS 51.
EHEU! QUAM PROCULA PATRIA!
PROBE LIBURNI PORTUM IN ITALIA,
JACET SEPULTUS.
TALI TANTOQUE VIRO, PATRUELI SUO,
CUI IN DECURSU LAMPADA
SE POTIUS TRADIDISSE DECUIT,
HANC, COLUMNAM,
AMORIS, EHEU! INANE MONUMENTUM,
IN IPSIS LEVINIAE RIPIS,
QUAS VERSICULIS SUB EXITU
VITAE ILLUSTRATAS,
PRIMAS INFANS VAGITIBUS PERSONUIT,
PONENDAM CURAVIT
JACOBUS SMOLLETT, DE BONHILL,
ABI, ET REMINISCRERE,
HOC QUIDEM HONORE,
NON MODO DEFUNCTI MEMORIAE,
VERUM ETIAM EXEMPLO, PROSPECTUM ESSE:
ALIIS ENIM, SI MODO DIGNI SINT,
IDEM ERIT VIRTUTIS PRAEMIUM!

Translated into English, the inscription reads:

Pause, traveller! If ever you have marvelled at a man endowed with an abundance of grace and talent, the very model of moral rectitude, give heed for a moment to the memory of Tobias Smollett, M.D. He was a person not meagerly endowed with qualities which we might readily praise and imitate in any man or citizen. Widely versed in letters, after he achieved a unique felicity of style that has commended him to posterity, he was snatched away by cruel death in his 51st year. Alas, he perished far from his native land, and lies buried now in the port of Leghorn (Livorno) in Italy. For this great man, my own cousin, I, James Smollett of Bonhill, have seen to the raising of this column, a monument of love. In the normal course of things it had been more fitting that I pass on to him the torch of life. This column stands on the banks of the Leven, the very place which heard his infant cries and was depicted in verses written before his death. Go now, traveller, and remember that this is not only a memorial to the memory of a dead man, but a precept for the living. Other men, if only they be worthy, can attain the rewards of virtue.

Translated by John P. Nolan

Though Smollett is best remembered for his epistolary novel *The Expedition of Humphrey Clinker* today, in Dorothy Wordsworth's time he was recognized not only for his literary work—as an author, a translator, and an editor—, but also for his study of medicine at Glasgow University, for which he would have had a command of Latin, and for his practice as a physician.

In 1773, when he and Boswell were in the area, Samuel Johnson was consulted on the inscription—whether it should be in English or Latin. Boswell's entry for Thursday, 28 October indicates that Johnson treated a recommendation (of Lord Kames) that the text should be in English because it could be easily understood "with great contempt, saying 'An English inscription would be a disgrace to Smollett.'" Boswell concurred: "I observed, that all to whom Dr Smollett's merit could be an object of respect and imitation, would understand it as well in Latin; and that surely it was not meant for the Highland drovers, or other such people, who pass and repass that way" (*Johnson and Boswell in Scotland*. Ed. Pat Rogers. New Haven and London: Yale University Press, 1993, pp. 292, 294).

The inscription is attributed (by Shairp) to three authors: Professor George Stuart of Edinburgh, John Ramsay of Ochtertyre, and Dr. Samuel Johnson.

APPENDIX 4

Dorothy Wordsworth's Trips to Loch Katrine and the Trossachs. (See also map on p. 31)

I. The first trip was from Tarbet across Loch Lomond by boat to ROB ROY'S CAVES (where they land briefly to get out and explore) and then to INVERSNAID. Then they walk along the road from INVERSNAID to STRONACHLACHAR (for which they did not have a name), passing, and taking note of, THE GARRISON. They pursue a road which they describe as "a mountain horsetrack" to STRONACHLACHAR and then up the west side of LOCH KATRINE to GLENGYLE, and the next day, walk three miles[1] down the east side of the lake to a ferryman's hut (most likely PORTNELLAN). There they get into a little boat, and the ferryman rows them to the foot of the lake. They notice BEN VENUE. They leave their boat in a bay, at anchor, and walk through a vale, to LOCH ACHRAY. They experience THE TROSSACHS.

They reverse this entire journey and return, by the same route, to INVERSNAID. They spend the night there, and the next day they are rowed across LOCH LOMOND to a point three miles above TARBET (which must have been INVERUGLAS). They walk to TARBET (Friday, 26 August to Sunday, 28 August; pp. 91–115).

II. The second trip starts at CALLANDER. They walk past LOCH VENACHAR (noticing BEN LEDI), past LOCH ACHRAY, taking special interest in the head of LOCH ACHRAY, and through the pass of THE TROSSACHS, to LOCH KATRINE. They walk up the side of LOCH KATRINE eight miles to the ferryman's hut. From there they row across the water to the opposite side of the lake to about a mile and a half above STRONACHLACHAR, and walk along the route that takes them past LOCH ARKLET, past THE GARRISON, to INVERSNAID.

They row across LOCH LOMOND to a point nine miles below GLEN FALLOCH (probably INVERUGLAS again). They walk up the east side of LOCH LOMOND to what I believe is INVERARNAN, in the glen of the RIVER FALLOCH. They cross the RIVER FALLOCH, then climb a hill to a mountain, following a path that only their Highland guide knew. They come down out of the mountain into GLENGYLE, at the head of LOCH KATRINE. They row to the ferryman's hut. The next day, they climb over the mountain and come down at the head of LOCH VOIL (probably the west end of it) and walk (as nearly as I can tell) through the Braes of Balquhidder to the burial place of Rob Roy, which would be BALQUHIDDER. They notice at the foot of the lake that "on the opposite side, which was more barren than that on which we travelled, was a bare road up a steep hill, which leads to Glen Finlas, formerly a royal forest" (p. 194). Then they walk down through STRATHYRE, along the shores of LOCH LUBNAIG, along the PASS OF LENY, to CALLANDER (Sunday, 11 September to Wednesday, 14 September; pp. 180–195).

1. Distances given in this appendix are Dorothy's own estimates.

APPENDIX 5

Robert MacGregor, dubbed Rob Roy because of his red hair, is the celebrated Highland figure whose identity is inseparable from the area of Inversnaid and the Trossachs. At the time Dorothy visited, his biographical image had not yet been fleshed out and popularized by Walter Scott's novel *Rob Roy* (1817), but he was decidedly a hero, and the facts of his life were passed on in a lively oral tradition. Born in 1671 at Glengyle, to a father who was chief of the Clan Gregor, Rob Roy was a well-known and respected cattleman, in a era when the Highland cattle were the primary source of income and livelihood. It was also a time when cattle were considered common property, taking someone's cattle was not illegal, and selling protection against theft was a means of earning a living.

In 1693 Rob Roy married Mary MacGregor of Comer, and they made their home at Inversnaid. He borrowed a considerable sum of money to increase his herd of cattle and build his droving business, but owing to the deception of his chief drover who was entrusted with the money and documents to purchase the cattle and bring them back, the enterprise failed and he was not able to make good on his loans. "As a result, Rob Roy MacGregor was branded an outlaw, his wife and family were evicted from their house at Inversnaid and this was then burned down.

It is at this time that he is supposed to have used what is now known as Rob Roy's Cave, but there is no evidence to substantiate this," (Mike Trubridge, *The Inversnaid Hotel and its Surroundings*. M.F. Wells (Hotels), 1992, p. 22).

Dorothy Wordsworth's use of the plural "Caves" suggests a misunderstanding about another nearby cave, said to have been used by Robert the Bruce (King of the Scots, 1306–29).

Two excellent modern sources, Nigel Tranter: *Rob Roy MacGregor* (New York: Barnes and Noble, 1995) and the film *Rob Roy* (dir. Michael Caton-Jones), shed contemporary light on the Scottish folk hero's story. Both deal realistically with the Inversnaid setting and the violation and abuse of Rob's wife there by Graham of Killearn, the Duke of Montrose's factor. The incident must not have been part of the lore the Wordsworths heard.

APPENDIX 6

The National Trust for Scotland reconstructs the background and setting in *The Hermitage Walk, Inver, by Dunkeld* (Edinburgh, 1990):

> The hermitage folly, or Ossian's Hall, was built in 1758 by the 2nd Duke's nephew, himself destined to become the 3rd Duke of Atholl. It was supposedly constructed in secrecy, as a surprise for the Duke, who had already set aside this woodland for planting with exotic trees.
>
> The exterior was originally much as it appears today, but had three sash windows overlooking the fall and was surrounded by a garden of fruit trees and flowering shrubs.
>
> In 1783 the interior was decorated as Ossian's Hall. The visitor entered first into a circular vestibule, to be confronted with a painting of blind Ossian the ancient bard, singing to a group of maidens. The sound of the waterfall could be heard, amplified by the acoustics of the building, but nothing was seen until the guide operated a secret pulley, whereupon the painting slid into a recess in the wall, allowing entry to an inner room. Here the walls and ceiling were covered with mirrors reflecting the waterfall, and creating the illusion of water pouring in all directions. Visitors described their 'shock' and 'amazement', though some did not enjoy the spectacle, especially the coloured glass, which was soon removed from the windows. Wordsworth, who appreciated the natural beauty of the place, was not impressed. Sadly the Hall was vandalised—first in 1821, when most of the damage was to fittings and furnishings, then in 1869, when it was blown up . . . The floor of Ossian's Hall was recently renewed and the remainder of the interior was refurbished in 1986.

William did not have good things to say about this mirrored hall for Ossian, and would "set free / The Bard from such indignity!" in his "Effusion, In the Pleasure-ground on the Banks of the Bran, Near Dunkeld."

INDEX

Modern spelling of place names, and variants and locations of inns, are in parentheses. Illustration numbers are in italics.

Scotland, vii, ix, 1–5, 7, 8, 10, 13, 14, 40, 41, 44, 46, 48, 49, 56, 58, 65, 67, 71, 74, 77, 85, 94, 102, 103, 106, 108, 111, 115, 117, 123, 125, 126, 128, 136, 141, 142, 143, 151, 158, 163, 164, 166, 168, 172, 173, 175, 177, 179, 184, 193n2, 196, 198, 204, 205, 217. *See also individual places.*
Scots, Mary, Queen of. *See* Hamilton, palace; Linlithgow, palace; Holyrood House
Selkirk, 207; Sheriff of, *see* Scott, Walter
Semple, Lord (house of), 76
Severn, River, 120
Shairp, John Campbell, 24, 26
Sinton, James (ed.), *Journal of a Tour in the Highland Western Islands of Scotland in 1800*, 118n1
Shakespeare, William, 51
Skiddaw, 44, 85
Skrine, Henry, 1–2, Work: *Three Successive Tours*, 2
Smith, Adam, 73n1
Smollett, Tobias, 2, 81, 154n1, 222, 223; birthplace, 81n1; monument (Renton), 2, 81, *61*; Works: "Ode to Leven-Water," 81n3; *The Adventures of Ferdinand Count Fathom*, 154; *Gil Blas* (translation), 154
Solway Firth, 41
Solway Moss, 217
Somerset, 10. *See also individual places*
Southey, Robert, 6, 14, 17, 18
Spenser, Edmund, 107, 126
Springfield, 41, *11*
Stephen, James, Work: "The Crisis in the Sugar Colonies," 46
Stoddart, John, Work: *Remarks on Local Scenery and Manners of Scotland* (Stoddart's Tour), 21, 22–3, 66n1, 83n2, 119n1, 169n1, 172n1,2, 181n1, 195, 198n1, 221
Stirling, 16, 195–96, 197, *168–71*; Castle, 23, 195–96, 197, *168*
Stirling Castle, *See* Stirling
Stirling, James. *See* Leadhills, miners' library
Stonehaven, 2
Strath Erne, 177
Strath Eyer, 192, 194
Strathyre, 179n1, 224
Stronachlachar, 95, 224

Tarbet, 5, 15, 89, 90, 93, 96, 114, 115, 116, 224; inn, 90, 91
Tay, River, 163–65, 173, 174, *130, 144*
Taynuilt, 133–34, 156, 158, *100*; Bunawe iron-furnace, 134n1, *100*; inn, 134, 156
Tees, River, 209
Teith, River, 195
Telford, Thomas. *See* Cartland Bridge
Tennant, Robert. *See* Saracen's Head, Glasgow
Teviot, River, 214–16
Thames, River, 77
"The Four" (Dunglass Castle), 76n1
Thirlmere (Lake District), 95
Thornhill, 45, *23*

Threlkeld, 39n1, 217, *208*; Salutation Inn, *208*, White Horse, 39
Tilt, River, 166
Tontine Hotel. *See* Glasgow, coffee-room
Tower Hotel. *See* Hawick
Tranter, Nigel, Work: *Rob Roy MacGregor*, 224
Trossachs, the, 2, 6, 15, 16, 21, 22, 91, 96, 97, 100, 103, 104, 106, 224, 225, *80, 157*
Trubridge, Mike, Work: *Inversnaid Hotel*, 93n2
Tummel, River, 20, 164, 165, 169–75
Turner, J.M.W., 62n3
Tweed, River, 20, 201–209, *189*
Tweeddale, Lord, 144, 145
Tyndrum, 131, 158, 159, 178; inn 3, 4, 158, 159
Tyson, Ann, 134. *See also* Bunawe, iron-foundry

Ulswater (Ullswater), 81, 90, 95, 119, 151, 178

Vallon, Annette, 9
Van Dyck. *See* Hamilton, palace

Walker, Carol Kyros, Work: *Walking North with Keats*, 119n1
Wallace, William, viii, 63n3, 67, 79n1, 221; Caves, 67, 221; statue, 221; Tower, 63, 79. *See also* Gibson, Mel; Wordsworth, William, Works: Composed at Cora Linn"
Wanlockhead, 48–50, 54, 57, 148, *25–9*
Waughs, Misses (of Carlisle), 117
Wedgwood, Thomas and Josiah, 18
Weem, 164, *131*, inn, *131*
Westmoreland (Westmorland), 7, 132, 149
White Hart. *See* Edinburgh
White Horse. *See* Thirlkeld
Wilkinson, Thomas, Work: *Tours to the British Mountains*, 193
Windermere, Lake, 82, 130, 139
Withering, William, Work: *An Arrangement of British Plants*, 163
Womack, Peter, Work: *Improvement and Romance*, 2
Woof, Pamela, Work: *Dorothy Wordsworth, Writer*, 13n
Wordsworth family: Christopher (brother), 17; Dorothy (niece), 19; Eve (mother), 105; John (brother), 18, 19, 20, 23, 40, 162n2, 214; John (nephew), 10, 19, 44, 138, 156, 218; Mary (sister-in-law), 1, 39, 57, 217; William (brother) *passim* and *see* Wordsworth, William
Wordsworth, Dorothy: brutal treatment of horse at Connel, 7–8, 140, 209; childhood 11–12; on churchgoing in Scotland, 58, 62, 98, 109, 110–11, 182, 185; comes upon the whisky hovel, 152; concern for horse, 6, 7–8, 39, 129, 136, 140, 142, 146, 147, 156, 165, 169, 170, 209, *111*; crafting and publication of "journal," 18–26; curiosity about Dorothy, 135, 148, 195; death of brother (John), 18, 22, 162; departure of Coleridge, 14, 15–17, 18, 115, 117, 118; disgust at King's House,